# Metaphor and Metonymy

Publications of the Philological Society, 42

**WILEY-
BLACKWELL**

# Metaphor and Metonymy

## A Diachronic Approach

Kathryn Allan

Publications of the Philological Society, 42

**WILEY-
BLACKWELL**

Blackwell Publishing was acquired by John Wiley & Sons in February 2007. Blackwell's publishing programme has been merged with Wiley's global Scientific, Technical, and Medical business to form Wiley-Blackwell.

*Registered Office*
John Wiley & Sons Ltd, The Atrium, Southern Gate, Chichester, West Sussex, PO19 8SQ, United Kingdom

*Editorial Offices*
350 Main Street, Malden, MA 02148-5020, USA
9600 Garsington Road, Oxford, OX4 2DQ, UK
The Atrium, Southern Gate, Chichester, West Sussex, PO19 8SQ, UK

For details of our global editorial offices, for customer services, and for information about how to apply for permission to reuse the copyright material in this book please see our website at www.wiley.com/wiley-blackwell.

Library of Congress Cataloging-in-Publication Data

Allan, Kathryn L.
  Metaphor and metonymy : a diachronic approach / Kathryn Allan.
  p. cm. – (Publications of the Philological Society, 42)
  Includes bibliographical references and index.
  ISBN 978-1-4051-9085-5 (alk. paper)
  1. Metaphor. 2. English language–Metonyms. 3. English language–Discourse analysis. 4. English language–Style. I. Title.
  PE 1445.M4A45 2008
  420.1'43–dc22

                                                              2008043503

ISBN 978-1-4051-9085-5

A catalogue record for this title is available from the British Library
Set in Times
by SPS (P) Ltd, Chennai, India
Printed and bound in Singapore
by Ho Printing Pte Ltd

*For Christian Kay*

# CONTENTS

# 1
# INTRODUCTION

Metaphor studies have long been challenged by questions about the nature of metaphor, and even after many centuries of study there is surprisingly little consensus about what actually constitutes metaphor. Dictionary definitions of the term vary: the *Oxford English Dictionary* (in a revised third edition entry) defines metaphor as 'A figure of speech in which a name or descriptive word or phrase is transferred to an object or action different from, but analogous to, that to which it is literally applicable'; the *American Heritage Dictionary* offers 'A figure of speech in which a word or phrase that ordinarily designates one thing is used to designate another, thus making an implicit comparison'. Definitions like these rightly reflect widely held popular beliefs about metaphor, but they are less successful at addressing the kinds of issue that metaphor theorists have explored in the past three decades. Many traditional ideas about metaphor, like those represented in dictionaries, have been disputed or discredited within the discipline by recent research. Metaphor is no longer regarded as a figure of speech only, and has been shown to be common and pervasive; and theories that all metaphorical mappings are based on objective similarity or comparison have been rejected as inadequate or simply mistaken. At the same time, there is no general consensus among cognitive linguists about how to define metaphor, and the growth of research on metonymy and its relationship with metaphor has further complicated the issue. Recently, with the increasing interest in electronic corpora and artificial intelligence, there have been renewed efforts to find some reliable and workable procedure for identifying metaphor, and at the heart of this issue is the need to find a generally acceptable definition of metaphor.

One complication in the debate is the existence of metaphors regarded by many as conventionalised to the extent that they 'die' or cease to be metaphorical. Work in cognitive linguistics, concentrated on system-wide 'metaphors we live by' (Lakoff & Johnson 1980), has diverted much attention away from this issue by shifting focus to the cognitive mechanisms that underlie metaphorical mappings, but there is still some uneasiness about the difference between more and less 'active' metaphors. By taking a diachronic approach to metaphor and metonymy, I would contend that it is possible to sidestep these issues and adopt a pragmatic, data-centred stance. The analysis presented in this book is focused on the target concept INTELLIGENCE, and starts from an examination of the etymological development of a group of lexical items from Old English (OE) to Present

Day English (PDE), in order to identify earliest meanings and stages in semantic change; these are nouns and adjectives signifying either cleverness or stupidity which can be applied to people. I then go on to look at three of the most productive source concepts in more detail; these are the SENSES, ANIMALS and DENSITY. Each group raises particular questions about the way in which metaphor can be motivated, and how mappings between concepts develop. In the main part of the book I present detailed individual case studies centred on the linguistic data for these concepts.


## 1.1 MOTIVATION

The approach adopted in this study is influenced by the work of scholars including Sweetser (1990) and Kay (2000), and is not concerned with a narrow classification of what constitutes metaphor and metonymy so much as with an exploration of the kind of factors that can motivate mappings of various kinds. Within the cognitive linguistics tradition, motivation has been an important focus of study, and recent publications such as Cuyckens et al. (2003) and Radden & Panther (2004) have been devoted to the topic. This has led to more explicit interrogation of the term 'motivation' within this field. In the introduction to the latter volume, which includes several papers on metaphor and metonymy, Radden & Panther discuss some of the 'characterizations' of motivation as it has been understood by different scholars, and suggest:

> In current functional and cognitive linguistics, the notion of moti-
> vation is understood in various ways, which are, however, not
> necessarily mutually exclusive... each of the ... characterizations
> contains important elements: non-arbitrary relationships between
> form and meaning (as opposed to arbitrary relationships), iconicity
> (as one type of motivation), and explanation ('making sense'
> through motivation). These and other elements need to be integrated
> into a unified theory of motivation. (Radden & Panther 2004: 2)

It is perhaps the idea of explanation that is the most relevant to this study, and it is this aspect which is played up by Radden & Panther in the discussion following this extract; they go on to say that 'the notion of motivation is closely related to that of explanation' (p. 11). Their discussion echoes the earlier comments of Kövecses, who suggests that the terms 'explanation' and 'motivation' are 'roughly synonymous' (1995: 182).

Any explanation of how a linguistic expression arises must take account of a wide range of factors, both intra- and extralinguistic. Studies of motivation within cognitive linguistics typically concentrate on extralin-guistic factors, and a major theme has been the consideration of the way in which thought is 'embodied'; a large number of metaphors and metonymies seem to be motivated by everyday physical experience, and are common to unrelated languages for this reason. For example, the connection between vision and understanding (discussed in Chapter 2) that is evident in linguistic expressions such as *I see what you mean* can be explained by the importance of vision as a primary means of information about the world, and this is common to all humans. However, while embodied experience has been shown to be central to conceptualisation and in itself can explain the mappings between source and target in some linguistic expressions, the metaphorical and metonymical differences that are evident across languages show that other factors can also be involved. Many scholars (e.g. Geeraerts & Grondelaers 1995; Holland & Quinn 1987) have discussed the central role of culture in any account of conceptualisation, and have pointed out that it is not possible to fully explain many real examples in language without considering the cultural context in which these occur. The mappings that are explored in Chapter 4 testify to this: although animal metaphors are found in many (if not all) languages, the same animal can represent different human characteristics in different societies. This probably reflects the different cultural models and traditions that are part of the social-cultural belief systems of these societies. The fact that animal metaphors themselves are common to many languages shows that in reality cultural and cognitive factors in motivation often interact; and this is also demonstrated by the data discussed in Chapter 3. There appears to be a general connection between density and stupidity in English that depends on the idea of the MIND AS A PHYSICAL ENTITY, which can be found in any language and can be explained by common cognitive processes; however, in many expressions such as *thick as mince* particular substances represent density, and the selection of these substances is likely to be culturally informed.

A more detailed analysis of each of these mappings is presented in the main part of this book, drawing attention to a number of motivating factors that can be involved in metaphorical/metonymical mappings. As Radden & Panther's typology of motivation demonstrates, these can be diverse. They identify several types of language-independent motivation, including experiential, perceptual and cognitive motivation (using fairly specific definitions for each), but comment that as well as these 'a fully fledged theory of motivation would … include cultural, social, psychological and anthropological factors as well as biological and neurological determinants' (2004: 31). Because of the enormous diversity of possible contributing factors posited by different scholars and the speculative nature of accounts of these factors, analyses of motivation have sometimes attracted criticism for their unscientific nature, but this kind of criticism perhaps mistakes the purpose of this type of work. Radden & Panther provide a helpful perspective on the value of studying motivation in the broadest sense:

> We ... regard the search for motivational explanations as a useful heuristic for linguistic research ... for many linguistic phenomena motivational accounts suggest themselves strongly – not in the sense of nomological-deductive explanations in the 'hard' sciences, but more in the spirit of what the German philosopher Wilhelm Dilthey characterized as 'understanding' (*verstehen*) in the humanities or cultural sciences (*Geisteswissenschaften*). (Radden & Panther 2004: 42)

The analyses presented here are very much in the same spirit. I do not intend to present a comprehensive, 'scientific' account of the motivation of a group of mappings; rather, I am interested in exploring the variety of both intra- and extralinguistic reasons for the emergence of particular mappings in a single semantic field. Essentially, what I hope to achieve in doing this is to highlight the diversity that characterises metaphor and metonymy in the broadest senses of the terms. Over 40 years ago, Max Black warned: 'Metaphor is a loose word, at best, and we must beware of attributing to it stricter rules of usage than are actually found in practice' (Black 1962: 28–9). I would suggest that this broadness in the way the term 'metaphor' is used reflects genuine complexity and diversity in the concept it denotes, and the same is true of metonymy.

## 1.2 BRIEF OUTLINE OF THE STUDY OF METAPHOR AND METONYMY[1]

### 1.2.1 *Early work on metaphor*

Historically, metaphor and related phenomena have attracted a general lack of enthusiasm from linguists. This is not to say they have been ignored: as far back as Aristotle, who is thought to have begun the tradition of studying figurative language, widespread interest in metaphor stretched into various disciplines, notably literary criticism and philosophy. But as modern linguistics emerged in the mid-nineteenth century, a growing determination that it be given the status of a science followed. Preoccupation with data that could be recorded precisely (phonetics received a great deal of attention) left little room for semantics, let alone figurative language that could not be accommodated easily in a typical grammar. Metaphor was considered to be 'a species of figurative language which needs explaining, or explaining away ... a kind of anomaly of language (Schön 1993: 137). Leonard Bloomfield's *Language* (1933) was typical of this period: in over 500 pages, there are only nineteen that deal with any form of semantics.

---

[1] The following is a brief summary only, and is intended to provide a background for the present study rather than a comprehensive account.

This left metaphor study to philosophy and literary criticism; and this is where almost all interest in the subject was rooted. In most early work, metaphor was seen by many scholars as 'a kind of decorative addition to ordinary plain language; a rhetorical device to be used at certain times to gain certain effects' (Saeed 1999: 303). Metaphor was most often discussed within guides to skill in rhetoric, and was rarely considered as its own justification. The writings of Henry Home (Lord Kames) in the eighteenth century are indicative of the work published in this era: in *Elements of Criticism*, first published in 1762, metaphor is considered along with other kinds of figurative language in a section entitled 'Figures' (Home 1993: 275ff.). Occasionally scholars did discuss the role of metaphor in language, but this comment by Shelley is very much in line with this idea of metaphor as a device used best by those with expertise in 'the art of rhetoric'.

> Their language [that of poets] is vitally metaphorical; that is, it marks the before unapprehended relations of things and perpetuates their apprehension, until words, which represent them, become, through time, signs for portions or classes of thought instead of pictures of integral thoughts: and then, if no new poets should arise to create afresh the associations which have been thus disorganized, language will be dead to all the nobler purposes of human inter-course. (Shelley 1891: 4–5)

His words demonstrate the view that metaphor is something 'special' or 'extraordinary' – although he talks about language being 'vitally metaphorical', he asserts that poets have an integral role in the creation of metaphor. He echoes Aristotle's famous phrase (in the *Poetics*): 'The greatest thing by far is to have a command of metaphor. This alone cannot be imparted to another: it is the mark of genius, for to make good metaphors implies an eye for resemblances' (quoted in Richards 1936: 89).

Naturally, therefore, 'literary' metaphor was deemed the most interesting and worthy of notice. As well as this, there was a prevailing attitude that metaphor was potentially a misleading and deceptive linguistic tool, and this idea can still be found. Max Black went as far as to say: 'Addiction to metaphor is held to be illicit, on the principle that whereof one can speak only metaphorically, thereof one ought not to speak at all... No doubt metaphors are dangerous ...' (Black 1962: 25, 47). Around the same time, a similar view was expressed by Colin Turbayne:

> I try to explode the metaphysics of mechanism ... by exposing mechanism as a case of being victimized by metaphor. Descartes and Newton I choose as excellent examples of metaphysicians of mechanism *malgré eux*, that is to say, as unconscious victims of the metaphor of the great machine ... All this is so in spite of the meager opposition offered by the theologians, a few poets, and fewer phi-

losophers, who, in general, have been victimized by their own metaphors to the same degree as their rivals. (Turbayne 1962: 5)

Though the majority of linguists would distance themselves from using terminology like 'dangerous' and 'misleading' in regard to metaphor, the idea that choice of metaphor can frame situations or people in different ways and influence the attitudes of others has certainly been taken on. It is also beginning to exert practical influential in a wider context. Currently, in the US particularly, political and media organisations are beginning to employ linguists (including Lakoff) to advise them of the best ways to 'market' themselves and their policies.

It was not until the early twentieth century, notably with I. A. Richards (whose interest lay mainly in literary criticism), that any detailed account of the workings of figurative language was attempted. In retrospect Richards's work on metaphor was groundbreaking, and the impact of his new perspective was far-reaching. He was one of the first to recognise that metaphor was not the unusual, extraordinary phenomenon that it had been widely regarded to be, describing it as the 'omnipresent principle of language', which 'we cannot get through three sentences of ordinary fluid discourse without' (Richards 1936: 92). He went on to say that metaphor was also common in scientific discourse and technical language. Perhaps his greatest contribution to the discipline, over forty years before Lakoff & Johnson published *Metaphors We Live By*, was his assertion that metaphor was more significant than a mere rhetorical flourish:

> The traditional theory noticed only a few of the modes of metaphor; and limited its application of the term *metaphor* to a few of them only. And thereby it made metaphor seem to be a verbal matter, a shifting and displacement of words, whereas fundamentally it is a borrowing between and intercourse of *thoughts*, a transaction between contexts. *Thought* is metaphoric, and proceeds by comparison, and the metaphors of language derive therefrom. To improve the theory of metaphor we must remember this. (Richards 1936: 94)

By bringing in the labels 'tenor' and 'vehicle' to distinguish between the two 'halves' of a metaphor (ie the concept being referred to and the concept being used metaphorically to refer to it), Richards created a useful terminology for future scholars. By simply attempting to look at the complexity of metaphorical expression, he cleared the way for more precise, more analytical investigations of metaphor.

The work of the philosopher Max Black in the 1960s has also been influential, and continues to be referenced by current scholars. Within the context of philosophy, Black was interested in the limitations of traditional theories in accounting for the way metaphor works, presenting a critique of the widely held *substitution view* (his terminology), and the closely related *comparison view* (Black 1962: 31–9). The substitution view holds that metaphorical expression is used as a substitute for some equivalent literal expression that the reader/hearer must 'decipher': Black's example is using 'Richard is a lion' to mean 'Richard is brave'. This is a standard definition for metaphor, found for example in the *OED* entry: 'The figure of speech in which a name or descriptive term is transferred to some object different from, but analogous to, that to which it is properly applicable; an instance of this, a metaphorical expression.' The comparison view is a slightly more sophisticated version of the substitution view, holding that metaphorical expression is simply condensed simile and can therefore be replaced by a literal comparison: to use Black's example again, 'Richard is a lion' stands for 'Richard is like a lion (in being brave)'. In his criticism of the substitution view, he claims that metaphor is reduced either to a convenient source of catachresis, existing to compensate for inadequacy in the lexicon, or to a mere decoration of language. Both of these are problematic, as Richards had previously noted:

> There are, however, many metaphors where the virtues ascribed to catachresis cannot apply, because there is, or there is supposed to be, some readily available and equally compendious literal equivalent … Except in cases where a metaphor is a catachresis that remedies some temporary imperfection of literal language, the purpose of metaphor is to entertain and divert. Its use, on this view, always constitutes a deviation from the 'plain and strictly appropriate style' (Whately). So, if philosophers have something more important to do than give serious pleasure to their readers, metaphor can have no serious place in philosophical discussion. (Richards 1936: 33–4)

Black is equally unconvinced by the comparison view: 'it suffers from a vagueness that borders upon vacuity' (1962: 37). In other words, there are no rules to guide a reader as to which characteristics are theoretically being compared, and often it is hard to find objectively recognisable, 'literal' resemblances. Building on Richards's suggestion that the ideas in metaphor 'co-operate in an inclusive meaning' (Richards 1936: 119), Black suggests that the alternative *interaction* view is a more realistic theory of the way metaphors function.

> … in the given context the focal word … obtains a new meaning, which is not quite its meaning in literal uses, nor quite the meaning which any literal substitute would have. The new context … imposes extension of meaning upon the focal word. And I take Richards to be saying that for the metaphor to work the reader must remain aware of the extension of meaning – must attend to both the old and the new meanings together. (Black 1962: 38–9)

In my opinion, the strength of this theory lies in its defined yet flexible nature: it applies (perhaps more or less obviously) to all types of metaphoric expression without requiring any amendment. Previous theories had all been demonstrated to be inapplicable or irrelevant in certain cases, but at last here was a simple yet convincing alternative. The interaction view of metaphor has gained the general approval of many subsequent scholars, and has informed much of the later work in the field, which picks up this idea that in some mappings only selected elements of the source are 'imported' while elements of the target are also retained. For example, Fauconnier & Turner's work on conceptual blending (1998; 2002; discussed in section 3.4.1) emphasises the way in which only certain features from a range of 'inputs' can combine to form a cognitively cohesive whole, i.e. a 'blend'. In their model, elements of more than one source or input can be involved in any blend, and metaphor is only one potential kind of input, alongside others such as metonymy, frames and cultural models.

After Black and during the 1960s and 1970s, semantics gradually began to be accepted as a viable part of linguistics, and linguists at last began to turn their attention towards figurative language as a valid and justifiable topic for study. The Bloomfieldian view that linguistics should be 'scientific' was still very much in evidence in much of the work done around this time (and continues to be important); but semantics was increasingly being taken more seriously, and this bred early attempts in what would now be termed 'cognitive linguistics'. In turn, this laid the foundations for later, more realistic examinations of what the term 'metaphor' constitutes and how it works. An increase of interest in meaning (bolstered by the work being done with componential analysis and prototype theory), and the resulting acceptance of metaphor as central in the development of polysemy, were factors that lent credibility to its study. The work of R. A. Waldron is indicative of this: in *Sense and Sense Development* he examines 'metaphoric transfer' in the context of diachronic meaning change (Waldron 1979: 162–85).

## 1.2.2 Metaphors We Live By, *and the work of Lakoff et al.*

It is in the last 20 years that metaphor has been recognised as a central element of linguistics, and perhaps the most significant influence on the field has been that of George Lakoff and Mark Johnson. Much of their work, both individually and collaboratively, has been important, but it is *Metaphors We Live By* that has had the greatest impact on study in linguistics, and has stimulated a wave of fresh interest in metaphor. Lakoff & Johnson looked beyond the role of metaphor in language and focused instead on its relationship to thought. The result is a coherent and convincing account of the way that metaphor underlies the fundamental structuring of concepts.

...metaphor is typically viewed as characteristic of language alone, a
matter of words rather than thought or action ... We have found, on
the contrary, that metaphor is pervasive in everyday life, not just in
language but in thought and action. Our ordinary conceptual system, in terms of which we both think and act, is fundamentally
metaphorical in nature ... Our concepts structure what we perceive,
how we get around in the world, and how we relate to other people.
Our conceptual system thus plays a central role in defining our
everyday realities. If we are right in suggesting that our conceptual
system is largely metaphorical, then the way we think, what we
experience, and what we do every day is very much a matter of
metaphor. (Lakoff & Johnson 1980: 3)

This assertion is followed up with the presentation of a number of the
metaphors that Lakoff & Johnson believe can be found in the structure of
certain concepts, alongside linguistic evidence for these.

The ideas presented in *Metaphors We Live By* are not all new.
The previous year, Michael Reddy had produced the same type of data
on the 'conduit metaphor' (Reddy 1979); and as I have already mentioned,
the basic notion of metaphor in thought can be traced back as far as
Richards. But the achievement of this book was the way it developed and
substantiated these theories. By picking up strands of research that had
hitherto been largely overlooked, and by adopting a fundamentally
different outlook at the outset, Lakoff & Johnson shifted the emphasis of
metaphor study and opened up new areas of inquiry. These included a new
interpretation of the terms 'live' and 'dead' when applied to metaphor.
Traditionally, the dominant view was that when a metaphor has become so
familiar that it is no longer striking to a reader/hearer it has 'died' and
passed into literal language (see e.g. Searle 1993: 122). Exactly at what point
this can be considered to have happened is debated. Brown suggests that it
is 'When the word becomes as familiar in its new context as it was in its old'
(Brown 1958: 142). MacCormac is more specific in his contention that
'when metaphors become so commonplace that one or more of the referents
adds a lexical entry in a dictionary, then we can be sure that the metaphor
has completely died and is now literal rather than metaphorical'
(MacCormac 1985: 77). A few scholars, before Lakoff & Johnson,
registered their unease about this issue – notably Richards, who talked
about the possibility of what might be termed 'remetaphorization'.

...however stone dead such metaphors seem, we can easily wake
them up ... This favourite old distinction between dead and living
metaphors (itself a two-fold metaphor) is, indeed, a device which is
very often a hindrance to the play of sagacity and discernment
throughout the subject. For serious purposes it needs a drastic
re-examination. (Richards 1936:101)

Lakoff & Johnson argued that 'dead' or conventionalised metaphors were actually the most important and interesting, since often they could provide linguistic evidence for the concepts that are used to structure speakers' views of the world, and their understanding of situations and experiences.

> Each of the metaphorical expressions we have talked about so far (e.g., the time *will come*; we *construct* a theory, *attack* an idea) is used within a whole system of metaphorical concepts – concepts that we constantly use in living and thinking. These expressions, like all other words and phrasal lexical items in the language, are fixed by convention. In addition to these cases, which are parts of whole metaphorical systems, there are idiosyncratic metaphorical expressions that stand alone and are not used systematically in our language or thought. These are well-known expressions like the *foot* of the mountain, a *head* of cabbage, the *leg* of a table, etc. ... They do not interact with other metaphors, play no particularly interesting role in our conceptual system, and hence are not metaphors that we live by ... If any metaphorical expressions deserve to be called 'dead,' it is these ... the systematic metaphorical expressions we have been discussing ... are 'alive' in the most funda-mental sense: they are metaphors we live by. The fact that they are conventionally fixed within the lexicon of English makes them no less alive. (Lakoff & Johnson 1980: 54–5)

The idea that conventionalised metaphors can be examined from a cognitive perspective, as a source of insight into the way concepts are structured, is now widely accepted within cognitive linguistics, and it has been taken up by many other scholars to become the focus of much of the current metaphor research within the discipline. It is this assumption that underlies this analysis of INTELLIGENCE metaphors, which is informed by the work of Lakoff & Johnson alongside subsequent research in the field.

### 1.2.3 *Metonymy*

Since Lakoff and Johnson's study, increasing attention has been paid to another figurative process that is also centrally important to conceptualisa-tion and human thought, and this is metonymy. As René Dirven points out in a discussion of early work on metonymy (Dirven 2002a), Jakobson discussed the importance of metonymy and the way in which it relates to metaphor in a 1956 paper, but subsequent research which developed theories of metonymy in more detail were not undertaken until much later, and for many years metonymy was considered to be far less interesting and important than metaphor:

> Jakobson was the first to pay equal attention to both metonymy and metaphor. This balanced view was probably still impossible at the

time of the metaphor revolution launched by Lakoff & Johnson's cannon shot known as *Metaphors We Live By* (1980). It took almost another twenty years to fully redress the balance between metaphor and metonymy... (Dirven 2002a: 1)

The view that metonymy is a relatively marginal figurative device which is conceptually less important than metaphor is no longer held to be viable by cognitivists. Recent studies have assigned it a much greater importance, recognising that 'it has become increasingly apparent that metonymy... may be even more fundamental than metaphor' (Panther & Radden 1999: 1).

   Much of the body of recent work focuses on the distinction between metaphor and metonymy, and metonymy tends to be defined in terms of the difference between the two, which remains problematic. To date, despite a number of studies, there is no widely accepted definition of metonymy which distinguishes it clearly from metaphor, and attempts to clarify the relationship between the two types of mapping have proved inconclusive (see Haser 2005: 13–52 for a detailed discussion). Much work in cognitive semantics focuses on the domain approach, where metaphor is seen as a mapping between two domains, and metonymy as an intra-domain mapping involving only one domain, or, following Croft (2002), as a mapping between two domains within the same domain matrix (see below). A fairly typical definition is given by Barcelona (who takes account of Croft's approach):

> *Metaphor* is the cognitive mechanism whereby one experiential domain ... is partially mapped onto a different experiential domain, the second domain being partially understood in terms of the first one ... Both domains have to belong to different superordinate domains ... *Metonymy* ... is a cognitive mechanism whereby one experiential domain is partially understood in terms of another experiential domain included *in the same common experiential domain.* (Barcelona 2002: 211–15)

Definitions of this kind are rooted in the theory of conceptual domains: knowledge of and about the world is mentally stored in groups of related concepts, and each of these concepts can only be understood in the context of that group (or, as Geeraerts puts it, 'chunk of experience': 1997: 97). In his discussion of domains, Langacker exemplifies this by citing the concept *knuckle*, which cannot be explained without the concept *finger*, in turn dependent on the concept *hand*, and so on (Langacker 1987: 147). A concept can therefore function as the domain for another concept while itself belonging to a 'superordinate' domain, thus belonging to a domain matrix. The distinction that is made between metaphor and metonymy is dependent on the possibility of demarcating the boundaries between domains (or domain matrices). However, this is widely acknowledged to be difficult and subjective. While some concepts such as colours make up a relatively restricted set, and can therefore be 'classified' into domains in a relatively straightforward and uncontroversial way, others are much more difficult to organise into domains, and such attempts can result in highly subjective classifications that appear to be of limited usefulness. As Croft (2002) points out, the notion of the domain is related to the theory of semantic fields, itself notoriously imprecise; Croft quotes Lyons's comment: 'What is lacking so far, as most field-theorists would probably admit, is a more explicit formulation of the criteria which define a lexical field than has yet been provided' (Lyons 1977: 267).

An alternative, and perhaps more traditional, approach to distinguishing between metaphor and metonymy relies on the difference between similarity and contiguity: metaphor is said to be a relationship of similarity, while metonymical mappings are those involving contiguity. By this criterion, metonymy has a largely referential function. While metaphor involves 'seeing one thing in terms of another', metonymy in language arises only from associations between concepts that are closely related in human experience. For example, referring to a monarch as *the crown* does not involve any kind of comparison, since it simply results from the close connection between the two entities, whereas referring to a person as 'the sun' (as in Shakespeare's *Romeo and Juliet*) is some kind of statement about that person. Although this distinction between metaphor and metonymy seems more promising than the domain approach, a number of scholars have pointed out that it too has limitations, and overall it appears to share the same basic problem as the domain approach (see Peirsman & Geeraerts 2006: 27–72). Feyaerts points out that referential function does not clearly distinguish metonymy from metaphor since both involve referential shifts, but that in cases of metaphor 'the referential shift is much bigger' (Feyaerts 2000: 76); again, this does not appear to offer a reliable or objective criterion for distinguishing between the two. The notions of contiguity and similarity are also problematic. Contiguity is itself an ambiguous concept which is defined in different ways by different scholars. If contiguity is defined as a relationship of conceptual closeness between source and target, this does not seem significantly different from the domain approach, since closeness between concepts involves the same kind of subjective judgement necessary to delimit boundaries between domains. Alternatively, some scholars avoid this issue by defining contiguity negatively as simply the opposite of similarity (e.g. Ullmann 1962; Feyaerts 2000). Similarity between source and target as the basis of metaphor has been much discussed and criticised in the past four decades, but it is uncontroversial to suggest that it is not equally obvious for all metaphorical mappings. For example, for image-based metaphors evidenced in expressions such as *he is a beanpole* there is obvious visual similarity between the source and target of the metaphor. This is not the case for primary metaphors such as SIMILARITY IS CLOSENESS, e.g. in the expression *that's not the kind of dress I had in mind, but it's close*, and it is much more difficult to argue that this metaphor is motivated by the same kind of relationship between source and target. This is discussed more fully in section 4.3.6.

In the last few years, some scholars have suggested that metaphor and metonymy are best seen as points on a cline; while there are some relatively straightforward examples of metaphor and some of metonymy, there are many problematic cases that seem to fall between the two. In fact, this suggestion was made by Jakobson in 1956, but has had little general impact until much more recently (see Dirven 2002b for a discussion). Radden suggests that:

> the traditional distinction between metaphor and metonymy can no longer be maintained. The classical notions of metaphor and metonymy are to be seen as prototypical categories at the end points of a continuum of mapping processes. The range in the middle of the metonymy-metaphor continuum is made up of metonymy-based metaphors, which also account for the transition of metonymy to metaphor by providing an experiential motivation of a metaphor. (Radden 2000: 105)

This view seems much more promising as a way of reconciling the difficulties involved in distinguishing between the two, and it is borne out by the data presented in this study. The SENSES mapping examined in Chapter 2 is problematic in terms of traditional ideas of metaphor, but does not fit neatly alongside uncontroversial instances of metonymy either. By contrast, in terms of motivation the DENSITY data in Chapter 3 and ANIMAL data in Chapter 4 appear to demonstrate much less problematic cases of metonymy and metaphor respectively.

## 1.2.4 *Use of corpora in the study of metaphor and metonymy*

Amongst the most recent body of research emerging from metaphor and metonymy studies, there is a recognition that much of the theoretical content of past work has lacked empirical evidence, and that there is potential for much more investigation of real usage; this is what is needed to test and explore further the relationship between metaphor and metonymy, and between different examples of each phenomenon. An increasing number of studies in various branches of linguistics employ a corpus-based approach. In Steen's volume on metaphor in literature, he comments that 'although philosophical and theoretical speculation have been rife across the centuries, attributing a crucial function to metaphor for the way we make sense of all sorts of phenomena, such ideas have only recently been put to the test in empirical research on the actual usage of metaphor by people (Steen 1994: ix). Later (p. 9) he goes on to criticise the non-empirical approach of Lakoff & Johnson:

...although the analysis of *language structure* is highly useful, it cannot serve as the whole basis for the study of *actual language use*. Language analysis may serve a function to derive all sorts of expectations and speculations about processing, but that is quite another matter, namely theory formation. Theories have to be tested, and the analysis of further language data cannot count as a serious test of predictions about individual metaphor use.

Some work combining a corpus-based approach with historical data has also been undertaken, notably by Geeraerts et al., and I believe that this sort of work has already yielded valuable insights into the way metaphor and metonymy work and develop, and will continue to do so in the future. Geeraerts & Grondelaers, in their study of the cultural traditions associated with anger, make the following statement:

> In the case of purely lexical research, the emphasis on the mechanisms of semantic flexibility that underlie the structure of polysemy (such as metaphor and metonymy) naturally entails a renewed interest in diachronic semantics ... to a large extent, the synchronic polysemy of lexical items is a reflection of their diachronic development. (Geeraerts & Grondelaers 1995: 177)

It is on this premise that the present work is based.

## 1.3 METHODOLOGY

### 1.3.1 *The* Historical Thesaurus of English *and the* Oxford English Dictionary[2]

This study is based on data from the *Historical Thesaurus of English* (*HTE*),[3] a project based in the department of English Language at the University of Glasgow to compile a thesaurus similar in structure to *Roget's Thesaurus*. The finished volume, to be published on paper and in electronic form in 2008 will contain lexical items from OE to PDE, classified by semantic field and presented chronologically with the first and (if no longer current) last recorded dates of usage as presented in the *OED*. These dates, as well as stylistic information such as dialectal or specialised usage, are taken from the *OED* (second edition) and supplemented by the *Thesaurus of Old English* (*TOE*), which provides additional information on lexemes that do not survive into the Middle English period. The *HTE* is, therefore, essentially a reorganisation of the *OED*, using the sense divisions and the definitions supplied at the various senses as the basis to reclassify lexemes into semantic fields. Using the *OED* for this type of research into meaning and meaning change raises particular theoretical and methodological questions about the nature of the data and the conclusions that can be drawn from it. Perhaps most fundamentally, the extent to which these definitions and sense divisions can be used uncritically must be considered.

In her discussion of the practice adopted by editors in writing definitions, Penny Silva notes that defining is a highly subjective and personal process, which it is difficult to explain in fine detail and to make any uniform rules about; the nature of word meaning makes it difficult to be in any way 'objective' about the definition process. Quoting John Simpson, the current editor of the *OED*, she observes that although patterns seem to emerge in the way *OED* editors approached definitions, 'no defining manual is able to codify all possible features without losing the "the spontaneity of lexicographical creation" (Simpson 27/12/97)' (Silva 2000: 83). In the kind of language that is used in *OED* definitions, it is clear that the editors of the first edition did not adopt any standard defining vocabulary of the type used by a small number of current dictionaries (for example, the *Oxford Advanced Learner's Dictionary*). This is in no way surprising – such a procedure would have been highly unusual at the time the first edition was compiled – but it makes it difficult to compare and contrast the definitions for lexemes with slightly different shades of meaning. As well as this, because *OED* was only minimally revised for the second edition, some of the language of the definitions reflects idiosyncratic or archaic word usage. For example, in the second edition, *noddy* (noun sense 1) is defined as 'a fool, simpleton, noodle', where *noodle* means 'a stupid or silly person'; this is not the most usual or frequent current sense of *noodle*, and the definition is shortened to 'a fool, a simpleton' in the third edition entry. Because the language of some definitions is oblique in this way, some types of searches in second edition entries are problematic; retrieving lexemes within a particular semantic field by searching through definitions for keywords is not reliable, and can miss large quantities of relevant data. However, *HTE* did not classify the *OED* data in this way. Rather than searching for keywords within particular semantic fields, *HTE* editors read the *OED* systematically, and this means that differences in the defining vocabulary used for broadly synonymous lexemes would not have led them to miss relevant data.

Aside from this, the evidence on which the *OED* bases its entries has also been criticised as problematic by various scholars. It is generally acknowledged that the evidence that survives for English in earlier periods is uneven; relatively few manuscripts from the Old and Early Middle English periods exist, and this means that it is difficult to compare the lexis of these periods with the lexis of later periods, where much more evidence is available. Defining lexemes for which there are few attestations can be problematic, and there are many examples of lexemes for which a meaning can only be suggested on the basis of a single example and (in some cases) comparison with potentially related forms or cognates. There are several definitions in the *OED* that explicitly note uncertainty about the meaning of a lexeme in a particular context, often using the expression 'Of uncertain meaning'.[4]

Where only a single attestation can be found for a lexeme or a particular sense of a lexeme, this may reflect an idiosyncratic use by a particular writer, i.e. a nonce-word, but in many cases it is more likely to reflect more frequent use, either in written sources that have not survived or in speech. Approximately one fifth of the lexemes in the INTELLIGENCE data are only attested once in the *OED*, but it seems unlikely that this is a problem for this study. Because of the nature of the data, it is comparatively unlikely that the meanings suggested in *OED* definitions are uncertain; only nouns and adjectives that can be applied to people are included in the data, and in most cases the meaning of the lexeme is clear from closely related forms or from the context in which the lexeme occurs. For example, there is only a single attestation for doddy-pate n c1500, but several for the related form doddypoll n 1401–1767. Even if this were not the case, the meaning is clear from the supporting quotation listed in the *OED*, from *The boke of mayd Emlyn* (c.1500): '[She] Made hym a fole, And called hym dody-pate.' In fact, although the *OED* only lists one supporting quotation for *doddy-pate*, a second attestation can be found in the *Early English Books Online (EEBO)* database, in two different editions of works by John Skelton dating from 1545 and 1568:

> ... he ratis He calleth them doddy patis He grynnes and he ...

This provides clear evidence that a single attestation in the *OED* is not necessarily evidence that a lexeme is a nonce-word. In this case, a second attestation can be found, and presumably this is only missing from the *OED* because it was not found by the editors of the first edition (and could be expected to be incorporated into the third edition; see Durkin 2002 for a discussion of the overall impact new evidence might be expected to have on *OED3*).

In some cases, single attestations in the *OED* must reflect nonce uses, but this does not seem problematic for a study of this kind. The observations and conclusions presented in this book are based on the analysis of a body of data, and each of the mappings explored in detail in the main chapters is evidenced by a number of lexemes that relate to a particular concept. The majority of these are not nonce-words, and are used for a period of time,

---

[4] One example is *ballow*, which is only attested once in 1612; this is defined as 'Of uncertain meaning; perh.: gaunt. Cf. *adj.*'

but even the nonce-words are significant, since these illustrate the productivity of a particular mapping.

The other criticism that has been levelled at the *OED* is that it is not truly descriptive in its use of source materials, and does not make equal use of all available evidence in all periods. Most commonly, it has been suggested that, despite the descriptive aims of the *OED*, it over-represents literary works at the expense of other genres such as scientific literature and newspapers (e.g. Kastovsky 2006: 266–7). Some scholars have also observed that the language of some writers, such as Dickens and Browning, is much better represented than that of others, such as Wilkie Collins and Blake (Brewer 2000: 56). Taylor asserts: 'it is a truism that ... the OED's reliance on literary quotations is problematic because it skews the representative character of the sampling' (Taylor 1993: 6), but as Brewer (2000) points out, it is very difficult to measure the extent to which this might be the case. It is undoubtedly true that some generally used lexemes were not included in the first edition because they were used most frequently in under-represented genres (although it is very difficult to prove this), and work on the third edition has shown that many of the earliest and latest quotations for lexemes or particular senses of lexemes can be ante- and postdated (see section 1.2.5 below for a discussion). However, although there are probably areas of lexis for which this is particularly a problem (such as scientific or technical vocabulary), it is doubtful that it has a significant impact on this study. The types of source material that are probably under-represented in *OED* quotations are unlikely to yield much data relating to intelligence which would be included in my corpus; scientific literature would not contain many INTELLIGENCE lexemes that were not medical terms, and newspapers from earlier periods are not rich in metaphorical or metonymical expressions for 'clever' or 'stupid'. It is still possible that the data is not comprehensive, but this does not invalidate the conclusions that have been drawn from the corpus that has been used. Neither the omission of antedatings or postdatings nor the over- or under-representation of particular authors or of particular text types are likely to have a huge impact on the present study. Fundamentally, I am drawing generalisations from a body of data extracted ultimately from the *OED* database via *HTE*; I am not looking at the frequency of incidence of metaphorical or metonymical expressions either diachronically or synchronically. For the reason, the representative nature of the *OED* data is not of such great concern as it might be for many other types of research.

### 1.3.2 *The INTELLIGENCE corpus*

The items in this corpus are taken from two sections of *HTE*, WISDOM and FOOLISHNESS. In line with *Roget's Thesaurus*, these are presented in two separate subsections, collected together under the heading INTELLECT, rather than in a single group. I have chosen to take them all together in this way because the focus of the book is the way in which INTELLIGENCE as a whole target concept is conceptualised, and this includes both CLEVERNESS and STUPIDITY. My corpus is made up of 1,075 *HTE* entries, made up of 464 nouns and 611 adjectives. Just over 11% of the total data dates as far back as OE; including expressions in specialised usage, such as those that are found in scientific language or are archaic, around 40% of the entries are labelled current.

A general point to be made about the data is that there is an imbalance between STUPIDITY and CLEVERNESS entries. Of the total of 1,075 entries that constitute the data, 648 (around 60%) signify stupidity, whilst 427 signify cleverness. There is an even more marked difference if the OE only data is removed from the calculation. There are 99 entries that are dated to the OE period without any subsequent evidence of use, leaving 976 entries dated after this time; of these 976, 624 (almost two thirds) are associated with stupidity, leaving 352 associated with cleverness. Possible reasons for this are discussed in section 1.4.1.

### 1.3.3 *Guide to the data*

At the end of each chapter in the main section of this book, i.e. Chapters 2, 3 and 4, the data relating to that chapter is presented in simple table form, divided into subgroups as presented in the chapter. Further data tables relating to core concepts that are mentioned in the book are presented at the back, alphabetically by core concept. The following section details the fields I have used in these tables, the information to which each one refers and, where appropriate, notes on why this has been included.

The first field in each table gives **record number**; in this book, I have cited all terms with part of speech and dates rather than using this ID, but it has been included for completeness. Field two contains **meaning,** i.e. either **clever** (with one or more subcategory, e.g. **clever – common sense**) or **stupid**. Field three is for **core concept,** and I have used various symbols in this field to indicate different relationships between concepts. For compound words, where each element relates to a different core concept, these are separated by 'and'; where two or more core concepts seem equally relevant to a source, I have used '&', and where two or more are equally possible and likely I have used 'or'. If an item has changed semantically before coming to be associated with INTELLIGENCE and this seems relevant, different core concepts to which it has been related are listed with the earliest first, separated by ' > '. If a core concept group is part of a larger, superordinate category, both are recorded with the superordinate category listed first, and separated by '–' , and where the core category group is uncertain this is preceded by '?'. The INTELLIGENCE terms themselves are in the third field, followed in the fourth by a part of speech label (either 'n' for noun or 'aj' for adjective).

Entries are presented in chronological order from earliest to latest, according to the date of the first and last record of usage. Where there are two entries with the same starting date, the one with the earliest final date will come first (i.e. entries with the same starting date marked current are listed last). As in *HTE*, dates up to 1150 are not preserved, but are simply labelled OE (Old English); entries with final dates after 1870 are marked current wherever possible, and all entries with final dates in the twentieth century are marked current. There are 11 fields in the database dedicated to dating, which allow entries to be labelled as OE and a possible three other dates. With the exception of the OE field, the date fields can all be preceded with 'ante' or 'circa', and this is recorded in a separate field (simply because the data were entered into an Access database which was easier to search for date ranges in this way). Dates are separated by ' – ' to show continued currency, and by ' + ' if there is a period of around 150 years or more between recorded use or in cases where one date is labelled to show specialised usage. Entries considered to be in current use are marked ' > ' in the final date field.

There are two further fields. Field sixteen contains **labels** referring to specialised usage, such as **slang** or **dialect**; if these apply to particular dates, these will also be given in this field. Field eighteen is for **derivation**, and was included in the original Access database to enable users to collect together all the terms with shared etymology by giving the roots from which terms are derived (this is discussed further below). Because Access does not accept the full range of symbols that are available in word processing packages, the symbol £ has been used instead of ə.

In this book, data items are underlined and given with part of speech label and dates of usage, e.g. in the form crafty < cræftig aj OE-1791 + 1876 >.

### 1.3.4 *Discrepancies between* HTE *and the* INTELLIGENCE *corpus*

At the time I collected my data, between October 2000 and January 2001, *HTE* had not been completed, and the sections I worked with had only been pre-classified (they would go on to be classified more finely and edited, checked, and then passed to Professor Michael Samuels for a final proof). Although I have edited the material to be included in the study using *HTE* guidelines, this may not correspond in all cases to the finished version of *HTE*, and there may be minor discrepancies of date or form. Moreover, I have not retained the classification into subsections with specific headings, since attending to these seemed in general to be unnecessary for my own investigation of the semantic field. However, I have used the broadest pre-classifications from the CLEVERNESS data, which give an indication of the type of intelligence connoted by each term (e.g. sharpness or shrewdness as opposed to common sense or genius). These are not discussed in detail in this volume, but they are included in the consideration of some groups where I have judged them to be relevant. There was nothing comparable to this set of divisions in the STUPIDITY data.

The main difficulty I encountered in using data from unfinished sections of *HTE* was the apparent lack of some terms that seemed to me to belong in these groups, and in several cases I intended to add these terms to my own data. However, I have not done this, since I believe that time did not allow me to review in any ordered or comprehensive way all the data that might be missing. It seemed preferable, and more theoretically justifiable, to work with the data as it existed at a particular stage of *HTE* whilst acknowledging that this may be incomplete. This is especially the case given the current revision of the *OED*, which will in turn affect *HTE* data and may lead to a number of insertions and changes in later editions; one of the areas that this may affect most is the inclusion of recent words. However, I do not believe that these omissions and discrepancies affect the observations made in this study, even though they may necessitate an adjustment in some percentages and statistics. As I have already stated, this study is not intended to be quantitative, and the figures I have included are only intended to give some impression of the balance between particular groups of data. This might serve to identify concepts that appear to be important diachronically or particularly productive at certain points in time, but it is certainly not an end in itself.

### 1.3.5 *Dating of entries*

Like all the information in the database, the dates that are attached to the individual entries are the dates given in *HTE*, with a few exceptions accounted for by the above explanation. These are based on written sources that are dated as precisely as possible, but this does not mean that they can be taken to be definitive. The dates given in any historical dictionary are always open to improvement,[5] and because of its unusual size and detail, the way in which it was compiled, and above all its age, the *OED* can be particularly problematic. The first edition was completed in 1928, and although the second edition was published relatively recently (in 1989), this was essentially the same work with the supplement integrated into it, and incorporated very little revision. This means that the huge body of research conducted since the first edition, spanning 75 years, has not been consulted, and some of this contains information that can improve the accuracy of *OED* dates. The *OED* is currently undergoing its first total revision, to create a new edition, and the datings of a considerable number of entries have been affected by new evidence. A comparison of a sample of *OED2*

---

[5] Definitive dates could only ever be given in a historical dictionary if it were based on a completely closed corpus comprising of all the surviving texts from a period or area; even in this case the evidence used would only be relevant to written, recorded language.

and *OED3* entries conducted by Durkin suggests that the dates given in *OED2* should be treated with care, since revisions affect a high proportion of items:

> Of the 245 *OED2* items with sixteenth-century first dates, 142 (58%) have the first date unchanged in *OED3*, while the remaining 42% have changed first dates, 61 (25% of the total) as a result of ante-dating, 41 (17%) as a result of redating of the existing first quotation, and one as a result of the existing first quotation being rejected ... I hope to have demonstrated some of the possible pitfalls in making uncritical use of dictionary data, especially where complex data such as that provided by the *OED* is to be used for statistical purposes ... Caution is therefore advisable when making use of such data for statistical purposes ... (Durkin 2002: 68–75)

While not all of the redatings discussed here involve long periods, a significant number do, and for one entry the first date has been adjusted by almost 350 years (although this is certainly exceptional). This is an important point in relation to the data used in this study, and any observations about the datings of individual items can only be speculative, based on the best evidence that is available. I have made only limited reference to the dates attached to particular items and groups, which are not discussed at length or in great depth here, but there is some consideration of what particular date ranges might imply: in Chapters 3 and 4 I have looked at the date ranges of the complete groups of data, and made various suggestions to account for these. Chapter 2 is the only one in which my argument is built on dating evidence, but this is well sourced and relates to the OE period rather than to any specific decade or even century.

## 1.3.6 *Data analysis*

My starting point in analysing the *HTE* data was to look closely at etymological information supplied in the *OED*. This was done for every entry in the data, as it seemed particularly important to avoid preconceived ideas about what constituted metaphor from the outset. From this initial analysis, some groups emerged in the data. A large number of items shared elements and roots, because these were either variant forms of one another or compounds: for example, *simple* and *silly* each had several variant forms; there is a large group of entries that derive from PIE *\*weid-* ( > PDE *wise, wit, vision*, etc; discussed in chapter 2); and there are 175 entries that are compounds formed from *head*. Beyond this, particular concepts were repeated in the data, and entries relating to these could be collected together. For example, the ANIMAL entries quickly emerged as a group, as did the VISION entries, and there were several other smaller clusters of entries like those relating to AGE and STRENGTH/WEAKNESS.

To label these recurring concepts, which I have taken to relate to motivation in the entries that are metaphorical or metonymical, I have used the label 'core concept'. This is a purposely general term, since it is appropriate to describe sources involving conceptual mappings but also concepts that might be regarded as being more 'literal' in nature, such as elements like brain that are found in compounds. These core concept labels are not mutually exclusive, and a large proportion of entries have been assigned to more than one core category. This might be the case if there has been a significant shift in meaning: for example, words derived from the Latin root *capere*, such as perceived aj 1400, are labelled both as SENSE – TOUCH, which seems to have been the core meaning of this root, and as SENSE – VISION, reflecting the semantic shift that affected many English derivatives of this root. Equally, entries might have multiple labels if they are compounds of two elements, or if it seems unhelpful to distinguish only a single core concept when a second might equally apply. In cases where there seems to be one motivating factor reflected in the most salient core concept, but if there is one (or more) other that might also be significant in the mapping, this is noted and discussed.

Obviously, a large number of entries that presented problems in this kind of classification. The etymological information presented in any dictionary will be incomplete, as there is often insufficient or problematic evidence from which to build up a picture of the roots of a lexical item, and the *OED* is no exception. For entries where no etymology is suggested, or where the etymology is doubtful, this has been indicated in the core concept field in the database.

It should be pointed out that, in most cases, I have split compound words into their parts and examined each one separately. This seems to be the most appropriate method of analysis in most cases, since the meaning of the majority of compounded entries in this corpus seems to be a sum of their parts (for example, this is clearly the case for almost all of the HEAD and BRAIN entries).[6]

It also enabled me (and would enable other potential users of the database) to run queries that pull out all the entries relating to a particular core concept – and this has been useful, as my study shows. The derivation field offers the opportunity of searching by particular lexical root, since these are given in a standardised form to link expressions with common derivation. The forms that I have used for these roots are the earliest forms from the source language where relevant, for example if there are several different derivatives from a single root as there are in the VISION group (with PIE *weid*- in common). In this and similar cases, I have also supplied the more immediate root to enable

---

[6] There are a few entries where the INTELLIGENCE meaning results specifically from the compounded form, and where this is the case I have categorised the entry accordingly and commented on the entry if the group to which it belongs is discussed.

searches that will recover only the most closely related forms (i.e. an entry in this field might read *videre* < \**weid-*, or *wit* < \**weid-*). In all cases I have used a PDE form unless this is misleading (e.g. *wise* rather than *wisan*), since this seems more useful to potential database users, who may not be familiar with these other forms. For the same reason, etymological information has not been given in this field if it does not seem relevant, and again in these cases I have supplied the most obvious form (in my judgement). At all times I have tried to supply all the information that will enable the most comprehensive list to be recovered when queries are run.

As described above, I have based my classification on etymology supplied by the *OED*. If there are two possible root senses, the one favoured by the *OED* is given; if there is no bias shown I have filed either in a general category which would accommodate both (if the senses are closely related) or under categories corresponding to each sense. In a few cases I have used the evidence of the other INTELLIGENCE data and my own judgement to decide which source meaning, or which aspect of the source meaning, is more likely to be relevant, and for any entries that are discussed this is noted. If there are a number of root senses supplied but OE clearly adopts only one, or one is attested significantly earlier than the others in OE, I have used that sense. If this is not the case, but several of the senses are possible sources for the INTELLIGENCE sense, the entry will be labelled 'etymology/ category uncertain' (and where appropriate, further comment will be made). I have tried not to make assumptions that are not evidenced: if a word appears with two senses from around the same time I have not presumed that one is earlier even if this would seem to be a natural conclusion. In some cases where the *OED* is unclear or uncertain about an etymology I have consulted the *Oxford Dictionary of English Etymology* (*ODEE*);[7] if this provides any clarification I have used it as further evidence and classified accordingly. If not, I have filed under 'etymology unknown'. Where there is no evidence of transfer from an earlier meaning, I have labelled entries INTELLIGENCE.[8] In many cases, it may be that additional information about etymology that might affect this classification is available in sources I have not consulted for every entry in the group, such as Holthausen's *Altenglisches Etymologisches Wörterbuch*. However, had I conducted more detailed research on all the items in the data (including those that are not discussed at any length or may not be mentioned in the main section of the book), this would have necessitated

---

[7] It should be stated that Onions's research in *ODEE* is not independent of the *OED*, but in some cases it provides more detailed supplementary evidence. This is especially the case for lexical items starting with letters early in the alphabet, since these were published earliest by the *OED*, and further evidence on their etymological history was available by the time Onions's work was completed.

[8] As with all of the other core category groups, this label may be used alongside others, e.g. for compound words, where there has been significant semantic change etc.

also the evaluation of competing etymologies, and hence entailed primary etymological work, which is not the focus of this study. This does mean that a small number of the etymologies may be disputed elsewhere, or that a small number of items may have been excluded from the core category groups to which reference is made. In general, though, I am confident that this is unlikely to invalidate the main arguments presented here.

If a word has a recognisable root but its INTELLIGENCE sense clearly emerges form its use in a specific context (e.g. light-weight n 1885 > , which is obviously a figurative use of the technical sense in boxing), I have categorised it according to its sense in this context (more or less specifically). Similarly, if a sense emerges centuries after its root sense with no continuation of use but has clearly been influenced by some other usage/context, I have tried to consider this.

For OE words, if a later descendant is listed in the *OED*, I have used the etymological information supplied by the *OED*. If not, I have used Bosworth & Toller's *Anglo-Saxon Dictionary*[9] to check for other meanings. If the word appears to have a concrete and abstract meaning, I have not assumed that the concrete meaning is the earliest, unless there seems to be evidence of this (e.g. gebeorglic aj OE appears to come from the noun *beorg* which has the concrete sense 'mountain' but no corresponding abstract sense). If I cannot go any further back than OE, I have put the word in a general core category group, i.e. either CLEVER or STUPID; if it is in the *OED* and there is an OE sense but the etymology is listed as obscure, unknown or uncertain, I have used this information in my categorisation. I have not marked length in any OE words in this volume or in the database, partly because, as far as possible, I have tried to avoid using symbols in the database for simplicity of use.


## 1.4 THE DATA: SOME PRELIMINARY COMMENTS


### 1.4.1 *STUPID VS. CLEVER*

As noted in the previous section, there is a significantly higher number of items that signify stupidity than cleverness in the data. This is in line with the general observations made by a number of linguists about derogatory vocabulary. Ullmann comments: '*Pejorative* developments are so common in language that some early semanticists regarded them as a fundamental tendency, a symptom of a "pessimistic streak" in the human mind' (1962: 231); he goes on to say that whilst the opposite kind of semantic change can also be observed, ' *"ameliorative"* developments ... on the whole ... seem to be less frequent' (p. 233). Waldron specifically discusses this trend in

---

[9] By this I mean Bosworth & Toller's 1898 edition, together with Toller's 1921 supplement and Campbell's 1972 addenda and corrigenda.

relation to the vocabulary of INTELLIGENCE, and suggests that this is a semantic area that is particularly prone to pejoration.

> The group of epithets denoting human cleverness, a quality which may easily be mistrusted by those who are exploited by it, shows a continuous trend towards pejoration. *Crafty* meant 'strong, power-ful, mighty' in OE but this sense became obsolete after the four-teenth century. There is a secondary sense in OE 'skilful, dexterous, clever, ingenious', which persists until the nineteenth century. The negative 'wily, cunning' appears in LME and co-exists with the favourable meaning, until in PresE it remains as the dominant sense ... [The] earliest adjectival sense [of *cunning*] in ME is 'learned, skilful', a meaning which is still recognized, if only as an archaism ... the current bad sense is first recorded in 1599. Again and again we find the same story: *artful* means 'learned, wise' in the seventeenth century; later this meaning narrows chiefly to 'skilful in practical ways', which gradually passes over into 'deceitful, cunning' ... *Sly*, which is from Scandinavian ... is yet another example of the same type of development. (Waldron 1979: 158–9)

These observations are mirrored by my own findings, and there are 56 entries in the INTELLIGENCE data, relating to various kinds of cleverness, that are marked 'derog' (i.e. derogatory).

Aside from this, some of the variation in forms that can be found in the STUPIDITY entries – which can account for the fact that some roots are productive and yield a number of entries – may also be associated with the fact that many of these terms are slang. Intuitively, it would seem that these are more likely to be used flexibly.[10] Having said that, in practice there is more variation in forms in the CLEVERNESS entries, and in fact the root that exhibits the greatest number of variant forms is PIE *weid-*, discussed in Chapter 2.

The balance in the OE data, which is the opposite to that in the rest of the group, may be explained by considering the nature of OE texts. Obviously, it was extremely expensive to produce any texts in OE, and to a certain extent this constrained the types of material that were copied. Most tended to deal with religious material, either the Bible itself or devotional or instructional texts. By nature, and because of the relatively formal register in which they tend to be written, these are unlikely to contain much in the way of colourful or creative terminology to describe stupid people; rather, they focus to a great extent on wisdom, either the wisdom possessed by divinities and saints, or that which humans should strive for in discipleship to God, and for this reason CLEVERNESS expressions are well represented in this body of texts. The *HTE* pre-classification that divides the entries into

---

[10]  e.g. *wido* for 'wide boy' and similar cases.

specific types of cleverness indicates that these entries are associated predominantly with particular kinds of intelligence: 68 entries are labelled CLEVER-WISE,[11] and there are no entries at all relating to common sense.

## 1.4.2 *The core concept groups*

This book is not intended to be a comprehensive analysis of all the core concepts involved in the conceptualisation of intelligence; assuming this were possible, it would be an enormous undertaking, and would involve extensive and meticulous research in numerous disciplines, including etymology, history and psychology. My intention in surveying the INTELLIGENCE data is to give an overview of the issues involved, and to try to gain insights into the workings of metaphor by the observation of empirical data. I will not examine all of the data, or discuss each of the core concept groups I have identified in detail (although I will refer to many of these within other sections).

Below is a list of all the labels I have used in the core concept field of the database. A number of these, which are not mentioned in this book, require further examination, and are best thought of as useful working labels rather than as suggested core concept groups. All the groups to which reference is made are emboldened; full tables of these are given in alphabetical order by core concept in appendices at the end of the volume. The core concepts that are dealt with in detail in Chapters 2, 3 and 4 are the SENSES, DENSITY and ANIMALS respectively. More detail about each of these is given in section 1.4.6.

**AGE**
**ALIVE/ANIMATE**
**ANIMAL**
**ANIMAL** − **BIRD**
**ANIMAL** − **BIRD** − **BUZZARD**
**ANIMAL** − **BIRD** − **COCK**
**ANIMAL** − **BIRD** − **CUCKOO**
**ANIMAL** − **BIRD** − **DAW**
**ANIMAL** − **BIRD** − **DOTTEREL**
**ANIMAL** − **BIRD** − **DOVE**
**ANIMAL** − **BIRD** − **EAGLE**
**ANIMAL** − **BIRD** − **GOOSE**
**ANIMAL** − **BIRD** − **LOON**
**ANIMAL** − **BIRD** − **SPARROW**
**ANIMAL** − **BIRD** − **WIDGEON**
**ANIMAL** − **FISH**
**ANIMAL** − **FISH** − **COD**

---

[11] One of these expressions was in two subgroups of the *HTE* classification, and is therefore labelled both WISE and INTELLIGENT in my database.

ANIMAL — FISH — LOACH
ANIMAL — FISH — MULLET
ANIMAL — FISH — SMELT
ANIMAL — INSECT
ANIMAL — INSECT — BEETLE
ANIMAL — INSECT — NIT
ANIMAL — INSECT — SNAIL
ANIMAL — MAMMAL
ANIMAL — MAMMAL — APE
ANIMAL — MAMMAL — BOVINE
ANIMAL — MAMMAL — DONKEY
ANIMAL — MAMMAL — PUPPY
ANIMAL — MAMMAL — SHEEP
ANIMAL — MAMMAL — SHREW
ANIMAL — MAMMAL — SQUIRREL
ANIMAL — MAMMAL — VERMIN
BEAUTY
BIRTH/CREATION
BODY PART
BODY PART — SEXUAL
BRAIN
BRAVERY
CARE/CONSIDERATION
CLOTHING/FOOTWEAR
COHERENCE
COLOUR
COMPLETION
CONTACT
CONTAINER
CONTAINER — EMPTY/FULL OF NOTHING
COUNT/RECKON
COURAGE
DECEIVE/CONFUSE
DENSITY
DENSITY — EARTH/TURF
DENSITY — FOOD
DENSITY — FOOD — GRAIN
DENSITY — FOOD — MEAT
DENSITY — FOOD — GENERAL
DENSITY — FOOD — MISC
DENSITY — WOOD
DILIGENCE
DIVIDE/SEPARATE

DIVINE/SUPERNATURAL
DRUNK
EASINESS
EXPERTISE
FACIAL EXPRESSION/FEATURE
**FAT**
FIERCE/CRUEL
FLEXIBLE/YIELDING
**FRUIT/VEG**
GENTLE/MILD
**GOOD/HAPPY**
**HARD/SOFT**
**HEAD**
**HEALTH — PHYSICAL/MENTAL**
**HIT/STUNNED**
**HUMAN**
**HUMBLE/ORDINARY**
HURT/INJURE
IDLE/WEARY
INFERIOR/SUPERIOR
**INTELLIGENCE**
JUDGEMENT
KNOWLEDGE
**LIQUID/SEMI-LIQUID**
**LOOSE TEXTURE**
**LUMP**
**MIND**
MISCELLANEOUS
MOVEMENT
MUDDLE
NATIVE/INHABITANT
**OBJECT**
OCCUPATION
OPEN
PERSONAL NAME
PICK UP/CHOOSE/GATHER
PLEASING/AGREEABLE
POWER/ABILITY
PROVIDED
**PURE/CLEAN**
QUALITY
QUANTITY
READY/PREPARED

RIGHT/LEFT
**SENSE — GRASP (TOUCH)**
**SENSE — HEARING**
**SENSE — SMELL**
**SENSE — TASTE**
**SENSE — VISION**
**SENSE — VISION — LIGHT/CLEARNESS**
**SENSE/FEELING**
**SHAPE**
**SHARP/PIERCING**
**SIZE**
SKILL
SLEEP
SMOOTH/LEVEL
SOLID/STEADY
**SOUND**
SPACE/DISTANCE
**SPEECH**
**SPEED**
**STRENGTH/WEAKNESS**
SUITABLE/APPROPRIATE
TEACHING/ADVICE
THOUGHT
UP/DOWN
USELESS/INVALID
**VALUE**
**WEALTH/PROSPERITY**
WEARY/FATIGUED
**WEIGHT**
WORLD

## 1.4.3 *The 'hierarchy' of core concepts*

The core concept groups that I have identified to classify the data vary in nature and generality. Some are closely aligned to very basic metaphorical sources like SIZE or CONTAINER, and these correlate with a large number of other core concepts in the data as well as constituting core concepts in themselves. Others, like the DENSITY group, are much more restricted and may rely to a greater extent on culture-specific influences (perhaps understandably, these tend to have been recognised and researched less). Correspondingly, these sources vary in their implications for the way intelligence is conceptualised. Some core concepts, whilst providing the motivation for a group of items in their own right, seem to be involved in the motivation for other groups as well; others are more narrow in their influence, and do not seem closely aligned with any other groups. This reflects Lakoff's observations about the inheritance hierarchies into which mappings fall. Lakoff suggests that the sources of metaphorical mappings can be organised into a hierarchy according to the extent to which they can combine with other sources and influence other mappings. The most basic and general mappings, like the SENSES group, are situated at 'higher' positions at the top of the hierarchy, while more specific, highly elaborate mappings which tend to be more culturally informed, like the DENSITY group, are placed in 'lower' positions. Mappings at the top of the hierarchy feed into those nearer the bottom, which 'inherit the structures of the "higher" mappings' (Lakoff 1993: 222). Primary metaphors, as classified by Grady (1997; discussed in section 2.5), fit into this classification at the top level, whilst the complex metaphors that can be broken down into several 'elements' operate at lower levels.

### 1.4.4 *Associations between core concepts*

As described in section 1.2, the term *core concept* is used because in many (and probably most) cases, expressions are motivated by more than one source concept, and examples of this are explored in the following three chapters. For several groups, this results from the nature of the sources themselves, rather than from the targets. Some concepts are bound up with one or more others, so that sometimes referring to a single concept 'automatically' implies others. This means that a network of associations can be drawn upon very economically (though this may not be done purposely or consciously).

For example, one concept that is very important in the way intelligence is conceptualised is SPEED.[12] In fact, there are few entries amongst the data that relate to this directly – only 15 entries in my classification – but the concept underlies a high number of expressions by being necessarily bound up with many other core concept groups. One of these is WEIGHT, which contains some entries derived from objects that are large and unwieldy, and one aspect of the burdensome nature of these objects is that they cannot be manoeuvred quickly. As this implies, for these entries large SIZE is also bound up with these other concepts. Aside from this, within ANIMAL there

---

[12] The table of entries relating to SPEED as a core concept is included in the appendix at the end of this volume. As the relevant column indicates, several of the entries, including all those derived from *quick*, do not have SPEED as their original motivation, but have been categorised in this group because of semantic shifts. *AHD* also suggests a semantic connection between the concept SPEED and *smart*. I have classified expressions derived from this item in SHARP, since this is the earliest sense suggested by the *OED* and indicated that *smart* follows the same kind of semantic path as *sharp*. *AHD* also draws attention to this and then goes on to make a link with SPEED: '*Smart* is a word that has diverged considerably from its original meaning of "stinging, sharp," as in *a smart blow*. The standard meaning of "clever, intelligent," probably picks up on the original semantic element of vigor or quick movement.'

are several entries including those in the subcategories BOVINE and SNAIL (discussed in Chapter 4) that are from animals recognised to be slow moving, and this naturally results from the direct relationship between speed and motion.

### 1.4.5 *MIND, HEAD and BRAIN*

The three groups that are the main focus of this study have been chosen because they represent particularly productive source concepts for INTELLIGENCE terms and are very different sorts of mapping (as I have described above). However, there are other core concepts to which a significant number of the entries in the database are related, and in fact these account for more entries than either ANIMALS or DENSITY. These are the MIND, and the HEAD and BRAIN.[13]

The first of these, which underlies a large group of entries, is the concept that I have labelled MIND. This is a problematic group: changing beliefs about the self have meant that the mental faculty is a particularly fuzzy concept, and terms used to refer to this have had varying denotations and connotations at different times in history. In modern popular consciousness, there is a dichotomy between the emotions and the intellect, which are held to be separate and often irreconcilable; in practice the distinction is not always sustainable, but it nonetheless exists as a powerful model. A person's emotional side is metonymized by the heart, and characterised as being illogical and unconnected to sense or reason. This contrasts with their mind or intellectual side, metonymized by the head or brain, which is logical and ruled by reason. However, this has not always been the popular view: traditionally there was a far more integrated concept of the intellect that did not divide the two aspects of the self. The range of *OED* definitions for *mind* (and other terms in the same semantic field such as *soul* and *will*) reflects this, and gives some indication of the broadness of the term at different times and the difficulty of attaching any clear limits corresponding to modern ideas to its earlier uses.[14] For example, in OE one sense of *mind* was closely connected with memory; the *OED* also lists the meaning 'The action or state of thinking about something; the thought *of* (an object)', with an earliest quotation dating to 971. A slightly later definition, with supporting quotations from c1340 to the present, gives a related but distinct meaning for the term:

---

[13] These have been labelled separately in the database so that they can be referenced individually, although they are very close conceptually.

[14] The term *intellect* fits in with a more clearly divided idea of the self, and correspondingly seems to surface much later than these others. The first supporting *OED* quotation is from Chaucer, dated to c1386, and this is given under the main definition, 'That faculty, or sum of faculties, of the mind or soul by which one knows and reasons (excluding sensation, and sometimes imagination; distinguished from *feeling* and *will*); power of thought; understanding. Rarely in reference to the lower animals.'

The seat of a person's consciousness, thoughts, volitions, and feelings; the system of cognitive and emotional phenomena and powers that constitutes the subjective being of a person; also, the incorporeal subject of the psychical faculties, the spiritual part of a human being; the soul as distinguished from the body.

The somewhat blurred boundaries that terms in this semantic field can have are mirrored in languages other than English: Buck notes the difficulty of distinguishing between the concepts referenced by a number of terms in a range of Indo-European languages. In his *Dictionary of Selected Indo-European Synonyms* he includes two separate categories, MIND (section 17.11) and SOUL/SPIRIT (section 16.11), but comments that there is not an entirely clear distinction between these:

> 'Mind' is intended here as the seat of intelligence, parallel to 'soul, spirit' (16.11) as the seat of emotions. But, as already remarked in 16.11, the two groups overlap. Several of the words there listed may cover also the 'mind', and conversely many of those in this list cover mental states in the widest sense, that is, may be used with reference to feelings as well as thoughts, Lat. *mēns*, Skt. *manas-*, Grk. μοπ (rarely), OE *môd*, NE *mind*, etc. (Buck 1949: 1,198)

Many of the OE terms that are found in the data, and their reflexes in ME and/or PDE, reflect this kind of general meaning. Because of this, in order to avoid any false distinctions, I have placed all of these in a single core concept group labelled MIND, which contains a sizeable proportion of the data, 116 entries (over 10% of the total INTELLIGENCE corpus). Within the group there is a high level of repetition of roots, and this is partly due to the proportion of OE data. Thirty-six entries appear in OE only, and many of these are compounds of the same roots, combined in a variety of ways. For example, the data contains both gleawferhþ aj OE and ferhþgleaw aj OE, as well as both gleawmod aj OE and modgleaw aj OE; many of the entries have parallel formations with a different first or second element, including hygefæst aj OE and hohfæst aj OE, and wiswylle aj OE and wishycgende aj OE. More than half of the total entries, 57, are from forms related to *wit*; these are also included in the SENSE – VISION group, since they are ultimately descended from PIE *weid-*, for which Watkins suggests the meaning 'to see'.[15] Other particularly productive roots are *mind* (including the OE form *(ge)mynd*), which yields 13 entries, *sense* (from Latin *sens* and ultimately PIE *sent-*, for which Watkins suggests 'to head for, go'), which yields 11 entries, and OE *hyge* (and variant form *hycge*).

Most of the entries in MIND are compounds with modifying elements that relate to a second core concept, as in the PDE noun form *x-mind* and

---

[15] In the *OED* entry for *wit* (v1), **weid-* is glossed 'to see (?orig to find)'.

adjective form *x-minded*. I would suggest that the simplest reason for the formation of linguistic items with a MIND element, and the predominance of these rather than non-compounded forms (especially in the later data), is to make the meaning of these expressions more explicit. Many of the specific entities that are sources in different core concept groups are found in more than one metaphorical mapping, and by referring metonymically to the respect in which the source is being mapped to the target a particular expression can be disambiguated. In the case of the INTELLIGENCE metaphors, the target is ultimately a person, so by using this kind of modified compound it is clear that mental abilities are being referred to, rather than any other aspect of the person such as appearance (for example). In most cases, metaphorical sources tend to become conventionally associated with particular targets over a period of time, but this may not always be the case. If an expression is coined that reflects a novel mapping, or if its source is a specific example of a more generic group (as is the case with the DENSITY items), it may not have become conventionalised, and the second element may clarify the meaning. However, it should be pointed out that the *x-mind* form[16] is itself a conventionalised formula, and is found even with sources that are very strongly associated with intelligence and also occur in expressions without a second element. Apart from this type of compound, the MIND group also contains entries that are composed simply of an expression for the mind, which can be affixed positively (e.g. with *-ful* or *-y*, as in andgietful aj OE or witty < (ge)wittig aj OE-1784 + 1886) negatively (e.g. with *un-* or *-less*, as in unwita n OE or heartless aj 1382–1611). A few entries have more than one affix, such as unandgitfull aj OE. In all of these entries, terms associated with the mind will automatically imply cleverness rather than stupidity unless modified negatively.

The same is true of entries that are formed with a HEAD or BRAIN element. The mapping of the abstract entity MIND to a physical organ or body part represents one of the most basic elements of the way intelligence is conceptualised in English, as well as in many other languages. This is a metonymy in which the physical organ related to thought, the brain, or the body part in which the brain is enclosed, the head, is used to stand for the less concrete concept of the mind or intelligence. The use of the physical in metaphorizing the mental can be seen in most of the core concept categories I have identified, though exactly what is mapped to the physical varies. For example, for the SENSES group, ideas are mapped to physical objects; CONTAINER, and related groups including DENSITY, additionally map the mind itself to a physical object.

---

[16] The OE entries have more flexible composition, but essentially most of these are similar in the way that they are formed from a MIND element with a modifying element (either preceding or following) that relates to another concept, as in the examples above.

Again, the majority of items in this group, which has a combined total of 203 entries, are of the noun form *x-head/-brain* or the derived adjective form *x-headed/-brained* (obviously *head* or *brain* can be substituted with a different expression for the same entity, e.g. *dome* or *skull* for 'head'). The modifying first elements in these items appear to be able to come from any other core concept group. Only nine entries in the HEAD and BRAIN group do not conform to this same pattern, and these are motivated by this core category without any other source. Five of these are simple expressions for the head or the brain;[17] the remaining four are suffixed, one (the only noun) with *-ist*, one with *-y*, and two with the negative *-less*. The latter, brainless aj c1470 > and headless aj 1526 >, both signify stupidity, while all the others bar one signify cleverness. This can be explained by the relationship between the head or brain and the mental: because these parts of the body are the most closely associated with thought and knowledge, they can be used to stand for the mind and intelligence in general, and in this capacity they will naturally have a positive meaning if unmodified, just as is the case with the MIND entries.[18] The one exception to this rule is noll n 1399 + 1566 The core meaning of *noll* is given in the *OED* as 'The top or crown of the head; the head generally'. Despite having this neutral meaning on its own, all of the phrases and compounds in which *noll* is found, including those within my data, are negative – for example, it is commonly collocated with the epithet *drunken*. The meaning 'a stupid person' seems to result from this frequent association with negative qualities, and in particular with expressions signifying stupidity.

Although one might expect that the more direct relationship between the brain and cognition than between the head and cognition might be reflected in the data, in fact the opposite is true. There are a far greater number of HEAD entries than BRAIN entries: 174 compared to only 29, i.e. more than six times as many. As well as this, the earliest entry in the BRAIN group is brainless aj c1470 >, whereas the earliest attested HEAD entry is found in OE (heafod n OE). One possible explanation for this is a lack of awareness of the role of the brain historically among non-experts, though evidence suggests that the majority of ordinary English-speaking people have probably known about the existence of the brain and its integral role in

---

[17] One of these is a plural form, the brains n 1925 >.
[18] Cf. Glucksberg & Keysar's (1993) observations about 'most salient part', also discussed in Ch. 4 below.

mental processes for several centuries.[19] However, this does not mean that it had acquired the level of familiarity that seems to be desirable in metaphorical mappings. Moreover, it seems to me that it is natural to think of the head as a reference point in assessing or commenting on a person's intelligence. Obviously the head contains the brain, but as well as this it is physically visible, and all our key impressions about a person's intelligence are gained from the face, from expressions and in particular the eyes. All of the senses apart from touch are related to organs located visibly on the head, and again the eyes must be particularly significant given the strong conceptual link between vision and perception, discussed in Chapter 2. The linguistic data in this study, for the most part, reflects ordinary and widespread usage rather than technical language, and therefore it should represent the way in which intelligence is regarded in general rather than by specialists. Perhaps in this context, and for the above reasons, the head is conceptually more salient than the brain.

### 1.4.6 *Focus of the study*

The main section of this book focuses on three groups of data, each related to a core category: these are the SENSES, ANIMALS and DENSITY. I have chosen these for two main reasons. First, they are all quantitatively important in the INTELLIGENCE data, and make up the three largest core concept groups (with the exception of MIND and HEAD, discussed above). As I have already stated, my research is not intended to be quantitative in itself, but I have used quantity as a useful indicator of the importance of particular concepts as sources for the metaphorisation of intelligence. However, perhaps more importantly than this, these groups are evidence of three very different mappings, and between them give some sense of both the diversity and the complexity that metaphor and metonymy can exhibit and the range of factors that can influence mappings.

Chapter 2 deals with a group of mappings that are recognised to be key to the way intelligence is understood in a number of languages, and these are

---

[19] Evidence suggests that the brain was recognised to have a key role in thought processes at least as early as 450BC, when research was conducted by a Greek physician, Alcmaeon; but it is not until much later that this was generally acknowledged to be scientific fact. A number of other theories have been posited at various times. These include (in 335BC) Aristotle's theory that the brain merely assisted the main organ of thought, which he believed was the heart; three entries in the data, heartless aj 1382–1611, hearty aj 1382 and simple-hearted aj c1400–1711, relate to this idea, though not necessarily to Aristotle's views on the subject. In 170BC Galen proposed that the brain was a glandular organ designed to control the bodily humors, and this theory was particularly influential in medieval thinking. However, even if its workings were not accurately understood, the brain seems to have been widely acknowledged as the seat of intelligence by the middle ages; at this time a ban on human dissection and the study of anatomy precluded much further study in Europe, although some primitive surgery was still conducted. (The summary given here is based on information about the history of neurology from http://www.pbs.org/wnet/brain/history/.)

related to the SENSES. These mappings are recognised to be primary metaphors because of their experiential basis; their very basic nature means that they can combine with others to result in more complex, compound mappings. For example, the core category group GRASP seems to incorporate the idea of the CONTAINER metaphor as well as TOUCH, and in the ANIMAL group there are several bird entries that are influenced by the idea of lack of VISION.

The DENSITY group, discussed in Chapter 3, is evidence for a slightly different kind of mapping that involves both metaphor and metonymy. Fundamentally, the mapping is motivated by the metonymical link between intelligence and the head or brain, so that the physical make-up of the brain becomes an indicator of intelligence (or rather, lack of intelligence). However, the core concept DENSITY also seems to be strongly culturally informed, in that the specific entities that are found as sources for particular terms tend to be selected for familiarity and depending on other shared entities within a society. As well as this, elements of the mapping between DENSITY and INTELLIGENCE are shared with other metaphors. It is therefore informed by other mappings, but in itself it seems more specific and narrow in its influence on other metaphors and on language in general; for example, it does not generate verb expressions in the way that the senses group does.

The final group that is examined in detail, in Chapter 4, is the ANIMAL group. The items in this group exemplify a general tendency to link humans and animals (an even more generally, animate beings) through anthropomorphism and zoomorphism. Unlike the SENSES entries, which display the systematic connection that is made between physical and mental perception, ANIMAL metaphor are found in a wide (and potentially unlimited) range of semantic fields that relate to humans. Because of this, particular ANIMAL metaphors will always have an additional motivation relating to another concept. In every case it is some characteristic associated with the animal that is mapped, rather than animality in itself; but at the same time the mapping is grounded in a tradition of human-animal thought that appears to be a common and perhaps inevitable by-product of the way the brain is designed.

Other issues related to the data will be considered within the following three chapters, in the context of these groups.

# 2

# SENSES

## 2.1 Introduction

Since the emergence of cognitive linguistics as a discipline, its theories have become increasingly important within semantics, and have been shown to be useful in analyses of diachronic as well as synchronic material; Blank & Koch note that 'some of the favourite subjects of cognitive semantics (metaphor, metonymy, polysemy etc.) deal precisely with the synchrony/ diachrony-interface' (1999: 10). Despite this, detailed studies marrying cognitive and historical semantics have been relatively rare, although there are some notable examples. Eve Sweetser has examined etymological data whilst taking account of current theories and findings (see especially Sweetser 1990), and Dirk Geeraerts has explored historical material within a cognitivist framework (e.g. Geeraerts 1997); more recently, scholars including Sylvester (e.g. 2006), Tissari (e.g. 2003) and Blank & Koch (e.g. 1999) have continued to work in similar area, and have shown the importance and potential of historical material for developing cognitivist theories. In general, however, the influence has mostly been in one direction, and historical approaches have had considerably less influence on cognitive theories of semantics than vice versa.

Within the body of work of this kind that has been attempted, one of the best-known and most thorough studies is Sweetser's analysis of the metaphorical link between intellection and the senses (1984; 1990), which focuses most sharply on the pervasive connection between vision and intellection/perception. This has subsequently become one of the best-documented conceptual metaphors, and studies have been conducted into a variety of languages, though rarely if ever with the same attention to etymology. Sweetser claims that the mapping is ancient, and can be traced back through the roots of language. In her examination of some of the most common polysemous words she uses comparative techniques in considering Proto-Indo-European roots and their descendants in other languages.

> Such large-scale conceptual metaphors are of the highest importance for synchronic and diachronic semantic analysis. Through a historical analysis of 'routes' of semantic change, it is possible to elucidate synchronic semantic connections between lexical domains; similarly, synchronic connections may help clarify reasons for shifts of meaning in past linguistic history. (Sweetser 1990: 45–6)

It is this type of methodology that I believe is required in understanding conceptual metaphor, but I would contend that the etymological evidence should be reassessed in light of recent theories about metaphor acquisition and metonymy. In this chapter I will attempt to reconsider the senses as source concepts, and I will argue that new findings (especially Christopher Johnson's theory of conflation) have implications for the way in which we discuss the mechanisms of particular metaphorical and metonymical relationships.

## 2.2 DATA

The senses have long been recognised as pervasive contributors to our perception of mental perception itself. Vision and touch, particularly, are integral to our vocabulary about knowing and understanding, and this in part accounts for the amount of research into the connection between them that has been, and is still being, undertaken within a variety of disciplines. This is reflected in my own data: nearly a fifth of the words included in my database have connections with the senses (204 words –18.98%).[1] Of these, around 70% (141 words) are used to signify cleverness; to use the notation of Componential Analysis, most of the vocabulary here is [+ intelligence], i.e. focusing on the senses as conduits of knowledge rather than on a lack of the senses as an impediment to cognition.

It should be noted again here that, where there has been significant meaning shift through time, a word may be included in the database in more than one category. In this particular section this only affects two entries: perceived aj c1400 and perceiving aj c1410–1645 are both derived from PIE *kap-, meaning 'grip', which developed to be used simultaneously of vision and general intellection in the fourteenth century. One further entry, nimble-witted aj 1613/6 >, is found in two categories, in this case because it is a compound of *nimble*, from PGmc *nem- meaning 'assign, allot, take', and *wit*, from PIE *weid-, which will be discussed below.

---

[1] As noted in Section 1.3.6, I have classified the data by 'core concept': this is a purposely general term, since it includes both metaphorical and metonymical sources but also concepts such as those represented by one element in a compound word that might be regarded as more 'literal' in motivation, for example *brain*. Included in the core concept SENSES IS LIGHT, which I regard as a special extension of VISION (this is discussed below). I have also identified a further group of data, the core concept of which I have termed SENSE/FEELING, but this has not been included here. Since words within this particular group are not related to particular physical senses (e.g. vision or touch), it is difficult to determine whether they can correctly be associated with the physical senses or are more sensibly identified with some kind of abstract 'mental' sense (or, as seems most likely, whether they carry a generalised meaning with elements of both). It should also be pointed out that words can be classified with more than one core concept if they have undergone significant meaning shifts. For example, words derived from the Latin root *capere*, such as perceived aj c1400, appear both in SENSE-TOUCH, following the meaning of this root, and in SENSE-VISION, reflecting a semantic shift.

## 2.2.1 *VISION*

Quantitatively, vision is by far the most important sense, accounting for 157 entries, around 77% of the SENSES data, and just under 15% of the total data. The striking feature of this group is the very limited number of root forms from which the entries are derived. The most productive of these roots is the reconstructed PIE root *weid-; including compounds, 106 words can be traced back to this root, through various later forms. The *OED* suggests that five of these have come through French from Latin *videre*, and that the remainder are from OE *witan* and related forms (*(ge)wit, wis, wissan,* etc.; it is often difficult to be clear about exactly which form is the direct source of a particular item, but roughly half are from a -*t*- form and half from an *s* form). 58 of the entries are current.

Two other root forms are particularly important in the VISION group. The first is OE *gleaw* (from PIE *ghel-*), which has 12 related entries, only one of which survives beyond the OE period. The other is OE *seon* (from PIE *sek^w-), from which *see* and *sight* are derived, and this is responsible for 11 entries dating from a1425 onwards; seven of these are current. There is further repetition of sources in the remaining 28 entries, but not to the same extent: four are from OE *blind* (from PIE *bhlendh-*); two are from OE *dwæs*; two are from OE *sceawian* (from which PDE *show* is derived, and which can be traced back to PIE *(s)keu-*); two are derived from Latin *illuminare*, from *lumen*, and one from the related Latin *lucere* (both ultimately from PIE *leuk-*); two are derived from Latin *perspicere* (from PIE *spek-*); two are compounds of *eye* (from PIE *ok^w-); two are from Latin *capere* (from PIE *kap-*; the sense progression of these items is discussed above); two appear to be forms of PDE *gowk*; two forms are from *opaque* (from Latin *opacus*); three are compounds of *clear*.[2] Two entries are from *understand*, which has been shown convincingly to be connected with light by Hough.[3] There are two entries with no repetition of sources, hlutor aj OE, and dim aj 1892 >, and *bright* appears in the data as a complete entry twice (bright aj 1741 > and bright aj 1824 + 1885 >) because it carries two distinct senses representing different types of intelligence.[4]

---

[2] This includes clear-eyed aj 1530 >, which has already been mentioned as a compound of *eye*.

[3] This has been a major source of controversy in recent years. Despite the fact that *understand* is one of the most central terms connected with the mental, there does not seem to be any comparable expression with a similar source relating to position or posture. This is borne out by the INTELLIGENCE data, in which there are no items that can be obviously grouped alongside these entries. However, Hough (2004) argues that *understand* is a LIGHT metaphor that has become conventionalised by making reference to other OE compounds of *stand* that mean 'shine'.

[4] The duplication is a result of the classification in *HTE*, in which different types of 'cleverness' are placed in different subsections. I have preserved it here because there are different citation dates for each sense, and I feel that it is misleading to merge the entries, even though I recognise that this is a somewhat clumsy solution.

It is difficult to comment at length on the implications of this level of lexical production from a few sources, but I am convinced that it must be significant. To a certain extent, the higher number of related forms must merely be the result of natural processes of language change. Some variation in forms is due to the variety of routes through which individual words, or individual morphemes, have entered English, and this accounts for the orthographical difference, and in part for the semantic difference, between *wit* and *vision*; the fact that they have the same root in PIE *\*weid-* is academic in this respect. The huge number of very similar forms varying only in affixes, many of which have very limited periods of usage (cf. witful aj c1205–1614, witty aj 1340–1611, witted aj 1528–1606, wittiful aj 1590) may occur simply because English in the late Middle and Early Modern periods was less standardised than in later periods, and therefore greater variation in affixed forms from the same base was generally tolerated. As well as this, there are a huge number of compounds in this group which share an element: for example, there are 23 entries that are modified compounds of *witted* alone.[5]

Despite these considerations, there would still seem to be an unusually large number of single-root derivations, and the number of words derived from PIE *\*weid-* seems fairly exceptional. In my opinion, it is certainly possible that this reflects the centrality of vision in the conceptualisation of intelligence. New words are coined from an established root form either because a need arises – perhaps because there is no available vocabulary for the particular part of speech required – or because a writer or speaker chooses not to use lexemes that are already available to him/her. This might happen for a number of reasons: for example, established forms may have picked up connotations that the writer wishes to avoid, or he/she may feel that a more appropriate or 'grander' stylistic effect can be created by use of a different formation. Whether it is the case that the coining occurs as a matter of necessity or choice, it still demonstrates the perceived 'aptness' of the root to express a particular concept, and in turn this must mirror the import of this concept. In this case, this must offer some indication of the way in which vision is key to human understanding of intelligence.

In its turn, this cumulation of single-root vocabulary must lead to a snowball effect: the very fact that this root is frequently exploited must attract further exploitation. This applies to the compound words as well, since the initial use of a word or element in a compound very often lays a foundation for the appearance of more, similar compounds.[6]

---

[5] One of these is the entry witted (with prec. modifier) 1377>; this represents a general tendency to make compounds from this element, including some nonce-words mentioned in the *OED* but not included in this data such as *two-third-witted*.

[6] The same sort of effect is evident in other areas of my data; see especially the DENSITY group, in which very few specific substances are found in a relatively large number of vocabulary items and come to be conventionally associated with INTELLIGENCE.

A further aspect of the data that should perhaps be commented on is the balance between CLEVER and STUPID words in this group of data. As I have already commented, in the data as a whole there are far more STUPID than CLEVER words, but this is not reflected in the OE data, which is made up of 41 CLEVER words and only 10 STUPID words. A large proportion of the OE words come from the *weid- root, 33 in total, and of these 27 signify cleverness. This is certainly a result of the nature of sources surviving from this period: most of these are biblical or related texts, many on the theme of wisdom (as discussed in chapter 1, section 1.2).

Overall in the VISION group, there are more words denoting cleverness than stupidity: out of the total 157 entries, 110 are linked with cleverness, and 47 with stupidity. As I commented above, this is consistent with the focus on the senses as conduits of intelligence. Predictably, because vision and blindness are clear opposites, there is clear symmetry in the data in that vision is always associated with cleverness and lack of vision with stupidity.

## 2.2.1.1 LIGHT

Within the VISION group, 34 entries are more specifically connected with LIGHT, although in many cases it is difficult to make a clear distinction between VISION and LIGHT as sources; for example, clear is from Latin clarus, which the OED defines as 'bright, clear, manifest, plain, brilliant, illustrious, famous, etc.'. Of the entries, 16 occur in OE, and 12 of these are compounds derived from PIE *ghel- (of which only one survives beyond the OE period, glew < gleaw aj OE-c1290). The rest are from a variety of sources. Three derive from PIE *leuk-, three from dim (<OE dim), and three from clear (< Latin clarus); two each are from dwæs, clear, bright and opaque; and the final entry is hlutor aj OE. The data is symmetrical in that bright and semantically related lexemes always equals clever and dim/dark and semantically related lexemes stupid, Although there are more entries signifying cleverness (a total of 21), there are still a number associated with stupidity (13); this is a similar bias to that found in the VISION data as a whole.

The particular motivation for the LIGHT group, as a subgroup of VISION, is discussed below.

## 2.2.2 TOUCH

In this section there are 32 items, making this the second largest group within the SENSES data (accounting for 15.69%, and just under 3% of the total data). Again, there is some duplication of roots, though not on the scale of the VISION group. The most productive root is PIE *kap- (< Latin capere), which accounts for 11 entries, dating as early as c1300 but mainly from the fifteenth and sixteenth centuries onwards, and four of these are current with this particular meaning.[7] A further six entries are from *clever*[8] (from PIE *\*gleubh-*), one dating from 1716 and the rest from the mid-nineteenth century, and all but one in current use; five entries are from OE *numol* (from PGmc *\*nem-*), with reflex *nimble*;[9] five are from Latin *prehendere* (*pre* + PIE *\*ghend-*). The five remaining entries are compounds, phrases or derivatives of *feel*, *fetch*, *reach*, *take* and *tact*. All but eight entries signify cleverness, and of these, six are compounds with the negative prefix *un-*.

I have labelled this core concept GRASP(TOUCH), because in all cases the words here are more specifically connected with grasping. I would contend that this is a special case of touching which incorporates the concept of possession or enclosure. This is discussed at more length below.

### 2.2.3 *TASTE*

There are 12 entries in this section.[10] Ten of these have a common PIE root, *\*sap-*; this level of productivity can be partly accounted for by the fact that they have come into English by different routes. According to the *OED*, sapientipotent aj 1656 and sapientipotent n 1675, and insipid aj a1700–a1834, come directly from Latin (although insipid aj a1700–1834 does have a French cognate earlier than the English form); sapient aj 1471–1868 and sapient n 1549–1600 + 1827 come either directly from Latin *sapientem* or via OFrench *sapient*; sage aj 1297–1872 and sage n a1400–1862, and the later compound sage-like aj 1879, come through French and Common Romanic from Latin; and savvey/savvy aj 1905 > comes through French much later.

---

[7] Two of the words in this group sit somewhat uncomfortably with the rest of the data, and may not be best included in this core concept group. heavy aj c1300 > and heavy-headed aj 1590 > clearly relate better to some kind of concept of weight and perhaps slowness; this development of meaning, (which fits in with the MIND AS A CONTAINER metaphor, i.e. 'holding' weighty contents), is shown in the core concept field of the database. Despite this, I have included them here, since it is interesting that they share a root with this group.

[8] The etymology of *clever* is doubtful, but the *OED* and other sources tentatively attribute it to ME *cliver*, which is found only once before the sixteenth century in English but has cognates in Old Frisian and material found in Jutland. The explanation given in the *OED* for its semantics is as follows: 'The early example suggests relation to ME *clivers* "claws, talons, clutches", in the sense "nimble of claws, sharp to seize", and the 16–17th c. examples (also of *cleverly*) show it connected with the use of the hands, a notion which still remains in the general sense of *adroit*, *dexterous*, having "the brain in the hand".'

[9] *Nimble* occurs twice in the database, once in the entry nimble < numol aj OE–1483 and again in the entry nimble aj 1604 >. As with *bright*, discussed earlier, this is because in each case a slightly different type of cleverness (as distinguished by the *OED*) is represented. It is HTE policy to preserve the distinctions made by the *OED* wherever possible; the splitting of the senses is further justifiable because of the gap between the end and beginning of the date ranges.

[10] There in one entry in this section that is duplicated: *sage* (n) appears with two slightly different senses, 'wise' and 'wise derog', and different date ranges, following the *OED*'s classification.

This variation in direct source forms, and the range of cognates available in other languages, show that the 'intelligence' sense of the root was very well established before any forms had appeared in English; this perhaps makes it less theoretically sound to suggest TASTE as a core concept for this group. Having said that, this study is concerned with the ultimate sources of intelligence vocabulary and the motivation behind their processes of change, so I do not believe that this invalidates the categorisation I have adopted. Moreover, the fact that there are entries in this section related in concept but not in root, and more generally that *taste* (and other vocabulary in the same semantic field) has other current senses related to mental processes, makes it more plausible to make the connection.

## 2.2.4 HEARING

This is noticeably the smallest group in the SENSES data, with only six entries, all of which express stupidity and two of which have questionable etymology. The most central current adjective to express lack of ability to hear, *deaf*, is listed in the *OED* with a limited period of use with this particular meaning, ie deaf aj c1440–1482, although intuitively I suspect that there are shades of this in the expression 'Are you deaf?'. However, from comparative evidence, an older connection with the mental does seem plausible, and it may even be possible that the physical meaning is not the earliest (or at least no earlier than the mental meaning). The *OED* suggests the following etymology:

> A Common Teutonic adj.: OE. *déaf* = OFris. *dâf* (WFris. *doaf*), OS. *dôf* (MDu., Du., MLG. *doof* (*v*), LG. *dôf*), OHG. *toup* (*b*), (MHG. *toup*, Ger. *taub*), ON. *daufr* (Sw. *döf*, Da. *döv*), Goth. *daufs* (*b*) :– OTeut. *\*dauþ-oz*, from an ablaut stem *deuþ-, dauþ-, duþ*, pre-Teut. *dheubh-*, to be dull or obtuse of perception: cf. Goth. *afdaubnan* to grow dull or obtuse, also Gr. τυφλός (:—θυφ-) blind.

The important point is that the earliest reconstructed meaning appears to be more generally related to lack of perception/intelligence than the more specific PDE *deaf*. This is line with the reconstructed semantics of several of the other main sense-perception verbs, discussed below.

There is also some data on lack of ability to speak, within a group I have labelled SPEECH, and although this seems to me to be a separate concept it may be worth noting here. Although there is not a great deal of cross-over between the two groups within the data – only one entry, surd aj 1601–a1676, is from Latin *surdus*, which can mean 'deaf' or 'dumb' and is therefore classified into both groups – the two concepts do seem to fall together occasionally, presumably because they are often linked. There are 28 entries in the SPEECH group; the most important root for these is *dumb*, discussed below, from which ten entries are derived (two of these date back to the mid-sixteenth century, and the rest from around the beginning of the nineteenth).

## 2.3 MOTIVATION

The senses have long been recognised as central to our perception of perception itself, and the motivation for the mapping between physical and mental in this case is well-documented and seems relatively straightforward. It is a textbook case for cognitive metaphor theory (perhaps even a cornerstone example), since it demonstrates the way in which our physical being cannot be separated from the way we conceptualise, and consequently affects language. From very early experience, humans have access to knowledge and understanding through the physical senses, and as a result the process (gaining knowledge/understanding) and the end result (being knowledgeable/having understanding) are inextricably linked, to the extent that one affects the way the other is perceived. Put simply, the way in which we are able to access knowledge affects our perception of what it is to be intelligent.

As I have already outlined, there is a huge difference in the quantity of data relating to each of the senses, and this can be understood better if one considers these individually.

### 2.3.1 VISION

This is without doubt the most recognised and studied source field within the SENSES group, and has been variously expressed as KNOWING or UNDERSTANDING IS SEEING. The bias towards VISION in the data is explained by Sweetser in terms of human reliance on available, apparently 'shared' input:

> ... vision is connected with intellection because it is our primary source of objective data about the world. Child language studies (e.g. Clark 1976) have shown that visual features are among the most marked in children's early discrimination of one category from an-other; and, as mentioned earlier, cross-linguistic studies of eviden-tials show that direct visual evidence is considered the strongest and most reliable source of data. This is reasonable, since vast numbers of objects in daily life do not give forth auditory stimuli, and it would be impossible for the child to constantly taste, smell, or touch every object to be encountered. As the child matures, social under-standing of appropriate distance also develops; it may not merely be dangerous to touch or taste, it may be socially inappropriate to get that close. Vision gives us data from a distance ... Vision is also identical for different people – that is to say, two people who stand

in the same place are generally understood to see the same thing. (Sweetser 1990: 39)

Vision also appears to be the most 'general purpose' of the senses. Viberg comments on the way in which the verb *see* can 'extend its meaning to cover the other sense modalities' in English (1983: 140), and he compares this to verbs in other languages with a prototypical meaning 'see' that can extend to mean other ways of perceiving. This is discussed at more length below.

Apart from the experiential reasons for the status of vision, it is crucial to be aware of its cultural significance. Western society assigns vision such a privileged status that it has been described as 'ocularcentric' (Jay 1993: 4), and this is evident in all sorts of ways historically: preoccupation with signs and symbols, belief in the authority of the written word and, in modern times, dependence on visual media such as TV and film. It must be that, as well as reflecting it, this perpetuates and intensifies the way we value and trust the visual over (for example) the auditory. Of course, this is almost impossible to measure in any meaningful way.

## *2.3.1.1* LIGHT

LIGHT is generally accepted to be closely connected to VISION, and is very often included within this group – for example, Sweetser lists light alongside the eyes and facial movement as an example of 'The physical nature of sight' as a source concept (1990: 32), and Lakoff & Johnson present metaphors of light and vision together under the heading UNDERSTANDING IS SEEING; IDEAS ARE LIGHT SOURCES; DISCOURSE IS A LIGHT MEDIUM (1980: 49). I regard it here as a special case of VISION, with a sort of extended version of the same motivation. If it is preferable for one to be able to see in order to gain information, then light is preferable to darkness since it facilitates vision. If one is *bright* then presumably this will enable one to see, in order to have access to knowledge or understanding, and perhaps it may also enable others to do the same.

It is also important to note that this metaphorical connection fits into a network of correspondences or oppositions between qualities perceived as positive and negative, which are often associated with one another more or less consciously. Lakoff & Johnson refer to this 'system of overall external systematicity' in discussing spatial metaphors (1980: 18); similar links are also proposed by Hertz, though perhaps more philosophically, within his study of the dichotomy between left and right.

> All the oppositions presented by nature exhibit this fundamental dualism. Light and dark, day and night, east and south in opposition to west and north, represent in imagery and localise in space the two contrary classes of supernatural powers: on one side life shines forth and rises, on the other it descends and is extinguished. The same with the contrast between high and low, sky and earth ... The same

contrast appears if we consider the meaning of the words 'right' and 'left'. The former is used to express ideas of physical strength and 'dexterity', of intellectual 'rectitude' and good judgement, of 'up-rightness' and moral integrity, of good fortune and beauty, of jur-idical norm; while the word 'left' evokes most of the ideas contrary to these. (Hertz 1960: 96–9)

In his discussion of morality metaphors, Lakoff suggests that the states and qualities equated with morality as opposed to immorality are grounded in physical experience, and can be understood if one considers the corollaries of bodily wellbeing. He identifies a number of these states, which are all connected with the generally positive as well as with the moral.

In the basic physical sense, 'well-being' is constrained as follows: Other things being equal, you are better off if you are
*healthy* rather than sick,
*rich* rather than poor,
*strong* rather than weak,
*safe* rather than in danger,
*cared for* rather than uncared for,
*cared about* rather than ignored,
*happy* rather than sad, disgusted or in pain,
*whole* rather than lacking,
*beautiful* rather than ugly,
if you are experiencing *beauty* rather than ugliness,
if you are functioning in the *light* rather than the dark, and
if you can stand *upright* so that you don't fall down.
These are among our basic experiential forms of well-being. Their opposites are forms of harm. Immoral action is action that causes harm, that is, action that deprives someone of one or more of these – of health, wealth, happiness, strength, freedom, safety, beauty, and so on. (Lakoff 1996: 250).

A number of the core concept groups in the INTELLIGENCE data appear in this list, and in fact, this perhaps offers some form of explanation for a number of apparently 'miscellaneous' entries which are either isolated or in very small core category groups. BEAUTY is found only in beautiful-minded aj 1865; PURE/CLEAN has two entries, clean aj c1400 > and cleanly aj c1540–1712; there are five entries relating to WEALTH/PROSPERITY. A further 13 entries are connected with either physical or mental HEALTH; 14 can be grouped under STRENGTH/WEAKNESS; 23 relate in various ways to COMPLETION (similar to wholeness); as I have discussed already, 33 are connected with LIGHT. There are other core categories I would place alongside these which appear to have similar justifications: ALIVE/ANIMATE (12 entries) is an obvious addition; VISION (158 entries) certainly belongs, since light is primarily related to well-being because it enables vision; and arguably the BIRTH/CREATION group (17 entries) can be included since it is connected with life. Including all of these categories, 264 entries – well over a fifth of the total data – can be associated with this very general, positive 'experiential wellbeing' motivation.

There is an exception to this general pattern, which can be accounted for by examining the meaning development of the lexical root. There are six entries (one of these uncertain), all meaning stupid, derived from *silly*, which can be traced back to OE *gesǣlig*. This is clearly a positive term that one would expect to mean 'clever' – it is listed in *TOE* in the sections 08.01.01.03, 'Good feeling, joy, happiness', and several of its subsections, 15.01.05, 'Possession of wealth', and 16.02.01.10.02.01, 'A blessing, invocation of divine favour', and so fits in with the other 'experiential wellbeing' data. However, its history has several stages, partially similar to the development of *innocent*: very roughly,

> happy/blessed > innocent > helpless/pitiful/weak/unsophisticated > foolish/stupid

(based on Samuels 1972: 66, which analyses the semantic development of this term in a more detailed diagram; this is given in full below in Chapter 4, section 4.7). This accounts for its use as an adjective expressing non-intelligence.

## 2.3.2 TOUCH

The desire to touch things seems to be to be one of the most basic of human responses to the external world. Even before babies can recognise it, touching and holding on to things is a reflex, and as they mature this becomes more conscious.

As mentioned briefly earlier, most of the items within this group are related, not only to touch, but specifically to grasping or physically holding/ taking. In fact, this metaphorical link tends to be most commonly discussed in these terms; for example, Lakoff & Johnson discuss UNDERSTANDING IS GRASPING (1999: 124–5), and Grady (1997: 297) lists this as a primary metaphor (see section 2.5 below). However, in the light of the other senses data and because this mapping does not seem to be irreducible (Grady's criteria for identifying primary metaphor), I am not sure that this is the most helpful way to describe the link, which can be broken into simpler constituent 'parts'. At its most general level, it is an ontological metaphor, exemplifying the human tendency to objectify abstract concepts, since ability to have hold of an idea implies that this is a bounded physical entity.[11] In this sense it represents a very typical concrete/abstract

---

[11] See Barnden (1997) for a discussion of this metaphor: . It is also expressed more specifically as the primary metaphor KNOWLEDGE IS PHYSICAL CONTENTS OF THE HEAD by Grady (1997: 298).

relationship between source and target, perhaps itself the most basic of all mappings.

It also seems to me to be consistent with, if not closely related to, some kind of CONTAINER metaphor, since there is an element of encircling something completely with the hands rather than only having contact with it (having it *in* one's grasp). This may be linked to the idea of control: if one is holding a physical object one can manipulate it, and similarly if one really understands an idea one can make use of it intellectually.

It is noted above that almost all of the entries in this group signify cleverness rather than stupidity, and that of the STUPID words there are only two entries that are not negated compounds (as with the entries derived from *gesælig* discussed above, this can be explained by their semantic development). This seems to me to be a consequence of the source concept: the opposite of *vision* is *blindness*, and the opposite of *hearing* is *deafness*, but there is no central opposite concept of *touch* or *grasp*, and correspondingly no basic lexical term to express this. Having said that, there are perhaps echoes of the idea to be found in words or phrases expressing stupidity that do not appear in *HTE* data: for example, *handless* in Modern Scots originally denoted a lack of ability to work with the hands but has developed to mean 'stupid', since the most basic function that this part of the body performs is holding/grasping; the example 'I'm all thumbs at algebra' (Lakoff 1994) further supports this.

Most of the words in this group connote understanding rather than knowledge or intellectual prowess. *Clever* is a notable exception, which could be because it is not a prototypical member of this group. Despite the centrality of the term, its etymology is somewhat obscure, and there is general uncertainty about its origins, although most etymologists mention ME *clivers*, 'claws'. Both *OED* and *MED* cite the same single quotation of *cliver* (aj) from ME and give similar tentative meanings (*MED*: '?Expert in seizing'), and *OED* says the following:

> Early history obscure: app. in local and colloquial use long before it became a general literary word. A single example of *cliver* is known in ME., but the word has not been found again till the 16th c., and it appears not to have been in general use till the close of the 17th, since Sir Thos. Browne specially mentions it as East Anglian, and Ray explains it among his dialect words. Outside Eng., Koolman gives EFris. *clüfer* (from *clifer*), clever, skilful, alert, ready, nimble, and *klöver*, *klever* is used in same sense at Ribe Stift in Jutland (Molbech). The early example suggests relation to ME. *clivers* 'claws, talons, clutches', in the sense 'nimble of claws, sharp to seize', and the 16-17th c. examples (also of *cleverly*) show it connected with the use of the hands, a notion which still remains in the general sense of *adroit*, *dexterous*, having 'the brain in the hand'. Cf. also CLE-

VERUS. *Clever* appears to have come into general use about the time that *deliver*, formerly used in the sense 'expert', became obsolete, but there is no trace of any influence of the one upon the other. The sense-development has analogies with that of *nimble, adroit, handy, handsome, nice, neat, clean.*

Sweetser comments on the close association of touch with emotional perception, and suggests that this is a corollary of the fact that 'there is not a simple and tidy way to divide physical perception from emotion' (1990: 44). My own difficulty in classifying a group that I have labelled SENSE/FEELING testifies to this. These have been separated from the rest of the physical SENSES data, as particular words have such general meanings that it is impossible to say whether they should be presented as having earlier physical meanings; nevertheless, they should perhaps be considered alongside this group.

## 2.3.3 TASTE

Although there is little data in this section and almost all of this is from a single root, the link between TASTE and mental states or processes can be found in other parts of speech and phrases. For example, one can have *good* or *bad taste*; something can *leave a bad taste in one's mouth*; one can *taste freedom* or *victory*. Having said that, TASTE is a far less common source of any kind of intellection vocabulary. The main reason for this must surely be its lack of suitability as a source of information, which Sweetser refers to in her discussion of VISION (1990: 39, quoted above). It is clearly impossible, and might even be dangerous, to taste everything, aside from the fact that this is likely to be unproductive and inappropriate. As well as this, it is the most personal of the senses, since one has a high level of control over what one chooses to taste, and nobody apart from the taster can be involved in the process of tasting. The prevalent abstract meaning of *taste*, 'personal preference or discernment', reflects this.

An interesting feature of the data is that no entries are modified compounds except for one, insipid n a1700–a1834, and in all cases the presence of taste (either the ability to taste or the presence of flavour) is equated with intelligence. In other words, *taste* is itself a positive, rather than a neutral term, in the same way that *to have taste* implies 'good taste'. Viberg notes that this is the case in various languages, and that the opposite can be observed in SMELL vocabulary.

> When taste and smell appear as copulative expressions, an evaluative element is often present. In one of the languages in the sample, namely Oromo (= Galla), there are no neutral verbs for taste and smell, as shown in Table 23. You must always choose between two verbs: *mi'aau* 'taste = good'/*haðaau* 'taste = bad' and *urgaau* 'smell

– good' / *ajaau* 'smell = bad' ... In English, the verbs *taste* and *smell* are freely combined with *good* and *bad* ... Parallel examples are found in Swedish. But in absolute constructions where no modifier is used, the verbs are not completely neutral. *Lukta* 'smell' implies 'bad' (as in English) and *smaka* 'taste' implies 'good' (unlike English) ... (In English, the adjectives *smelly* and *tasty* differ in the same way.) This seems to reflect a very general tendency. For *smell*, I examined what happens if you use the verb in an absolute construction in most of the languages in the sample. And it turned out that a bad smell was implied. (Viberg 1983: 152–5).

### 2.3.4 HEARING

As indicated above, there is very little data on HEARING compared with the other senses. In the literature, this metaphorical link is most often described as UNDERSTANDING IS HEARING or something similar, with an emphasis on comprehension rather than (for example) academic learning. Although all the words in this section express stupidity, there are certainly other verbs and phrases in current usage that fit in with this mapping and can be more 'positive'. To hear someone, for example in the phrases *I hear you* or *Do you hear what I'm saying?*, is to understand them; to *listen* to someone is to try to understand them and to be receptive to their ideas. Sweetser discusses the way in which 'physical auditory reception ... [is] linked with heedfulness and internal "receptivity"... and hence also to obedience' (1990: 41).

The same distinction between *hear* and *listen* is mirrored in the vocabulary of vision – there is a difference in the kind of attention indicated by *looking* compared to *seeing* – but there still seems to be a discrepancy in the extent to which vision and hearing are trusted as sources and conductors of knowledge. As with smell and taste, the usefulness of hearing is limited by the fact that not everything has a sound; but this does not seem a convincing argument on its own since it would be difficult to compare the number of entities that cannot be heard with those that cannot be seen. As I have already mentioned, Sweetser points out that 'Vision is also identical for different people – that is to say, two people who stand in the same place are generally understood to see the same thing' (1990: 39). The same does not seem to be believed of hearing, or at least not to the same extent; intuitively people seem to trust auditory data less (attested by the lack of a hearing-related term equivalent to *eyewitness*, for example). On the one hand this seems illogical: hearing capability can certainly vary enormously from individual to individual, but then so can vision. In terms of any interpretive element, the same is true: one's impressions when listening to music, for example, are personal and subjective, but this is also the case when it comes to appreciating visual art.

On the other hand, it is true that one has more control over vision than over hearing. Although one can 'tune in' to a stimulus either visually or aurally, vision involves particular physical factors, since in order to look at something the body must be oriented in a certain way and the eyes must be opened and directed at the stimulus, whereas hearing does not have any similar restrictions, but is 'mainly a mental activity' (Sweetser 1990: 41). Conversely, one can be reasonably confident that another person sees something if these physical 'conditions' are being met so that they are apparently looking at the stimulus; but it is more difficult to assess whether or not someone is listening and therefore hearing, since no change of position or expression are required.

This may go some way to explaining why, in general, hearing tends to be associated with a much narrower field of mental experience than vision, and therefore is not linked with intelligence to the same extent.


## 2.4 PROTO-INDO-EUROPEAN

At a basic level, the mapping between INTELLIGENCE and the SENSES appears to be one of the simplest and easiest to account for, and this appears to be the underlying assumption in most of the literature, where it is presented as fairly typical and unproblematic. Each of the senses provides a source concept that maps onto the target, KNOWING or UNDERSTANDING, thus resulting in a 'classic' link between a 'concrete' physical ability and a more 'abstract' mental process.

However, this seems to me to be something of an assumption, and one that is not borne out by the evidence. Sweetser's assertion that 'There is a set of basic IE roots which seem to have referred to vision as far back as their history can be traced' (1990: 33) seems to me to be accurate, but misses an important point: as far as they can be reconstructed with any certainty at all, most of these roots seem to have referred to mental processes as well. It may be the case that 'Vision verbs commonly develop abstract senses of mental activity' (p. 33), and this is certainly what one would assume intuitively, but it does not appear to be evidenced by the etymologies of some root words in the data.

In her study, Sweetser considers the roots of perception verbs connected with vision only, and within this group she does not include all of the most central English verbs – for two of the PIE items, all the reflex verbs listed are from other languages. As a starting point, I have examined the five most quantitatively important PIE roots in the corpus, each of which yields more than ten entries. In order of productiveness, these are:

PIE *weid-( > PDE *wit, vision* )
PIE *ghel-( > OE *gleaw* > EME *glew* )

PIE *sek^w-( > OE seon > PDE *see, sight*, etc. )
PIE *kap-( > L *capere* > PDE *perceive, conceive* )
PIE *sap-( > L *sapere* > PDE *sage, sapient* )

*ghel-* is unusual in this group in that none of its reflexes survive into PDE, and only one survives past the OE era until 1290, glew < gleaw aj OE-c1290. Of the others, *weid-* (discussed above) is the root of 106 entries, the greatest number by far, accounting for one tenth of the INTELLIGENCE data. *ghel-* yields 12 entries, *sek^w-* and *kap-* each yield 11, and *sap-* is the root of 10. In total then, these five roots have 151 derived entries, almost three quarters of the SENSES data (204 entries).

Both Sweetser and the *AHD* give the meaning of *weid-* as 'to see'. Pokorny's entry for this root gives a 'physical vision' meaning first, and lists the mental meaning alongside this as a meaning originally of the perfect tense form 'have seen, know':

> 2. *u̯(e)di-* ‚erblicken, sehen‘ (ursprüngl. Aorist), Zustandsverbum *u(e)idē(i)-*, nasaliert *ui-n-d-*, Perf. *u̯oid-a-* ‚habe gesehen, weiß‘, woher die Bedeutung ‚wissen‘ auch auf andere Formen übertragen wurde; aus der Bedeutung ‚erblicken‘ stammt ‚finden‘; *u̯id-to-s* ‚gesehen‘, *u̯id-ti-*, *u̯id-tu-* ‚das Wissen‘, *u̯idâ*, *u̯idiom*, *u̯id-* ‚Wissen‘, *u̯eidos-* n. ‚das Sehen‘; Partiz. Perf. *u̯eid-u̯ôt-s*, f. *u̯idus-î* ‚wissend‘. (Pokorny 1959: 1125)

In almost all the languages listed there are reflexes which show the meanings 'see' and 'know', including some that Pokorny overlooks: both Latin *video* and Greek οιδα can be used with a mental sense (see Lewis & Short 1996 and Glare 1982; Liddell & Scott 1996).

Sweetser also makes a brief reference to PIE *sek^w-*, asserting that '*sek^w-* is the ancestor of Hittite *sakk-/sekk-* "know,"'[12] as well as of Eng. *see*' (1990: 33). However, these do not seem to be the only reflexes that indicate a conflated sense of mental and physical. The *AHD* gives the definition 'see, perceive'; Pokorny (identifying the root as *sek^u̯ -*) is more general, listing various possible meanings, and drawing attention to the fact that this root shares a source with the preceding entry, which has the basic meaning 'follow'.

> ‚bemerken, sehen; zeigen‘, ursprüngl. ‚wittern, spüren‘ und (jünger) ‚sagen‘; identisch mit 1. *sek^u̯-* . (Pokorny 1959: 897)

For *ghel-* and *kap-*, I have not been able to find evidence to support a mental meaning as central as the physical meaning. *kap-* has the Latin

---

[12] There is some disagreement about this root in modern literature, and it may be that some of the items that have been traditionally linked to this are not actually related. Lehmann draws attention to various possibilities suggested by different scholars, but says: 'Hitt *sakuwa* n pl *eyes* is probably related, and also *sakuwai- observe* ... though ... not to Hitt *sak(k)- know*' (1986: 291).

reflex *capax*, which can mean 'mentally perceptive', and *percipere* derives from this. *sap-* (Watkins uses *sep-*), by contrast, is recognised by both *AHD* and Pokorny as meaning 'taste' and 'perceive', and has reflexes in Latin, Oscan, Middle High German and Old Icelandic relating to the mental sense.

Other roots have reflexes in the data that are comparable in etymology. *ghend-* ( > Latin *prehendere*) has a few reflexes with the meaning 'mentally grasp', but several more with related mental meanings such as 'guess', 'suspect' and 'presume' (Pokorny 1959: 437–8); similarly, PGmc *nem-* ( > PDE *nimble*) has various senses connected with counting, reckoning and checking, which seem to go beyond the purely physical (Pokorny 1959: 763– 4). *(s)keu-* ( > PDE *hear, show*) is listed as

> I. **keu-, skeu-** dehnstufig *kēu-* ,worauf achten (beobachten, schauen)', dann ,hören, fühlen, merken'... (Pokorny 1959: 587).

This clearly incorporates a mental meaning, and I believe that it is important to bear in mind when considering Sweetser's observations about the direction of possible semantic change. If the earliest senses of any basic hearing verbs do not separate the physical and the mental, this indicates that there is a perceived connection between hearing and intellection in general. If this is the case, the type of change she observes is less surprising at the very least.

> An interesting feature of the hear-heed semantic change is that the opposite direction also seems to be possible: words meaning mental attention or understanding can come to mean physical hearing. Thus, Lat. *intendere* 'stretch out, direct one's attention to,' comes to mean 'take heed of, understand' in later Romance languages – OFr. *entendere*, Sp. *entender*, and It. *intendere* all mean 'understand.' But in French the semantic development did not stop there, and *entendre* in Modern French has the primary meaning 'hear' (ousting OFr. *ouïr*, the legitimate heir of Lat. *audire*). Something similar may be going on in the domain of vision: in at least one case, a verb seems to have shifted from the realm of intellection to a possible (if not completely) physical meaning, namely *recognize*, which derives from the Latin root *gno-* 'know.' Thus, although the patterns of semantic change which I am describing do seem to be primarily one-way (concrete → abstract, or physical → mental), nonetheless some verbs may shift in the opposite direction along these same axes. (Sweetser 1990: 35)

The probable meaning of *(s)keu-* also shows the crossover between physical senses that can be found in the semantic development of a number of roots, including *sekʷ-* (above). Interestingly, this is also evident in other lexemes that are not found in the data but are semantically related, the most striking of which is perhaps the Latin root of *taste* (according to the *OED*):

> ME. *tasten*, a. OF. *tast-er* to touch, feel (12th c.), in 13–14th c. also to taste, mod.F. *tâter* to feel, touch, try, taste, = Pr., OSp. *tastar*, It. *tastare* to feel, handle, touch, grope for, try (Florio):–Com. Romanic or late pop.L. \**tastare*, app. from \**taxtāre:*–\**taxitāre*, freq. of *taxâre* to touch, feel, handle (Gellius, etc.): see tax *v.*

Additional etymologies in the same semantic area back up the idea that the traditional idea of a concrete source to abstract target may not always be accurate. The *OED* gives information for *dumb a (n)* which points to metaphorical extension in the opposite direction:

> A Com. Teut. adj.: OE. *dumb* = OS. *dumb* (MDu. *domp, dom*, Du. *dom*, LG. *dum*), OHG. *tumb, tump* (MHG. *tump, tum*, early mod.G. *thumb*, mod.G. *dumm*), ON. *dumbr* (Sw. *dumb*), Goth. *dumbs*. In Gothic, Old Norse, and OE. only in sense 'mute, speechless'; in OHG. it shared this sense with those of 'stupid' and 'deaf'; in the other langs. and periods, generally in sense 'stupid', though early mod.Ger. had also that of 'deaf': see Grimm. These diverse applications suggest as the original sense some such notion as 'stupid', 'not understanding', which might pass naturally either into 'deaf' or 'dumb'.

It seems plausible that *deaf* followed a similar etymological path:

> A Common Teutonic adj.: OE. *déaf* = OFris. *dâf* (WFris. *doaf*), OS. *dôf* (MDu., Du., MLG. *doof (v)*, LG. *dôf*), OHG. *toup (b)*, (MHG. *toup*, Ger. *taub*), ON. *daufr* (Sw. *döf*, Da. *döv*), Goth. *daufs (b)* :– OTeut. \**dauþ-oz*, from an ablaut stem *deuþ-, dauþ-, duþ*, pre-Teut. *dheubh-*, to be dull or obtuse of perception: cf. Goth. *afdaubnan* to grow dull or obtuse, also Gr. *τυφλός* (:—*θυφ-*) blind.

In general, it is not possible to be certain that sense – intellection lexis is the result of a clear, physical to mental, source to target metaphorical mapping. At best this seems simplistic, and at worst, inaccurate; although it is intuitively satisfying it does not appear to reflect subtleties in the etymological data.

## 2.5 PRIMARY METAPHOR AND CONFLATION THEORY

Above, I discussed the motivation for this group of metaphors. At the core of this is the idea that experiences from very early childhood are significant to the extent that, perceptively, they become inseparable from intellectual processes. This is consistent with two complementary theories that have been proposed recently: the first of these is about metaphor at its simplest, most irreducible level, and the second concerns the way in which concepts are initially acquired. Both theories form part of the Integrated Theory of Primary Metaphor (Lakoff & Johnson 1999: 46ff.), which pulls together the work of Joe Grady, Chris Johnson, Srini Narayanan and Giles Fauconnier and Mark Turner. The first part is Grady's (1997) theory that there are a number of very simple, irreducible metaphors, 'primary metaphors', which are motivated by various kinds of early experience. Grady's theory of primary metaphor was a direct product of Lakoff & Johnson's work, and was formulated to account for the parallels that can be observed across mappings, and the way in which targets only selectively import features of the sources that are mapped to them. Grady observed that many of the mappings that had been identified and discussed in the literature could be broken down further, and could be logically interpreted as complex, 'secondary' metaphors that combined more basic, 'primary' mappings. For example, he analyses THEORIES ARE BUILDINGS and observes that this can be explained as a combination of ORGANISATION IS PHYSICAL STRUCTURE and VIABILITY IS ERECTNESS. By describing the metaphorical link in this way, the 'poverty' of the mapping – i.e. the fact that certain elements of buildings, such as windows, are not mapped over to corresponding elements of theories – can be accounted for.

Furthermore, Grady proposes that these basic primary metaphors link particular kinds of sources and targets. As the motivations for these mappings, sources are simple, 'generic' experiences that are directly linked to the way in which human physically interact with their surroundings, e.g. having a body that operates as a container, or experiencing different temperatures. Grady describes primary target concepts as 'the most fundamental aspects of our cognitive machinery' (1997: 134), and gives as examples abstract concepts relating to relations, degree, time, etc., for example quantity or similarity, as well as others relating to consciousness and the emotions, for example thought or anger. The links between source and target appear to be natural to the extent that they are made involuntarily:

> Primary metaphors ... appear not to fit a typical characterisation of conceptual metaphors as tools for constructing, grasping, and communicating about difficult, abstract concepts. Instead the target concepts of these mappings refer to experiences which appear, based again on several types of observations, to be fundamental aspects of cognitive function ... it seems likely that metaphorical associations between source and target concepts are inevitable ... it seems impossible for there *not* to be significant interactions between concepts that are tightly correlated within recurrent experience-types. Metaphor, on this account, would be a fundamental and necessary

by-product of the interaction between cognitive structures and experience in the world. (Grady 1997: 173)

Since Grady first posited this theory, primary metaphors have been shown to underlie a huge number of secondary mappings, both conventionalised and novel, and a number of the primary metaphors that he lists are relevant to the core concept groups identified in the INTELLIGENCE data. KNOWING/UNDERSTANDING IS SEEING is one of these (Grady 1997: 296).

A second theory, proposed by Chris Johnson, follows on from this. Johnson suggests that in early language learning children acquire certain lexical meanings, reflecting mental concepts, that do not correspond exactly to those that adults would identify. Rather than extending the sense of a word metaphorically in the way that the Metaphorical Acquisition Hypothesis suggests, i.e. by learning one (probably concrete) meaning first and subsequently transferring this to another (probably abstract) context, some lexical items appear to be learned with a more general meaning. This is only separated into the different senses traditionally identified as the source and target of the metaphor later in the child's development.

> Polysemous verbs conventionally exhibit a number of different but closely related senses or conventional usages in the input to the child. While there might be a good reason to distinguish these in adult language, the evidence for distinctions between them might be scarce or non-existent in the input that is meaningful and useful to very young children. In cases of metaphorical polysemy ... the task is further complicated by the experiential correlations that can motivate metaphors. If these correlations are properties of children's earliest learning experiences with the forms, then the assumption that source domain meanings are earliest becomes potentially problematic, given the delimitation problem. Children may initially fail to distinguish different senses because their properties may overlap, resulting in conflation. The different senses might become differentiated from one another only later in the acquisition process. (Johnson 1999a: 128)

Having examined a corpus of data made up of seven children's usage of *see* in context, he identifies vision verbs as exemplifying this phenomenon, and suggests that there is a stage during which the physical sense and the mental sense are combined or 'conflated' for the child. At this stage the visual and mental senses are assimilated into 'a single inclusive meaning that involves vision as well as the states and changes of awareness that naturally accompany it' (Johnson 1999a: 183); it does not appear that the child has any practical need to separate these any more finely, and from analysing the way adults use *see* in interaction with children, it appears that they may not even have the evidence to do this. All of the seven children recorded for the corpus use *see* with a conflated sense for a significant period of time before more clearly 'metaphorical' usages can be identified. Johnson gives the following examples of overlap utterances where both a visual and mental element contribute to the meaning: '*I don't see where this one goes, See what else fell down Mommy?, I see what happens, See what I can make ...*' (p. 183).

The significance of Grady's theory for the link between vision and intellection seems to reach far beyond the particular verb he investigates, *see*. He suggests that the centrality of this verb in the semantic field means that its usage is like a 'blueprint' for the way in which other vision vocabulary can be used.[13]

> Since see is one of the two earliest vision verbs to be learned by children (look being the other), there is a sense in which the constructional grounding of mental see in visual see in fact grounds the whole KNOWING IS SEEING metaphor as a linguistic convention for children. That is, because the pattern of see + WH-complement directly encodes the kind of correlation between mental and visual experience that motivates the metaphor, it sets a developmental precedent for visual vocabulary to be applied to the mental domain. (Grady 1997: 126)

Most importantly, conflation theory has consequences for the way adults use vision vocabulary. Even though the physical and mental senses are conventionally separated into literal and metaphorical, early experience sets an important precedent for later usage; and the way in which vision as a concept is understood initially must affect one's understanding thereafter, even if intuitively or subconsciously. Lakoff & Johnson discuss this in relation to their 'Integrated Theory of Primary Metaphor', and suggest that there is a physiological reason: neurological research (in particular Narayanan 1997) suggests that concepts and semantic fields are represented in specific areas of the brain, and that during the conflation period, neural links are made between these areas. In other words, the way adults conceptualise is underpinned by the physical architecture of the brain.

The result of these theories combined is that the VISION group (and I would argue the SENSES data as a whole) is motivated by innate early experiences, to the extent that it may even be an unavoidable by-product of physical existence. In other words, to go back to Lakoff & Johnson,

> We acquire a large system of primary metaphors automatically and unconsciously simply by functioning in the most ordinary of ways in the everyday world from our earliest years. We have no choice in

---

[13] Similarly, the evidence of the ANIMAL and DENSITY groups suggests that when a link has been made between two concepts that is cognitively 'convincing' and therefore successful, this can attract other lexical items to follow the same metaphorical pathway.

this. Because of the way neural connections are formed during the period of conflation, we all naturally think using hundreds of primary metaphors. (Lakoff & Johnson 1999: 47)

An important question is whether there are other concepts apart from vision that initially have some kind of conflated sense. This seems more difficult to prove, but it does seem plausible, especially as regards the other senses; presumably, as alternative methods of accessing information these work in a similar way. Having said that, I believe that the sense hierarchy set out by Viberg is relevant here, and may reflect the level to which each of the senses is bound up with intellection or any other mental function. Viberg (1983) investigated perception verbs in a number of languages from several different families, and found patterns in the way in which these could be extended semantically over the languages he studied. Basically, particular verbs of certain senses could be used in a fairly general way to cover other sense modalities but others were restricted in possible meanings, and this could be expressed in a hierarchy where verbs could extend their meaning downwards (i.e. left to right in the following diagram) but not upwards:

$$\text{sight} > \text{hearing} > \text{touch} > \begin{cases} \text{smell} \\ \text{taste} \end{cases} \qquad \text{(Viberg 1983:147)}$$

Vision is unique in this hierarchy, since it is the only sense that can extend to cover all the others; this may be connected with its status as the most 'used' of the senses in terms of cognizing,[14] since it is the most 'general-purpose' tool of perception by this measure. Landau & Gleitman make a similar point in their study of the way blind and sighted children use vision verbs, in which they conclude: 'to a young child, *look* means "explore with the dominant modality used for apprehending objects," distinct from such terms as *touch* that refer merely to manual contact' (Landau & Gleitman 1985: 69). Consequently, it may be the case that since the other senses are not bound up with cognizing to the same extent that vision is, they may not be learned as conflated concepts in the same way. It is impossible to make any final statement about this until further work in child language acquisition is undertaken.

## 2.6 EVIDENCE IN NON-INDO-EUROPEAN LANGUAGES

If one accepts the experiential basis for the sense metaphors that has been suggested by Lakoff et al., and if one further accepts Conflation Theory, it

---

[14] I do not mean by this that vision is actually used more than other senses, or even that individuals are more aware of visual perception that of other types of perception (though this may be true). I am referring to its distinct role as what Sweetser calls 'our primary source of objective data about the world (1984: 40), which is discussed in section 2.3 above.

would seem to be a logical progression to look for evidence of the same conceptual link in languages completely unrelated to English, i.e. those with non-Indo-European roots. In other words, if it is true that we conceptualise intelligence in terms of our primary means of access to knowledge about the world, the senses, and if in practice the physical and mental processes involved are inseparable, then it follows that one would expect to find the same link in other languages, since all humans have the same physical make-up. Of course, this is in part an over-simplification, since it would be naïve not to take into account the role of culture and tradition, which must affect language in complex and often unpredictable ways. Nevertheless, one would hope to find significant parallels.

Comparison of language families, in any comprehensive way, is an extremely difficult and problematic task, especially when dealing with semantics. However, the emergence of several cross-linguistic resources in the last few decades affords much easier and more thorough comparison of this aspect of language than was previously possible, especially for the non-comparative linguist. Two of the most ambitious of these are Ehret's 1995 work on Proto-Afroasiatic, and Tryon's 1995 *Comparative Austronesian Dictionary* (organised in a similar way to a thesaurus), both similar in layout and methodology to Pokorny, my primary source for Proto-Indo-European. This makes them particularly suitable for my purposes.

There are still major difficulties in using comparative evidence in this way. The best, most comprehensive sources deal with a range of lexical features, and this can mean that none of these are dealt with at length. For example, both Ehret and Tryon present evidence for proto-roots, but neither is explicit about the criteria they have used to arrive at a meaning for any of these roots, nor do they offer any discussion of cases where this has been particularly uncertain (although obviously there is a considerable element of doubt in all cases). It is also unclear whether any distinction between literal and figurative has been made; it is possible that certain meanings have been omitted because they are not regarded as established or conventional usage, or because they are found only in particular contexts. However, it seems likely that this might render the evidence presented here incomplete rather than inaccurate.

For each of the senses, I have attempted to look at all relevant lexical items and list any comparative evidence that supports a link between this sense and intellection or cognition (see section 2.9 below). In order to limit quantity, I have listed only relevant entries or parts of entries;[15] obviously in the resources themselves, much more information is given. For Proto-Afroasiatic, Ehret lists the evidence from Semitic, Egyptian, Cushitic, Chadic and Omotic, though not for every root; for Austronesian, Tryon includes information from 40 languages, again selectively.

---

[15] I have changed the formatting of these entries for presentation here; some underlining and emboldening have been added to compensate for loss of visual clarity.

The evidence that can be found in both families is very patchy. There are few roots that have reflexes supporting the mental–physical link in more than a few languages, but the number of roots for which there is indication of a link is high. Moreover, it does seem to be system-wide: in section 2.9 I have included vocabulary that does not correspond exactly to that found in my own data, because this appears to demonstrate the presence of the concept of physical vision, or of some conflated sense of physical-mental vision, within a wider semantic field. In the VISION section this can be seen clearly. For Afroasiatic root 729, a direct link between *see* and *know* is indicated, but roots 219 and 730 also seem significant, since they suggest a conflated physical–mental sense of perceiving (awareness and attentiveness generally involve both types). Similarly, sections 15.510, 17.130, 17.140, 17.190 and 17.210 all seem to indicate a direct correlation, but the other sections listed here are also important: 15.550 SHOW includes Madurese *pa-tau* 'cause to know', which again suggests conflation, whilst 17.340 and 17.350 (within section 17 MIND, THOUGHT) indicate that vocabulary for clearness and visibility has the same polysemous nature as in English. 17.380 EXPLAIN contains vocabulary associated with visibility and also with openness, which presumably relates to making things visible.

HEARING is also fairly well represented in both families, at least with a more general mental meaning, and again, there are several examples of conflated or closely semantically related vocabulary which support a system-wide connection. Amongst the Afroasiatic languages, the 'hear–heed' connection that Sweetser draws attention to is represented, and this seems similar in nature to the conflated sense of *see*. For example, attentiveness is a combination of hearing/listening and understanding, since it implies intent to understand through physical hearing, and this conflated sense is associated with hearing in roots 219, 728 and 1015. In Austronesian, hearing and believing are connected (section 17.150), and the same link between deafness and dumbness that can be found in English also appears to be made, as in section 4.960. Lack of ability to speak is also found in relation to stupidity, in section 17.220, though only in Spanish (and conceivably as a result of contact).

TOUCH seems less well attested; from the evidence I have found, there is not as strong a connection as in IE, but this could be affected by the difficulty of determining whether *feel* is being used to mean physical touching or not in the sources. In Afroasiatic, root 145 produces reflexes meaning both 'touch' and 'experience', but only one of each; in Austronesian the link between physical and mental is better (and more convincingly) attested in section 15.720 FEEL.

Just as in Indo-European, there appear to be less central links between intellection and the remaining senses TASTE and SMELL (if these do exist). In Egyptian (Afroasiatic root 145) there is a word that can mean both 'taste' and 'experience', whilst in several Austronesian languages there are items polysemous for 'smell' and perceive'.

It should also be pointed out that there are a few examples of crossover between the senses. In section 15.720 FEEL (Austronesian), touching, feeling (presumably physically, since this is alongside other sense verbs) and hearing are alongside one another; 15.310 appears to show a link between touching and tasting, although it is less clear here whether 'feel' is meant physically or mentally; and similarly it is difficult to tell whether 11.160 is related to physical grasping and shows crossover between touching and vision. 15.310 demonstrates the general way vision can be linked with other senses as a general mode of perception as it can in English and other languages (Viberg 1983: 140–41), in Port Sandwich 'eat look-s.th.'.

Although I have carried out only a relatively cursory investigation of non-IE languages, and make these suggestions about sense – intellection vocabulary cautiously, my observations do correspond to comments made by Viberg. This is especially noteworthy because some of the languages included in his study were from language families other than the ones on which I have focused.

> Related to the meanings considered by Kryk are several cognitive meanings that are assumed by the perceptual verbs in English: *understand* ('I see'), *experience* ('taste freedom'), *suspect* ('smell treason', 'smell a rat'). Actually, it seems to be fairly common that the closest equivalent to some of the cognitive verbs in English such as *know, understand,* or *think* is covered by a verb of perception through semantic extension. Especially *see* and *know* seem to be covered by one word in a number of languages (e.g. several Polynesian and Australian languages, Kobon). (Viberg 1983: 157)

## 2.7 ONTOGENY AND PHYLOGENY

From the evidence I have considered, there appears to be an interesting parallel between the ontogenetic and the phylogenetic development of the meaning of certain VISION roots. Recently the connection between ontogeny and phylogeny in linguistic development (and the idea that one may recapitulate the other) has been lent credibility by studies into the evolution of language, but few of these have considered semantic development, concentrating instead on mechanical and performative aspects of phonology (see e.g. MacNeilage & Davis 2000; Lieberman 1998). This is entirely understandable, given that there is some concrete evidence about physical features of the vocal tract (albeit evidence that may be interpretable in a variety of ways). Meaning, on the other hand, is very much more difficult even to conjecture about, especially because all the early historical 'evidence' that is available is based on guesswork, no matter how well informed. From recent studies, it is clear that semantic change may not be random or impossible to account for, but it is still not readily predictable; correspondingly, when one is dealing with very ancient data, it is not possible to be sure that nothing in the development of a particular root has been overlooked, or even that a major piece of evidence is no longer available (such as material from a language that is no longer in existence, or any record of a particular item of vocabulary).

As well as this, and perhaps more significantly for this study, semantic reconstruction tends not to take account of the influence of culture on language. The 'ocularcentricity' of western society is doubtless the product of the close conceptual connection between vision and intellection, resting on the motivation that I have discussed, and this may be universal in human experience. However, it is probable that this cultural emphasis on the visual has, in turn, affected the strength of this link in people's perception, even if only subconsciously.[16]

Despite these difficulties, the idea that ontogeny may recapitulate phylogeny in this case may be worth serious consideration. This has been suggested in a previous study, but with the assumption that the 'literal' meanings of sense vocabulary come first historically; Sweetser (1990: 18) suggests that this is mirrored in the way children learn physical meanings of words first. The idea is further discussed, and refuted, in the light of new research about child language acquisition, by Johnson (1999b: 157–8), but with the same assumption about historical semantic extension. From the data I have examined, precisely the opposite of Sweetser's proposition may be true: rather than demonstrating an extension of meaning from the concrete and physical to the abstract and mental, both the ontogenetic and the phylogenetic processes involve the splitting of the concept into two separate meanings from a preceding conflated sense.

This is clearly problematic in terms of the way metaphor has traditionally been understood. The idea of an 'A to B' mapping depends to some extent on the presupposition that there is a time lapse involved; a lexeme has an earlier, literal meaning, and this is later extended to a figurative meaning, i.e. mapped onto another concept. However, in the case of the SEE-UNDERSTAND mapping, and potentially in other cases involving a conflation stage, this is not the way the metaphor is 'acquired'; rather, both meanings are learned together and separated later. The research presented here

---

[16] It is not impossible that this offers a partial explanation for some of the non-Indo-European data that I have considered. If it is the case that there are only traces of conflated sense-intellection words in other language families, this could be because this has not been such an important conceptual link in other societies as it is in the west. I make this suggestion very cautiously though; it is also possible that influence from western society accounts for any sense-intellection words in other cultures, although I would maintain that the distribution of lexical items in the data I have examined does not support this.

suggests that the diachronic situation may be similar, so that in some cases it may not be possible to evidence earlier literal meanings for lexical items that exhibit both concrete and abstract senses.[17]

Interestingly, the problematic relationship between 'literal' and 'non-literal' language has been observed by other scholars, and this provides an interesting backdrop to the difficulties posed by conflation theory. Tests on reader/hearer interpretation of literal and non-literal language indicate that there is no significant difference in the time taken to retrieve literal and non-literal meanings for lexical items that could be interpreted in more than one way (see Glucksberg 2001 for a full discussion). In this sense, the literal meaning of a lexeme is not necessarily the most basic or primary one, and this contradicts the intuitively 'different' status that is accorded to figurative language. Radden's suggestion that literal and figurative language form a continuum (with metaphor and metonymy on the same continuum at the figurative end) provides a helpful perspective that goes some way to resolving this tension, since it moves away from the idea that literal and figurative language are diametrically opposed (Radden 2002: 431).

## 2.8 CONCLUSION

In this chapter, I have presented information that seems to indicate that the connection between the SENSES and INTELLIGENCE may not be a straightforward case of metaphor as it is traditionally understood. If there are a number of instances of lexis for which the physical sense does not precede the mental sense developmentally or historically (and I believe these lexemes do exist), then it is perhaps misleading to discuss these in terms of source and target, since this implies extension from one concept to the other.

Explaining the SENSES group in terms of a group of straightforward mappings from (earlier) sources to (later) targets oversimplifies the relationship between the concepts involved at the very least. It seems to me that conflation theory offers a convincing explanation of the motivation behind the connection, especially when one considers this alongside the historical development of related vocabulary in Indo-European and other language families. Given that simple source-to-target mappings seem to occur neither

---

[17] It is important to note that the relationship between concrete and abstract domains in the SENSES group is constrained, and the notion of the 'A to B mapping' is helpful in drawing attention to this even if it does not always reflect the historical or synchronic development of particular mappings. Where there is a link between two domains, such as SEEING and KNOWING/UNDERSTANDING, it tends to be unidirectional; it is likely that there will be a number of lexical items that can be used to denote meanings in both domains, but, there will also be some that can only denote the abstract meaning, in this case knowing/understanding.

historically nor developmentally, I would contend that the connection between the concepts SENSES and INTELLIGENCE must be re-evaluated.

Chris Johnson highlights this problem in his explanation of the difference between this traditional view and his own theory.

> The Conflation Hypothesis predicts that children pass through an intermediate stage in which they produce uses of *see* that combine properties of its visual meaning with properties of its metaphorical mental meaning. The Metaphorical Acquisition Hypothesis does not predict any such intermediate stage, but rather, that *see* should be learned and used first in one type of context and then extended abruptly to a very different type of context. This second view of acquisition corresponds more closely to the standard idea of what metaphor is, and follows quite naturally from the representation of metaphor as a mapping between distinct conceptual domains. (Johnson 1999a: 182)

Other scholars have also made reference to the inappropriateness of this model of metaphorical extension in relation to SENSE-INTELLECTION vocabulary, and have drawn attention to the issue of whether two distinct domains are actually involved in the mapping, or whether there might be more accurate ways to analyse it. Goldberg (p.c.) suggests that the UNDERSTANDING IS SEEING metaphor is better described as a GENERIC IS SPECIFIC-type metaphor, COGNITIVE AWARENESS IS COGNITIVE AWARENESS GAINED THROUGH VISION, since this is better motivated and accounts more convincingly for certain uses of *see* that imply awareness rather than understanding. Presumably some of the examples of the use of *see* presented by Johnson as examples of conflation would fit into this category, such as the 'recognize' sense that he identifies in phrases like *I see that there's no more milk* (Johnson 1999a: 151). By contrast, Feyaerts treats the problem somewhat differently in his analysis of domain matrices and metonymic relationships, arguing that it is more accurate to describe the mapping as metonymical than metaphorical.

> ...who can say whether and why a particular description of a domain matrix is correct or not? Intuitively, I experience the conceptual relationship between SEEING and KNOWING to be of a different order than, for instance, the relationship between LIVING and TRAVELING, which essentially reduces to a structural comparison ('life is like a journey'). Although I admit that both concepts can be structurally mapped onto each other, involving ontological, image schematic and logical structures, I claim that this description does not exhaust the conceptual relationship between both concepts. An important aspect of this relationship is the causal-conditional contiguity of both experiences, which indicates that a metonymic extension (PERCEPTION FOR RESULT OF PERCEPTION) can be identified as well. This observation

seriously questions the hypothesis of two different domain matrices being involved in this extension pattern. (Feyaerts 1999: 319)

I would certainly agree with Feyaerts' assertion that the range of mappings that have been interpreted as metaphorical is extremely broad, and includes examples of radically different types of conceptual relationship. More generally, he highlights the problem of the domain approach as a way of distinguishing between metaphor and metonymy. Although I agree with his point that metonymical extension appears to be involved in the KNOWING IS SEEING mapping, I am uneasy with the notion that overall the SENSES group of mappings should simply be reclassified as examples of metonymy on the basis that in each case only one domain matrix is involved. This simply comes back to a subjective judgement about the boundaries between domains and domain matrices. As discussed in Chapter 1, this does not seem to be a reliable way to distinguish between metaphor and metonymy, and it perpetuates the notion that there is a line between the two types of mapping.

Having said this, I would not argue that the notions of domains or domain matrices should be discarded, since they have clearly shown themselves to be theoretically useful and valuable. The reason that there are not clear boundaries between domains is not because there is any inherent flaw in domain theory that can be remedied to provide more precise and objective boundaries between domains; rather, conceptual domains have fuzzy boundaries because they reflect the way encyclopedic knowledge is acquired and organised in human thought, and this is inherently messy. In Langacker's terminology, the concept represented by a lexeme is a 'point of access to a network' with an 'open-ended set of relations', which are all relevant to the concept but only some of which are activated at any one time the concept is 'used' (Langacker 1987: 163). Attempts to classify words and the concepts they represent into groups of any kind show that categories shade into one another, and are connected in complex and unpredictable ways. This is evident from small- and large-scale thesauri, including *HTE*. Users of such reference works might not always agree with the classificatory system employed, but this does not lead them to disregard such attempts to classify the lexicon as intrinsically useless or irrelevant; similarly, the fact that there may be differences in opinion about the boundaries of a domain does not mean that the notion of domains is invalid. In his discussion of the theory of semantic fields, Lyons points out that, 'vaguely formulated though it has been, field-theory has proved its worth as a general guide for research in descriptive semantics over the last forty years; and it has undoubtedly increased our understanding of the way the lexemes of a language are interrelated in sense' (1977: 267). Similarly, the idea of conceptual domains has proved itself to be useful, and the fact that it cannot be formulated into an explicit set of rules about which concepts belong to particular domains is not in itself a weakness. Rather, the impossibility of assigning clear boundaries to domains does mean that the relationship between metaphor and metonymy needs to be considered carefully. While there are some clear cases of metaphor which are generally agreed to involve more than one domain or domain matrix, and some clear cases of metonymy involving a single domain or domain matrix, there are also high numbers of mappings that are more controversial and appear to form an intermediate category, including primary metaphors and other metonymically motivated metaphors (see Goossens 2002 for further discussion of this type of mapping). This lends support to the idea that metaphor and metonymy are most helpfully viewed as closely related phenomena which form a continuum, with prototypical cases at the extreme 'ends'.

This is crucially important when examining the SENSES data, since it offers a different perspective on the mapping which is perhaps more compatible with the theory of primary metaphor; at the very least, it is helpful in drawing attention to the fact that the connection between the senses and intelligence is very different from the connection between source and target that is involved in some other kinds of metaphor. However, theories of the metonymical motivation for metaphors may not solve the problem of earlier and later meanings that is assumed by any kind of mapping from source to target, whether this is primarily metaphorical or metonymical, and this is something that requires further attention. It may be the case that because prototypical metonymies such as container for contents appear to exhibit a more general process than prototypical metaphorical mappings (i.e. between general classes of entities rather than specific entities only), one would not expect to find any evidence of time lapse between the source and target senses of lexemes with metonymically related meanings. Although scholars including John Taylor (e.g. 2002) have drawn attention to the potential for metonymy to motivate semantic change, there appears to be little work that examines the dating evidence for a range of metonymical mappings to find out how often it is possible to trace a clear time lapse between the source 'meaning' and 'target' meaning. This is something that could helpfully be explored in the future.

In summary, the SENSES data can only be viewed as the product of a metaphor if the term 'metaphor' itself is used in a broad enough sense to accommodate different types of mappings, including those that cannot be described in terms of a simple 'A to B' mapping over time, and to accommodate different types of motivation, including motivation which is metonymical in nature. In other words, both the highly diverse nature of metaphorical mappings and the relationship between metaphor and metonymy must be borne in mind. Any view that assumes that all metaphorical relationships are the product of a single type of mechanism, or that there is a clear difference between all metaphor and all metonymy, can only serve to hinder a more comprehensive understanding of conceptual relationships.

## 2.9 EVIDENCE FROM AFROASIATIC AND AUSTRONESIAN

### 2.9.1 VISION

## Afroasiatic

root 219 (Ehret 1995: 159): **\*-sim- "to pay attention to, take note of"** (Sem.,Eg., Ch. innovation: added sense, "to listen to")
SEMITIC A. *s amm* "to examine closely"; \*smʕ "to hear" (stem + \*ʕ part.; semantics unclear); \*smr "to guard" (stem + \*r diffus.; semantics: guarding involves looking all around)
EGYPTIAN *smt* "to hear" (stem + \*t dur.)
CHADIC \*ṣəmi "ear" (N; stem + \*y deverb.) (J: \*sɜm-)
OMOTIC Majoid: Nao *sem-* "to see"

root 672 (Ehret 1995: 345): **\*-ʕaaf- "to see"**
CUSHITIC EC: Sidamo *aaf-* "to know"
OMOTIC \*a:p- "eye" (Mocha *a:pó*; Bench *ap¹*; Yem *āāfā*) SOm \*a:f- "to see" (Ari *áaf-* "to find")

root 720 (Ehret 1995: 361): **\*-ʔil-/\*-ʔal- "to see"; \*ʔīl- "eye"**
CUSHITIC \*ʔīl- "eye"; PSC \*ʔiley- "to know" (stem + \*y in- choat. > dur.)
NOm: Mao \*al- "to know"

root 730 (Ehret 1995: 364): **\*ʔark'- "to notice, become aware of" (root #729 + \*k' intens. of effect)**
EGYPTIAN $^{C}rk$ "to perceive"
CUSHITIC \*ʔark'- "to see"

root 961 (Ehret 1995: 458): **\*-wâh- "to look"**
EGYPTIAN $wh^{C}$ "to investigate" stem + \*ʕ part.; semantics: "look *out* for"?; C.*wɛh*)

## Austronesian

section **15.510 SEE** (Tryon 1995 vol.4: 211–12)
JAV    Also 'know'.
KAU    Also *ion* 'perceive with the eyes or ears'.
RAP    *tike ʔa* 'see (contemplate)'; *take ʔa* 'see (discovering)'; *u ʔi* 'see (observe; focusing on object)'.

section **15.550 SHOW** (Tryon 1995 vol. 4: 215–16)

MAD   *tau* 'know'. *pa-tau* 'cause to know'.

TOL   *ve* (vb trans) 'show, inform, tell', *vər-ve-ai* (vb intrans),
        *vər-* intrans, - *ai* intrans.

MEK   *e-pa-kina(-i-a)* 'make (s.th.) appear'.

KIR   Causative form, from *oti* 'visible, clear, manifest'.

PON   With directional suffixes; causative form; see *sansal* 'clear,
        obvious'.

section **17.130 THINK ( = reflect)** (Tryon 1995 vol. 4: 358)

MAB   'do thinking about'; *mata -iŋgal* 'eye pierce', 'think about';
        *mata- ila pa* 'eye goes to', 'think about'; *mata- imīli*
        'eye returns', 'think back'.

KAU   'eye-his follow'.

KWA   -*atəriŋ* also 'listen'; -*auar* also 'recall'; -*arhi* 'concentrate'.

PON   Also *mʷuserēre* (vb intrans); hon.; *pēm* (vb intrans), also 'sense,
        feel'.

section **17.140 THINK (=be of the opinion)** (Tryon 1995 vol. 4: 360–61)

MAB   -*re keᵐbei* 'see like this'; -*so* 'say'.

PON   *leme* also 'believe'; *kupʷurēioŋ* also 'feel'.

section **17.160 UNDERSTAND** (Tryon 1995 vol. 4: 364–6)

**Arabic**: *faham*          **Sanskrit**: *arthi(n)-*          **Spanish**: *entender*

TAK   'hear, perceive' (15.410).

ADZ   'to hear, understand s.th.'.

MEK   *e-ikifa-lei-na* 'understand, comprehend'; Desnoës has *e-ia-iopi-
        na (ia* is modern *isa* 'see') 'understand, know, be aware of'; see
        NW Mekeo *i-iobina* 'know, understand'.

KWA   Also -*ata* 'see'.

KIR   *atā* also 'know'; *ōta* 'clear, understood'.

section **17.190 IDEA, NOTION** (Tryon 1995 vol. 4: 373–5)

MEK   *opo* means '(a) thought'. *oŋe* means 'mental image; idea'.
        See 17.110, note.

KWA   *nataien* 'be wise', also means 'crack', 'snap'; *narhīen* 'seeing'.

section **17.210 WISE** (Tryon 1995 vol. 4: 375–6)

**Sanskrit**: *vicakṣaṇa-* 'intelligent, wise'

KAU 'eye-his discern behaviour' (see 21.260).

section **17.220 FOOLISH, STUPID** (Tryon 1995 vol. 4: 377–9)

TAG Also *gāgo / -a, [lōko / -a]*, Spanish *loco / -a* 'crazy'; *gaguear* 'stammer'.

KIL Also verb phrase *i-tuli taiga-la* it-deaf ear-his 'he is a fool!'

KWA Also *nipʷana- rəpʷia* 'forehead smooth'; *-ata aua* 'see incorrectly'; *nukʷane-rəsəkai* 'head hard'; *nukʷane-rərənekən* 'head strong'.

section **17.340 CLEAR, PLAIN** (Tryon 1995 vol. 4: 396–8)

DOB 'it does contents' which can mean 'it is clear' or 'it is true'.

TAK 'outside-at-PERFECT' (12.060), i.e, '(it) is on the outside', i.e. 'it is plain'.

MAB 'be in the light with respect to' = be clear about.

YAB 'it-lie outside'.

MOT 'to be open, be clear, appear'.

MEK *e-malolo* is primarily used of clear water but can also be used of e.g. language. *ai ʔapa* is 'clear' of water, 'plain' of food.

MSH Also 'evident, understood'; *alikkaṛ.*

PON *tēte* also 'evident'; *sansal.*

WLE *xiřa* also 'obvious', *ffata* also 'real'.

section **17.350 OBSCURE** (Tryon 1995 vol. 4: 398 –400;

NB section 17 is 'mind, thought')

TAG *lābo ʔ + ma-* 'not clear'; also *tago ʔ* 'hidden from view'.

BLA 'not clear'; *ma-g-liduŋ* 'covered over, obscure'.

MUR Also *mobōt* (of sun, moon).

GOR *mo-olomo (wolomo + mo-)* (of vision/sight'); also *ǰā ʔo-onuh-e (ǰa* 'not' + *wonuhu* + *ʔo--oe),* of writing; *ʔo-onuh-e* 'can be seen clearly'.

BUR   *kabo* 'murky, cloudy, obscure'; *dofo mohede* 'not yet straight/clear'.

YAB   'it-lie inside'.

MEK   *e-upu* is primarily used of murky water but can be used of a topic or discourse. *e-pini* means 'complicated, difficult, involved'. East Mekeo *e-upu* corresponds with *e-kopu, e-kobu* in the other dialects.

SAM   Var. *faʔa-ninimo, faʔa-* CAUS, *nimo* (vb intrans) 'vanish, disappear'.

## section **17.380 EXPLAIN** (Tryon 1995 vol. 4: 404–6)

MGY   *zava* 'clearness, transparency'.

MAD   *tərraŋ* 'clear'.

BAL   See *tlatar* 'clear, plain'.

SAS   *təraŋ* 'clear', 'plain'.

TOL   *və-* CAUS, *kāpə* 'clear'; also *və-mətoto* (see 17.160); *və-nunure* (see 17.170).

BUA   *nɛr tato* 'explain out loud, give directions'; *tatɛkin* 'open something up, explain it'.

ADZ   'explain-talk in the open'.

KIL   *-luki* 'tell'; *-ulaim* 'open'.

MOT   $g^w au$-*rai-a* 'to speak about' ($g^w au$ 'to say, speak'), *maoro* 'straight, correct'. Also *ani-na ha-hedinari-a* 'to cause the meaning to be clear' (*ani-na* 'content, substance', *hedinarai* 'to be clear, appear'), and $g^w au$-*rai-ahedinarai* 'to speak about clearly'.

MEK   'make clever, wise'.

KWA   *-awahaŋ* 'set straight, advise'; *-ɸl* 'open up'; *-ni sas* 'say correctly'; *-oseri* 'unroll, unwind, solve, translate'.

KIR   CAUS of *oti* 'plain, clear'.

SAM   *faʔa-* CAUS, *ma-tala* (vb intrans) 'be open', *ma-* intrans, *tala* (vb trans) 'unfold, undo'.

## 2.9.2 TOUCH

## Afroasiatic

root 145 (Ehret 1995: 133): *-dap- "to touch, feel, put the fingers on"
SEMITIC pPS *dp "to touch; to put hands on"
EGYPTIAN *dp* "to taste, experience" (semantics: as in English *taste* ;
    C. *tōp*)

## Austronesian

section **11.160 GET, OBTAIN** (Tryon 1995 vol. 3: 547–9)
KIL    'take, get (it)'; also -*bani* 'find'.
MEK    Compare *e-aŋa* 'bite' (04.580); also *e-uŋe-pa* 'receive, accept'.
MSH    *lo* also 'see'.
WLE    *werᵢ* also 'see'.

section **15.720 FEEL** (Tryon 1995 vol. 4: 239–40)
TAG    *damdam* + *maka-/ma--an*; also *dama* + *-um-/-in* 'perceive'.
YAB    'feel, test'; also -*lᵢ* 'feel, stroke, caress', *-moasaʔ* 'touch,
       grope, finger, feel'.
KAU    *saa* for tactile sensation; also *poî-poŋ* 'search by feeling'; *hip*
       'sense, be aware of'.
MAR    *habo* 'feel with hand'; *haimi* 'sense'.
PAA    Also 'hear'.
MSH    Also 'experience, sense'; *uŋᵢ̣ri* also 'touch'.
PON    *tɔke* also 'touch'; *pēm* 'perceive, sense, think'; *kēn* also
       'experience'.
RAP    *hāhā* 'feel (examining, registering)'.

2.9.3 *Taste*

## Afroasiatic

root 145 (Ehret 1995: 133): **-dap- "to touch, feel, put the fingers on"**
SEMITIC pPS *dp "to touch; to put hands on"
EGYPTIAN *dp* "to taste, experience" (semantics: as in English *taste* ;
    C. *tōp*)

## Austronesian

section **15.310 TASTE** (Tryon 1995 vol. 4: 193–4)

MUR   *kinam (maŋ- -in)* also 'try'; *ili ʔ (maŋ- -in)* also 'experience'.

BAL   See 15.720, 'feel'.

TAK   'lick see' (04.590, 15.510).

MOT   *mami-na* 'feeling, taste (noun)'; *mami-a* 'to feel, test', *toho* 'to try'.

MEK   *ŋamuŋa* 'essence, flavour, spirit' from *ŋamu* 'root'? *ŋamuŋā e-opo* 'taste something'.

POR   'eat look-s.th.'.

## 2.9.4 *HEARING*

## Afroasiatic

root 219 (Ehret 1995:159): **\*-sim- "to pay attention to, take note of" (Sem., Eg., Ch.** innovation [emboldened in orig]: **added sense, "to listen to")**
SEMITIC A. *samm* "to examine closely"; *smʕ "to hear"
(stem + *ʕ part.; semantics unclear); *smr "to guard"
(stem + *r diffus.; semantics: guarding involves
looking all around)
EGYPTIAN *smt* "to hear" (stem + *t dur.)
CHADIC *ṣəmi "ear" (N; stem + *y deverb.) (J: *s₃-)
OMOTIC Majoid: Nao *sem-* "to see"

root 728 (Ehret 1995: 365): **\*-ʔânxʷ- to listen; ear" (root #723 + \*xʷ extend. fort.; \*m > /n/ ([ŋ]) / \_\_ \*xʷ)**
CUSHITIC *ʔânxʷ-/*ʔînxʷ- "to listen, pay attention to"
(Agaw "ear"; Append. 2)

root 1015 (Ehret 1995: 524): **\*-hʷăy- "to listen to, pay attention to" (Eg., Sem.** innovation: "pay attention **to" > "watch over," hence "protect"**
SEMITIC A. *haiman* "to guard, protect" (stem + *m n. suff. or
*m extend. + *n non-fin.)
CUSHITIC PEC *hayy- "wisdom, wise advice" (semantics:
hear > understand > be wise")
OMOTIC NOm *h₂ay- "ear" (Ometo *h₂ayts-; Bench *(h)ay* [4],
Mocha *wà:mo* < *way- + *m n. suff.; Yem *wèes-*
"to hear"; NOm n. + *s caus. as denom.)

## Austronesian

section **04.960 DUMB** (Tryon 1995 vol. 2: 622–4)
WOL  Also *oga; ka-moo-moo* 'dumb, mentally deficient'.
BUR  Also *geba te stori moo* 'person unable to speak';
*geba ebele-n* 'stupid person, simpleton'; *geba
ebafa-n* 'dumb, unteachable, unmannered'.
TAK  'senile'.

BUA $k^wa$ $ma$ 'not able to speak'; $k^wa$ $\eta\partial\eta\partial l\partial\eta$ 'able to make unintelligible sounds'; both mean 'foolish, stupid'.

KIL 'be foolish', the usual derogatory description of the deaf-and-dumb person. Also $to$-$mto$-$mota$ 'person-continuous-hiccough', 'person speaking in unintelligible gasps'.

### section **15.410 HEAR** (Tryon 1995 vol. 4: 201–2)

TAK 'hear, perceive'.

MEK $e$-$lo\eta o$ 'perceive, hear, know'; initial /l-/ is an accretion in East Mekeo, selective borrowing into North Mekeo and NW Mekeo gives $o\eta o$ 'hear, perceive', $lo\eta o$ 'know' in these dialects.

### section **17.150 BELIEVE** (Tryon 1995 vol. 4: 362–3)

**Sanskrit**: $pratyaya$-

DOB $\hat{P}a$-$re\eta in$ 'hear, believe', $\hat{P}ok^walay$ $m$-$re\eta in$-$ni$ 'don't believe him'.

MOT $here\beta a$ 'word', $abi$-$a$ $dae$ 'receive' ($abi$-$a$ 'get, hold', $dae$ 'go up'); also $kamonai$ $(heni$-$a)$ 'to hear, believe'; $abidadama$ $heni$-$a$ 'to believe, have faith in'.

### section **15.410 HEAR** (Tryon 1995 vol. 4: 201–2)

TAK 'hear, perceive'.

MEK $e$-$lo\eta o$ 'perceive, hear, know'; initial /l-/ is an accretion in East Mekeo, selective borrowing into North Mekeo and NW Mekeo gives $o\eta o$ 'hear, perceive', $lo\eta o$ 'know' in these dialects.

### section **17.150 BELIEVE** (Tryon 1995 vol. 4: 362–3)

**Sanskrit**: $pratyaya$-

DOB $\hat{P}a$-$re\eta in$ 'hear, believe', $\hat{P}ok^walay$ $m$-$re\eta in$-$ni$ 'don't believe him'.

MOT $here\beta a$ 'word', $abi$-$a$ $dae$ 'receive' ($abi$-$a$ 'get, hold', $dae$ 'go up'); also $kamonai$ $(heni$-$a)$ 'to hear, believe'; $abidadama$ $heni$-$a$ 'to believe, have faith in'.

section **17.160 UNDERSTAND** (Tryon 1995 vol. 4: 364–6)

**Arabic**: *faham*   **Sanskrit**: *arthi(n)-*   **Spanish**: *entender*

TAK   'hear, perceive' (15.410).

ADZ   'to hear, understand s.th.'.

MEK   *e-ikifa-lei-na* 'understand, comprehend'; Desnoës has *e-ia-iopi-na (ia* is modern *isa* 'see') 'understand, know, be aware of'; see NW Mekeo *i-iobina* 'know, understand'.

KWA   Also *-ata* 'see'.

KIR   *atā* also 'know'; *ōta* 'clear, understood'.

section **17.160 UNDERSTAND** (Tryon 1995 vol. 4: 364–6)

**Arabic**: *faham*   **Sanskrit**: *arthi(n)-*   **Spanish**: *entender*

TAK   'hear, perceive' (15.410).

ADZ   'to hear, understand s.th.'.

MEK   *e-ikifa-lei-na* 'understand, comprehend'; Desnoës has *e-ia-iopi-na (ia* is modern *isa* 'see') 'understand, know, be aware of'; see NW Mekeo *i-iobina* 'know, understand'.

KWA   Also *-ata* 'see'.

KIR   *atā* also 'know'; *ōta* 'clear, understood'.

section **17.170 KNOW** (Tryon 1995 vol. 4: 366–7)

TAK   'hear, perceive' (15.410)

YAB   Also *-liʔsu* '-see away'; *-ŋo su* '-hear away'.

MEK   *e-loŋo* also 'hear' (see 15.410, note). NW Mekeo *i-iobina.*

section **17.220 FOOLISH, STUPID** (Tryon 1995 vol. 4: 377–9)

TAG   Also *gāgo / -a, [lōko / -a],* Spanish *loco / -a* 'crazy'; *gaguear* 'stammer'.

KIL   Also verb phrase *i-tuli taiga-la* it-deaf ear-his 'he is a fool!'

KWA   Also *nip^w ana- rəp^w ia* 'forehead smooth'; *-ata aua* 'see incorrectly'; *nuk^w ane-rəsəkai* 'head hard'; *nuk^w ane-rərənekən* 'head strong'.

## 2.10 DATA TABLES

### 2.10.1 *SENSE-VISION*

Table 1

| Record no. | Meaning | Word | Part of speech | OE? | Plus/and | a/c1 | Date 1 | +/- | a/c2 | Date 2 | -/+ | a/c3 | Date 3 | Current? | Label | Derivation |
|---|---|---|---|---|---|---|---|---|---|---|---|---|---|---|---|---|
| 1 | clever-intelligent | gleaw | aj | OE | | | | | | | | | | | | gleaw < *ghel- |
| 3 | clever-wise | runwita | n | OE | | | | | | | | | | | | rune wit < *weid- |
| 4 | clever-wise | fyrnwita | n | OE | | | | | | | | | | | | fyrn wit < *weid- |
| 5 | clever-wise | Peodwita | n | OE | | | | | | | | | | | | Peod wit < *weid- |
| 7 | clever-wise | gleawlic | aj | OE | | | | | | | | | | | | gleaw < *ghel- |
| 15 | clever-wise | wiswyrde | aj | OE | | | | | | | | | | | | wise < *weid- word |
| 19 | stupid | dwæs | n | OE | | | | | | | | | | | | dwæs |
| 26 | clever-intelligent and wise | wisfæst | aj | OE | | | | | | | | | | | | wise < *weid- fast |
| 29 | stupid | ungewitful | aj | OE | | | | | | | | | | | | wit < *weid- |
| 30 | stupid | gedwæsmann | n | OE | | | | | | | | | | | | dwæs man |
| 31 | clever-wise | welbesceawod | aj | OE | | | | | | | | | | | | show < sceawian < *(s)keu- |
| 32 | clever-wise | besceawod | aj | OE | | | | | | | | | | | | show < sceawian < *(s)keu- |
| 36 | stupid | samwis | aj | OE | | | | | | | | | | | | wise < *weid- |
| 37 | clever-wise | (ge)sceadwis | aj | OE | | | | | | | | | | | | scead wise < *weid- |
| 44 | clever-wise | wissefa | n | OE | | | | | | | | | | | | wise < *weid- sefa |
| 46 | clever-wise | freagleaw | aj | OE | | | | | | | | | | | | gleaw < *ghel- |
| 48 | clever-wise | (ge)wittig | aj | OE | | | | | | | | | | | | wit < *weid- |
| 51 | clever-sharp | gearowitol | aj | OE | | | | | | | | | | | | gearo wit < *weid- |
| 54 | clever-wise | ealdwita | n | OE | | | | | | | | | | | | eald < *al- wit < *weid- |
| 55 | clever-wise | witega | n | OE | | | | | | | | | | | | wit < *weid- |
| 58 | clever-wise | forewitig | aj | OE | | | | | | | | | | | | fore wit < *weid- |

Table 1 (contd.)

| Record no. | Meaning | Word | Part of speech | OE? | Plus/ and | a/c1 | Date 1 | +/- a/c2 | Date 2 | -/+ a/c3 | Date 3 | Current? | Label | Derivation |
|---|---|---|---|---|---|---|---|---|---|---|---|---|---|---|
| 59 | clever-wise | gleawmod | aj | OE | | | | | | | | | | gleaw < *ghel- mod wise < *weid- |
| 60 | stupid | medwis | aj | OE | | | | | | | | | | wise < *weid- |
| 61 | clever-intelligent | ginnwised | aj | OE | | | | | | | | | | ginn wise < *weid- |
| 66 | clever-wise | modgleaw | aj | OE | | | | | | | | | | mod gleaw < *ghel- |
| 67 | clever-wise | gleawferhþ | aj | OE | | | | | | | | | | gleaw < *ghel- ferhþ |
| 68 | clever-wise | ferhþgleaw | aj | OE | | | | | | | | | | ferhþ gleaw < *ghel- |
| 70 | clever-wise | hreþergleaw | aj | OE | | | | | | | | | | hreþer gleaw < *ghel- |
| 71 | clever-wise | sundorwis | aj | OE | | | | | | | | | | sundor wise < *weid- |
| 72 | clever-wise | gleawhydig | aj | OE | | | | | | | | | | gleaw < *ghel- hyge |
| 73 | clever-wise | wishydig | aj | OE | | | | | | | | | | wise < *weid- hyge |
| 75 | clever-wise | wiswylle | aj | OE | | | | | | | | | | wise < *weid- will |
| 79 | stupid | ungleaw | aj | OE | | | | | | | | | | gleaw < *ghel- |
| 80 | clever-wise | wishycgende | aj | OE | | | | | | | | | | wise < *weid- hyge |
| 81 | clever-wise | hygegleaw | aj | OE | | | | | | | | | | hyge gleaw < *ghel- |
| 83 | stupid | unwita | n | OE | | | | | | | | | | wit < *weid- |
| 84 | clever-intelligent | hlutor | aj | OE | | | | | | | | | | hlutor |
| 93 | clever-wise | uÞwite < uÞwita | n | OE | – | c | 1200 | | | | | | | uÞ wit < *weid- |
| 95 | clever-wise | glew < gleaw | aj | OE | – | c | 1290 | | | | | | | gleaw < *ghel- |
| 97 | clever-wise | witter < witter | aj | OE | – | a | 1400/50 | | | | | | | wit < *weid- |
| 98 | clever-wise | wise < wisa | n | OE | – | c | 1440 | | | | | | | wise < *weid- |
| 101 | clever-wise | wisely < wislic | aj | OE | – | c | 1556 | | | | | | | wise < *weid- |
| 105 | clever-wise | wite < wita | n | OE | – | c | 1315 | + | 1701 | | 1762 | | | wit < *weid- |
| 106 | stupid | unwitty < unwittig | aj | OE | – | | 1670 | + | 1859 | | | | | wit < *weid- |
| 107 | clever-intelligent | witty < (ge)wittig | aj | OE | – | | 1784 | + | 1886 | | | | 1886dl | wit < *weid- |
| 109 | clever-shrewd | world-wise < woruldwis | aj | OE | – | c | 1205 | + | 1845 | | | ^ | | world wise < *weid- |
| 112 | stupid | witless < gewitleas | aj | OE | | | | | | | | ^ | | wit < *weid- |
| 113 | clever-wise | wise man < wis man | n | OE | | | | | | | | ^ | | wise < *weid- man |
| 115 | stupid | blind < blind | aj | OE | | | | | | | | ^ | | blind < *bhlendh- |

Table 1 (contd.)

| Record no. | Meaning | Word | Part of speech | OE? Plus/ and | a/c1 | Date 1 | +/- | a/c2 | Date 2 | -/+ | a/c3 | Date 3 | Current? | Label | Derivation |
|---|---|---|---|---|---|---|---|---|---|---|---|---|---|---|---|
| 118 | clever-wise | (the) wise | n | OE | | | | | | | | | > | | wise < *weid- |
| 119 | clever-wise | wise < wis | aj | OE | | | | | | | | | > | | wise < *weid- |
| 127 | clever-intelligent | understanding | aj | | c | 1200 | | | | | | | > | | under stand |
| 128 | clever-sharp | yare-witel | aj | | c | 1205 | | | | | | | | | ?yare wit < *weid- |
| 131 | clever-wise | witful | aj | | c | 1205 | – | | 1614 | | | | | | wit < *weid- |
| 132 | clever-wise | redewise | aj | | a | 1225 | | | | | | | | | rede wise < *weid- |
| 141 | clever-intelligent | skillwise | aj | | a | 1300 | – | a | 1340 | | | | | | skill wise < *weid- |
| 143 | clever-wise | wise to/unto | aj | | a | 1300 | – | | 1781 | | | | | | wise < *weid- |
| 144 | clever-wise | wiser | n | | a | 1300 | – | c | 1480 | + | | 1818 | > | | wise < *weid- |
| 152 | clever-wise | witty | aj | | | 1340 | – | | 1611 | | | | | | wit < *weid- |
| 160 | stupid | goky | n | | | 1377 | | | | | | | | | gowk |
| 162 | clever-intelligent | witted (with prec. modifier) | aj | | | 1377 | | | | | | | > | | wit < *weid- |
| 163 | stupid | (blind) buzzard | n | | | 1377 | | | | | | | > | | blind < *bhlendh- buzzard -ard |
| 169 | clever-wise/shrewd | prudent | aj | | | 1382 | | | | | | | > | | providens < pro- videre < *weid- |
| 170 | clever-wise | well-advised | aj | | c | 1386 | – | | 1611 | | | | | | ad- videre < *weid- |
| 171 | stupid | dull-witted | aj | | | 1387 | – | | | | | | > | | dull wit < *weid- |
| 185 | stupid | unwiseman | n | | | 1400 | – | c | 1520 | | | | | | wise < *weid- |
| 186 | clever-wise | perceived | aj | | c | 1400 | | | | | | | | | perceive < per capere < *kap- |
| 191 | clever-shrewd | worldly-wise | aj | | c | 1400 | – | | | | | | > | | world wise < *weid- |
| 194 | clever-sharp | perceiving | aj | | c | 1410 | – | | 1645 | | | | | | perceive < per capere < *kap- |
| 196 | clever-wise | prudent | aj | | a | 1425 | – | | 1579 | | | | | | pro- videre < *weid- |
| 197 | clever-sharp | sighty | aj | | a | 1425 | – | | 1579 | + | | 1869 | | 1869dl | see < sekw- |
| 200 | clever-intelligent | of understanding | aj | | | 1428 | – | | 1772 | | | | | | under stand |
| 201 | clever-wise and wise derog | wisdom(s) | n | | | 1432 | – | | 1831 | | | | > | | wise < *weid- |

Table 1 (contd.)

| Record no. | Meaning | Word | Part of speech | OE? | Plus/ and | a/c1 | Date 1 | +/- a/c2 | Date 2 | -/+ a/c3 | Date 3 | Current? | Label | Derivation |
|---|---|---|---|---|---|---|---|---|---|---|---|---|---|---|
| 203 | clever-sharp | seeing | aj | | | | 1440 | – | 1825 | | | | | see < sekw- |
| 204 | clever-wise | visable | aj | | c | | 1440 | – | | | | | | videre < *weid- |
| 209 | clever-wise derog | wizard | n | | c | | 1440 | – | 1697 | + | 1841 | | | wise < *weid- -ard |
| 210 | stupid | want-wit | n | | c | | 1448/9 | – | 1610 | + | 1900 | | | want wit < *weid- |
| 212 | clever-intelligent | well-witted | aj | | c | | 1450 | – | 1552 | | | | | well wit < *weid- |
| 215 | clever-wise | inwise | aj | | | | 1450/80 | | | | | | | wise < *weid- |
| 217 | clever-genius and intelligent | wit | n | | c | | 1470 | | | | | > | nn ai&hs | wit < *weid- |
| 220 | clever-wise | advised | aj | | | | 1475 | – | 1702 | | | | | ad- videre < *weid- |
| 221 | stupid | short-witted | aj | | | | 1477 | | | | | > | | short wit < *weid- |
| 244 | clever-intelligent | witted | aj | | | | 1528 | – | 1606 | | | | | wit < *weid- |
| 250 | clever-sharp | clear-eyed | aj | | | | 1530 | | | | | > | | clear < clarus eye < okw- |
| 251 | clever-sharp | quick-witted | aj | | | | 1530 | | | | | > | | quick wit < *weid- |
| 259 | stupid | blinded | aj | | | | 1535 | – | 1826 | | | | | blind < *bhlendh- |
| 262 | clever-wise derog | over-wise | aj | | | | 1535 | | | | | > | | over wise < *weid- |
| 263 | clever-intelligent | wits | n | | | | 1536 | | | | | > | nn ai | wit < *weid- |
| 281 | clever-sharp | quick-sighted | aj | | | | 1552 | | | | | > | | quick see < sekw- |
| 294 | clever-wise derog | self-wise | aj | | | | 1561 | – | 1836 | | | | | self wise < *weid- |
| 314 | clever-wise | bilwise | aj | | | | 1577 | | | | | > | | bill wise < *weid- |
| 321 | stupid | unilluminated | aj | | | | 1579 | | | | | > | | illuminate < *leuk- |
| 328 | clever-sharp | ready-witted | aj | | | | 1581 | – | 1869 | | | | | ready wit < *weid- |
| 335 | clever-sharp | sharpsighted | aj | | | | 1583 | | | | | > | | sharp see < sekw- |
| 336 | clever-sharp | perspicuous | aj | | | | 1584 | + | 1865 | | | | | perspicere < *spek- |
| 341 | clever-sharp | sharp-witted | aj | | a | | 1586 | | | | | | | sharp wit < *weid- |
| 345 | clever-sharp | clear-sighted | aj | | | | 1586 | | | | | > | | clear < clarus |
| 352 | stupid | wittol | n | | | | 1588 | – | 1721 | + | 1822 | | | wit < *weid- |
| 358 | clever-wise | wittiful | aj | | | | 1590 | | | | | > | | wit < *weid- |
| 360 | clever-sharp | inseeing | aj | | | | 1590 | – | 1611 | + | 1840 | | | see < sekw- |
| 369 | stupid | lean-witted | aj | | | | 1593 | | | | | > | | lean wit < *weid- |

Table 1 (contd.)

| Record no. | Meaning | Word | Part of speech | OE? Plus/ and | a/c1 | Date 1 | +/- | a/c2 | Date 2 | -/+ | a/c3 | Date 3 | Current? | Label | Derivation |
|---|---|---|---|---|---|---|---|---|---|---|---|---|---|---|---|
| 370 | clever-common sense | mother witted | aj | | | 1593 | | | | | | | | | mother wit < *weid- |
| 371 | stupid | blunt-witted | aj | | | 1593 | | | | | | | | | blunt wit < *weid- |
| 384 | stupid | fat-witted | aj | | | 1596 | | | | | | | ^ | | fat wit < *weid- |
| 391 | clever-genius | deep-seen | aj | | | 1597/8 | | | | | | | | | deep see < sekw- |
| 406 | stupid | wit-lost | aj | | | 1599 | | | | | | | | | wit < *weid- lose |
| 422 | stupid | woollen-witted | aj | c | | 1600 | – | | 1635 | | | | | | wool wit < *weid- |
| 430 | clever-sharp | insighted | aj | | | 1602 | | | | | | | ^ | | see < sekw- |
| 438 | stupid | gowk | n | a | | 1605 | | | | | | | ^ | og sc&nd | gowk ?gawk |
| 444 | stupid | beef-witted | aj | | | 1606 | | | | | | | | | beef wit < *weid- |
| 469 | clever-sharp | well-sighted | aj | | | 1613 | – | | 1656 | | | | | | well see < sekw- |
| 471 | clever-sharp | nimble-witted | aj | | | 1613/6 | | | | | | | ^ | | nimble < numol <*nem- wit < *weid- |
| 476 | clever-sharp | quick-eyed | aj | a | | 1616 | | | | | | | ^ | | quick eye < *okw- |
| 480 | stupid | buzzard-blind | aj | | | 1619 | | | | | | | | | buzzard -ard blind <*bhlendh- |
| 509 | clever-wise derog | wiseling | n | | | 1633 | – | | 1765 | | | 1914 | ^ | | wise < *weid- |
| 511 | stupid | thickwitted | aj | | | 1634 | | | | | | | ^ | | thick wit < *weid- |
| 521 | clever-sharp | perspicacious | aj | | | 1640 | | | | | | | ^ | | perspicere < *spek- |
| 522 | clever-sharp | far-sighted | aj | | | 1641 | | | | | | | ^ | | far see < sekw- |
| 532 | stupid | half-witted | aj | c | | 1645 | | | | | | | ^ | | half wit < *weid- |
| 538 | clever-wise derog | self-wiseling | n | | | 1649 | | | | | | | | | self wise < *weid- |
| 565 | clever-genius | eagle-wit | n | | | 1665 | | | | | | | | | eagle wit < *weid- |
| 572 | stupid | lack-wit | n | | | 1667 | | | | | | | ^ | | lack wit < *weid- |
| 593 | stupid | under-witted | aj | | | 1683 | + | | 1856 | | | | | | under wit < *weid- |
| 603 | clever-wise derog | wisdomship | n | | | 1692 | | | | | | | | | wise < *weid- |
| 632 | clever-sharp | clear-headed | aj | | | 1709 | | | | | | | ^ | | clear < clarus head |
| 639 | clever-sharp derog | over-witted | aj | a | | 1716 | | | | | | | | | over wit < *weid- |
| 641 | clever-wise derog | afterwise | aj | a | | 1719 | | | | | | | | | after wise < *weid- |

Table 1 (contd.)

| Record no. | Meaning | Word | Part of speech | OE? Plus/ and | a/c1 Date 1 | +/- | a/c2 Date 2 | -/+ | a/c3 Date 3 | Current? | Label | Derivation |
|---|---|---|---|---|---|---|---|---|---|---|---|---|
| 658 | clever-intelligent | bright | aj | | 1741 | | | | | > | | bright <*bher£g- |
| 670 | clever-wise derog | wiseacre | n | | 1753 | | | | | > | | wise <*weid- -acre |
| 672 | stupid | opaque | aj | | 1755 | | | | | > | | opaque |
| 673 | stupid | half-wit | n | | 1755 | | | | | > | | half wit <*weid- |
| 676 | clever-wise derog | wisehead | n | | 1756 | | | | | > | | wise <*weid- head |
| 691 | stupid | wittol | aj | | 1780 | – | 1869 | | | | | ?wise <*weid- |
| 738 | clever-highbrow derog | illuminati | n | | 1816 | | | | | > | | illuminate <*leuk- |
| 747 | clever-sharp | pellucid | aj | | 1822 | | | | | | | lucid <*leuk- |
| 754 | clever-precocious | bright | aj | | 1824 | + | 1885 | | | > | | bright <*bher£g- |
| 765 | stupid | unwitted | aj | | 1828 | | | | | | | wit <*weid- |
| 802 | stupid | opacity | n | | 1844 | | | | | | | opaque |
| 805 | clever-wise | wisdomful | aj | | 1845 | | | | | | | wise <*weid- |
| 816 | clever-wise and sharp | far-seeing | aj | | 1848 | | | | | > | | far see <sekw- |
| 869 | stupid | barren-witted | aj | | 1870 | | | | | | | barren wit <*weid- |
| 900 | clever-wise derog | wiseacredom | n | | 1885 | | | | | | | wise <*weid- -acre |
| 913 | stupid | dim | aj | | 1892 | | | | | > | | dim |
| 916 | clever-wise derog | wisebones | n | | 1894 | | | | | | | wise <*weid- bones |
| 917 | stupid | want-wit | aj | | 1894 | | | | | | | want wit <*weid- |
| 920 | clever-smart alec derog | wise guy | n | | 1896 | | | | | > | cq og us | wise <*weid- guy |
| 931 | stupid | thickwit | n | | 1904 | | | | | | | thick wit <*weid- |
| 933 | clever-smart alec derog | wisenheimer | n | | 1904 | | | | | > | us sl | wise <*weid- |
| 934 | stupid | wool-witted | n | | 1905 | | | | | | | wool wit <*weid- |
| 963 | stupid | nitwit | aj | | 1922 | | | | | > | cq | nit wit <*weid- |
| 965 | stupid | nitwit | n | | 1922 | | | | | > | cq | wit <*weid- |
| 966 | stupid | dim-wit | n | | 1922 | | | | | > | og us | dim wit <*weid- |
| 991 | stupid | nitwitted | aj | | 1931 | | | | | > | | nit wit <*weid- |
| 1004 | stupid | half-wit | aj | | 1938 | | | | | > | | half wit <*weid- |
| 1011 | stupid | dim-witted | aj | | 1940 | | | | | > | | dim wit <*weid- |
| 1051 | clever-shrewd | street-wise | aj | | 1965 | | | | | > | sl og & cf us | street wise <*weid- |
| 1069 | clever-smart alec derog | wise-ass | n | | 1971 | | | | | > | sl | wise <*weid- arse |

*2.10.1.1* SENSE–VISION–LIGHT

Table 2

| Record no. | Meaning | Word | Part of speech | OE? | Plus/ and | a/c1 | Date 1 | +/– | a/c2 | Date 2 | –/+ | a/c3 | Date 3 | Current? | Label | Derivation |
|---|---|---|---|---|---|---|---|---|---|---|---|---|---|---|---|---|
| 1 | clever-intelligent | gleaw | aj | OE | | | | | | | | | | | | gleaw < *ghel- |
| 7 | clever-wise | gleawlic | aj | OE | | | | | | | | | | | | gleaw < *ghel- |
| 19 | stupid | dwæs | n | OE | | | | | | | | | | | | dwæs |
| 30 | stupid | gedwæsmann | n | OE | | | | | | | | | | | | dwæs man |
| 46 | clever-wise | freagleaw | aj | OE | | | | | | | | | | | | gleaw < *ghel- |
| 59 | clever-wise | gleawmod | aj | OE | | | | | | | | | | | | gleaw < *ghel- mod |
| 66 | clever-wise | modgleaw | aj | OE | | | | | | | | | | | | mod gleaw < *ghel- |
| 67 | clever-wise | gleawferhþ | aj | OE | | | | | | | | | | | | gleaw < *ghel- ferhþ |
| 68 | clever-wise | ferhþgleaw | aj | OE | | | | | | | | | | | | ferhþ gleaw < *ghel- |
| 70 | clever-wise | hreþergleaw | aj | OE | | | | | | | | | | | | hreþer gleaw < *ghel- |
| 72 | clever-wise | gleawhydig | aj | OE | | | | | | | | | | | | gleaw < *ghel- hyge |
| 79 | stupid | ungleaw | aj | OE | | | | | | | | | | | | gleaw < *ghel- |
| 81 | clever-wise | hygegleaw | aj | OE | | | | | | | | | | | | hyge gleaw < *ghel- |
| 84 | clever-intelligent | hlutor | aj | OE | | | | | | | | | | | | hlutor |
| 95 | clever-wise | glew < gleaw | aj | OE | – | c | 1290 | | | | | | | | | gleaw < *ghel- |
| 115 | stupid | blind < blind | aj | OE | | c | 1200 | | | | | | | ∧ | | blind < *bhlendh- |
| 127 | clever-intelligent | understanding | aj | | | | 1377 | | | | | | | ∧ | | under stand |
| 163 | stupid | (blind) buzzard | n | | | | | | | | | | | ∧ | | blind < *bhlendh- buzzard -ard |
| 200 | clever-intelligent of understanding | understanding | aj | | | | 1428 | – | | 1772 | | | | | | under stand |
| 250 | clever-sharp | clear-eyed | aj | | | | 1530 | – | | | | | | ∧ | | clear < clarus eye < *okw- |
| 259 | stupid | blinded | aj | | | | 1535 | | | 1826 | | | | | | blind < *bhlendh- |
| 321 | stupid | unilluminated | aj | | | | 1579 | | | | | | | ∧ | | illuminate < *leuk- |
| 345 | clever-sharp | clear-sighted | aj | | | | 1586 | | | | | | | ∧ | | clear < clarus |
| 480 | stupid | buzzard-blind | aj | | | | 1619 | | | | | | | | | buzzard -ard blind < *bhlendh- |
| 632 | clever-sharp | clear-headed | aj | | | | 1709 | | | | | | | ∧ | | clear < clarus head |

Table 2 (contd.)

| Record no. | Meaning | Word | Part of speech | OE? | Plus/ and | a/c1 | Date 1 | +/- | a/c2 | Date 2 | -/+ | a/c3 | Date 3 | Current? | Label | Derivation |
|---|---|---|---|---|---|---|---|---|---|---|---|---|---|---|---|---|
| 658 | clever-intelligent | bright | aj | | | | 1741 | | | | | | | ^ | | bright < *bherÊg- |
| 672 | stupid | opaque | aj | | | | 1755 | | | | | | | ^ | | opaque |
| 738 | clever-highbrow derog | illuminati | n | | | | 1816 | | | | | | | ^ | | illuminate < *leuk- |
| 747 | clever-sharp | pellucid | aj | | | | 1822 | | | | | | | | | lucid < *leuk- |
| 754 | clever-precocious | bright | aj | | | | 1824 | + | | 1885 | | | | ^ | | bright < *bherÊg- |
| 802 | stupid | opacity | n | | | | 1844 | | | | | | | | | opaque |
| 913 | stupid | dim | aj | | | | 1892 | | | | | | | ^ | | dim |
| 966 | stupid | dim-wit | n | | | | 1922 | | | | | | | ^ | og us | dim wit < *weid- |
| 1011 | stupid | dim-witted | aj | | | | 1940 | | | | | | | ^ | | dim wit < *weid-; |

2.10.2 *SENSE-GRASP (TOUCH)*

Table 3

| Record no. | Meaning | Word | Part of speech | OE? | Plus/ and | a/c1 Date 1 | +/- a/c2 Date 2 | -/+ a/c3 Date 3 | Current? | Label | Derivation |
|---|---|---|---|---|---|---|---|---|---|---|---|
| 99 | clever-intelligent | nimble < numol | aj | OE - | | 1483 | | | | | nimble < numol < *nem- |
| 146 | stupid | heavy | aj | | c | 1300 | | | | | heavy < *kap- |
| 166 | clever-intelligent | well-feeling | aj | | c | 1382 | | | | | well feel |
| 186 | clever-wise | perceived | aj | | c | 1400 | | | | | perceive < per capere < *kap- |
| 194 | clever-sharp | perceiving | aj | | c | 1410 | − | 1645 | | | perceive < per capere < *kap- |
| 202 | clever-intelligent | capax | aj | | | 1432/50 | − | 1556 | | | capere < *kap- |
| 312 | clever-sharp | of a far fetch | aj | | | 1574 | | | | | far fetch |
| 344 | clever-genius | of (a) great/deep reach | aj | | | 1586 | | | | > | great deep reach |
| 361 | stupid | heavy-headed | aj | | | 1590 | | | | > | heavy < *kap- head |
| 372 | clever-intelligent | conceited | aj | | | 1593 | − | 1594 | | | conceive < con capere < *kap- |
| 374 | stupid | unconceiving | aj | | | 1593 | − | 1740 | | | conceive < con capere < *kap- |
| 377 | clever-intelligent | conceitful | aj | | | 1594 | − | 1607 | | | conceive < con capere < *kap- |
| 427 | clever-intelligent | apprehensive | aj | | | 1601 | − | 1697 | + | 1868 | ad- pre- hendere < *ghend- |
| 437 | clever-sharp | nimble | aj | | | 1604 | | | | > | nimble < numol < *nem- |
| 448 | clever-common sense | capable | aj | | | 1606 | | | | > | capere < *kap- |
| 467 | stupid | unapprehensible | aj | | | 1613 | | | | | ad- pre- hendere < *ghend- |
| 471 | clever-sharp | nimble-witted | aj | | | 1613/6 | | | | > | nimble < numol < *nem- wit < *weid- |
| 488 | clever-sharp | nimble-headed | aj | | | 1624 | | | | | nimble < numol < *nem- head |

Table 3 (contd.)

| Record no. | Meaning | Word | Part of speech | OE? Plus/and | a/c1 Date 1 | +/- a/c2 Date 2 | -/+ a/c3 Date 3 | Current? | Label | Derivation |
|---|---|---|---|---|---|---|---|---|---|---|
| 490 | stupid | unapprehensive | aj | | 1624 | – | 1840 | | | ad- pre- hendere <*ghend- |
| 568 | stupid | uncomprehensive | aj | | 1667 | | | | | com- pre- hendere <*ghend- |
| 640 | clever-intelligent | clever | aj | | 1716 | | | ∧ | | clever<*gleubh- |
| 644 | stupid | unperceiving | aj | | 1723 | + | 1803 | | | perceive<per capere<*kap- take |
| 674 | clever-sharp | uptaking | aj | | 1756 | | | | sc | ad- pre- hendere <*ghend- |
| 704 | stupid | unapprehending | aj | | 1794 | – | 1891 | | | clever<*gleubh- |
| 761 | clever-intelligent | cleverish | aj | | 1826 | – | 1844 | | | clever<*gleubh- |
| 789 | clever-sharp | nimble-brained | aj | | 1836/48 | | | | | nimble<numol <*nem- brain |
| 813 | clever-smart alec derog | clever-boots/-sides/-sticks | n | | 1847 | | | ∧ | cq&dl | clever<*gleubh- boots sides sticks |
| 848 | clever-intelligent | perceptive | aj | | 1860 | | | ∧ | | perceive<per capere<*kap- tact |
| 857 | clever-wise | tactful | aj | | 1864 | | | ∧ | | |
| 864 | clever-smart alec derog | clever-clogs | n | | 1866 | | | ∧ | cq&dl | clever<*gleubh- clogs |
| 905 | clever-smart alec derog | clever dick | n | | 1887 | | | ∧ | | clever<*gleubh- dick |
| 922 | clever-smart alec derog | clever-clever | aj | | 1896 | | | ∧ | | clever<*gleubh- |

2.10.3 SENSE-TASTE

Table 4

| Record no | Meaning | Word | Part of speech | OE? | Plus/and a/c1 | Date 1 | +/- | a/c2 | Date 2 | -/+ | a/c3 | Date 3 | Current? | Label | Derivation |
|---|---|---|---|---|---|---|---|---|---|---|---|---|---|---|---|
| 140 | clever-wise | age | aj | | | 1297 | – | a | 1872 | | | | | | sapere<*sap- |
| 182 | clever-wise | sage | n | | a | 1400 | – | | 1862 | | | | | | sapere<*sap- |
| 219 | clever-wise | sapient | aj | | | 1471 | – | | 1868 | | | | | | sapere<*sap- |
| 238 | stupid | wearish | aj | | | 1519 | – | | 1537 | | | | | | wearish |
| 274 | clever-wise | sapient | n | | | 1549 | – | | 1600 | + | | 1827 | | 1827jo | sapere<*sap- |
| 555 | clever-wise | sapientipotent | aj | | | 1656 | | | | | | | | | sapere<*sap-potent |
| 580 | clever-wise | sapientipotent | n | | | 1675 | | | | | | | | | sapere<*sap-potent |
| 617 | stupid | insipid | n | | a | 1700 | – | a | 1834 | | | | | | sapere<*sap- |
| 667 | clever-wise derog | sage | n | | | 1751 | – | | 1893 | | | | | | sapere<*sap- |
| 868 | clever-common sense | salted | aj | | | 1869 | – | | 1900 | | | | | | salt |
| 887 | clever-wise | sage-like | aj | | | 1879 | | | | | | | | | sapere<*sap- |
| 936 | clever-shrewd | savey/savvy | aj | | | 1905 | | | | | | | > | | sabe<sapere<*sap- |

## 2.10.4 *SENSE-HEARING*

### Table 5

| Record no. | Meaning | Word | Part of speech | OE? | Plus/and | a/c1 | Date 1 | +/- | a/c2 | Date 2 | -/+ | a/c3 | Date 3 | Current? | Label | Derivation |
|---|---|---|---|---|---|---|---|---|---|---|---|---|---|---|---|---|
| 148 | stupid | daff | n | | | c | 1325 | – | | 1616 | + | | | 1876 | | 1876di nd | ?daft ?deaf |
| 206 | stupid | deaf | aj | | | c | 1440 | – | | 1482 | | | | | | | deaf |
| 302 | stupid | deaf/dumb as a beetle | aj | | | | 1566 | | | | | > | | | | | deaf dumb beetle |
| 426 | stupid | surd | aj | | | | 1601 | – | a | 1676 | | | | | | | surd |
| 630 | stupid | dunny | n | | | | 1709 | | | | | | | | | | ?dun |
| 807 | stupid | dunch | aj | | | | 1845 | – | | 1927 | | | | | | | dun dunch |

# 3

# DENSITY

## 3.1 Introduction

The second group of INTELLIGENCE data I will examine is made up of entries related to DENSITY, ie the property of having physically close texture. This is a notably different kind of source concept from the other two large groups that are presented here, and in the context of the other data it appears to be a much more specific and narrow concept than either of these. As has been shown in the preceding chapter, the senses are integral to the way INTELLIGENCE is understood, whereas density seems intuitively to be much more marginal. At the same time, the DENSITY group contrasts sharply with the ANIMAL data in Chapter 4. Animals are metaphorically related to humans in a relatively predictable and systematic way to refer to a range of characteristics including intelligence, but there does not appear to be an acknowledged habitual mapping between physical textures and human characteristics that is comparable with this ANIMAL mapping.

Correspondingly, DENSITY as a source concept has received little attention from any area of language study; in fact, its metaphorical link with INTELLIGENCE only seems to have been picked up in a single isolated account (in an article that provided the initial impetus for the present study). This gives a preliminary description of the evidence and motivation for the mapping.

> ...to express the abstract idea of stupidity in Modern English, we consistently draw on the more tangible domain of texture, that is the texture of material objects: we talk about a *head made of concrete*, *impenetrable stupidity* (which nothing can pierce through); we refer to a person as being *thick, dense, cloth-headed, wooden-headed*, or even, in the vernacular, *as thick as two short planks*...the metaphor can be expressed as a proposition...: Stupidity is close texture. (Kay 2000: 277)

The lack of attention to the DENSITY metaphor elsewhere is a surprising oversight. From the data presented here, it appears to have been a relatively important conceptual source for several centuries, accounting for a good number of expressions. My impression is that even though it may not be at the core of the way intelligence is conceptualised to the same extent as the senses or animals, it is still highly productive as a means to metaphorise stupidity. This is evidenced by the appearance of recent expressions like *thick as shit* or Scottish English *thick as mince* (discussed further below). As well as this, the DENSITY group provides an interesting parallel to the SENSES data, since the mappings involved in each are motivated by metonymy. This is discussed in more detail in section 3.4.

It may be that one reason for the omission of research into the mapping is that the DENSITY group represents a particular kind of metaphor, and one that does not sit well against that background of metaphor research conducted in the past. Early enquiries into metaphor, within philosophy and later literary criticism, dealt mainly with creative and novel metaphor found in literature and fairly high-register genres. Neither afforded much attention to low-register colloquial language, and it is with this kind of language that the DENSITY group is associated. Twenty-one entries (around 24%) in the group are labelled either 'slang', 'colloquial' or 'dialectal', based on the somewhat erratic labelling in the *OED*. Without examining each of the quotations for each entry it is difficult to ascertain whether this figure is accurate, but it may be meaningful that more than half of the entries in the group, 50 entries, share some etymological history with these 21.[1] Although I would not argue that this figure is a precise reflection of the number of entries that should be identified with low-register or spoken language, it does indicate that in this case *OED* labelling may not be consistent or comprehensive.[2]

Within the Lakoffian tradition and cognitive linguistics generally, there has been more work on spoken language and slang. The bulk of attention, however, has been concentrated on a fairly limited set of metaphors, which can be clearly shown to be motivated cognitively and experientially, and which are conceptual in that they underlie the way a whole concept is structured. This has allowed room for the thorough investigation and deconstruction of particular mappings in a way that was not previously attempted, and to a large extent the approach has demystified the mapping process by endeavouring to root it in real human experience. Conversely, however, it has drawn attention away from metaphors that are more culturally conditioned, and which affect conceptualisation in a smaller scale. I would contend that the DENSITY group reflects a metaphor of this kind, and it is for this reason that it has been largely ignored.

## 3.2 DATA

The interesting thing about the DENSITY group is that the source concepts from which individual entries derive are unexpectedly specific, and there are a very limited number of these. I have identified three broad groups by source, WOOD, EARTH and FOOD, and around 70% of the entries are connected

---

[1] To gain this information I ran a query in the database, specifying any of the same relevant derivation words in the 'derivation' field. For example, one of the entries that is labelled *slang* is grout-headed aj 1578–1694 + 1847/78; a query using *grout* in the 'derivation' field finds a further two entries with this element.

[2] It should be noted that labelling will be substantially revised in *OED3*.

with one of these (possible reasons for this are discussed below). There is no particular bias towards either nouns or adjectives within the group.

All of the entries in this group signify stupidity; there are no expressions at all in the data that are related to cleverness, including negated compounds,[3] and correspondingly, every one of the entries is related to close texture as opposed to loose texture. Moreover, there does not seem to be a binary and symmetrical opposition between DENSE mapping to STUPID and NON-DENSE mapping to CLEVER, as there is in many of the other source concepts relating to properties, including STRENGTH/WEAKNESS, HEALTH, COMPLETION and SPEED. Part of the reason for this may be that it simply is not a symmetrical concept; there is no single word that is commonly used to express the opposite of density without introducing another seme,[4] and this may indicate that there is no central antonymous concept. There are a very few words in the data that might arguably be associated with loose texture; the most straightforward of these is Scots and dialectal fozy aj 1894>, defined in the *OED* as 'spongy, loose-textured' (and classified as LOOSE TEXTURE), but like the DENSITY entries this also signifies stupidity.

### 3.2.1 *General terms*

There are surprisingly few general terms within the data. Of the total of 89 entries in the group, only 18 are derived from general terms, all of which are adjectives meaning 'dense'. Almost all of these, 14 of the entries, are variants of *thick* (mainly in compounds), and of the remaining entries two are from *gross* and a single entry each derive from *dense* and *crass*.

One of the entries in this section is also listed under WOOD/TREE, and deserves comment. This is the simile as thick as two planks aj 1974>. My own intuition and the comments of others suggest that the formula *as thick as —* is common and still highly productive, demonstrating the continued use of the DENSITY mapping. Some of the current conventional phrases that have been drawn to my attention are *thick as a brick*, *thick as (pig/dog) shit*, Scottish English *thick as mince*, and Irish *thick as a ditch*;[5] a number of occasional uses have also been recorded. The first *OED* quotation supporting thick aj 1597>, from Shakespeare's *The Second Part of King Henry the Fourth*, is a simile of this form: the character Falstaff says: 'his Wit is as thicke as Tewksburie Mustard' (line 262). Partridge lists a much more recent example, *thick as a docker's sandwich*, from a 1973 Morecambe and Wise Show (Partridge 1984: 1219), and Brewer's *Dictionary of Phrase and Fable* lists *as thick as a doorpost*. This continuing productivity seems to me to be further evidence

---

[3] The opposite situation can be found in, for example, the SENSES group, where a number of entries are formed from lexical roots found elsewhere in the group with a negative prefix.

[4] *Roget's Thesaurus* places *density* next to *rarity*, but as the *OED* points out, this is usually associated with air. In addition, its use is not widespread or common.

[5] www.clichesite.com, accessed 28 Feb. 2008.

that the phrase 'dead metaphor' is not appropriate, since it calls into question the assumption that highly conventional metaphors like this have simply become new linguistic forms and no longer have associations with the original source concept. It does not seem possible to prove that terms like this, with image-based origins, still call up mental images of physical entities for speakers; but given that new and original phrases with the same motivation can be coined, it seems unhelpful to dismiss this possibility entirely. As Richards points out, 'however stone dead such metaphors seem, we can easily wake them up' (1936: 101). As well as this, the appearance of phrases of this type lends credence to the idea that in certain cases simile can be one stage in the process of linguistic metaphorisation (discussed below in section 3.4.3).

### 3.2.2 WOOD

There are 34 entries in the WOOD group, and most of these derive from a small number of roots. Seven entries, five of them compounds with a HEAD element, are from *block*, and a further six are from *log* (four of these are more specifically from the later *logger*[6]); again, in all but one of these *head* is the second element of the item. There are also five entries that derive from *wood*. The remaining 16 entries have a range of roots, and apart from two entries that contain a general term for wood, timber-headed aj 1666 and timber-head n 1849, all of these derive from terms for pieces of wood. One entry, as thick as (two) plank(s) aj 1974 >, is exceptional in this group, since it is not from a term specifically denoting a large chunk of wood. Of the others, two entries each derive from *stock*, *stub*,[7] *chuckle*, *nog* and *chump*. The remaining items are hulver-head aj a1700, stump n 1825 >[8] , and the curious phrase as sad as any mallet aj 1645.

---

[6] According to the *OED*, this developed as 'app. a word invented as expressing by its sound the notion of something heavy and clumsy', in a parallel way to *log*, though the dictionary does not say that *logger* is a direct descendant of *log*. As well as this, contrary to the intuitions of a number of people with whom I have discussed the DENSITY data, the expression *loggerhead* is attested earlier with the meaning 'a stupid person' than to refer to any kind of blunt instrument. It therefore seems unlikely to have been motivated by the idea of a blunt instrument knocking against something clumsily, as in the phrase *at loggerheads* (cf. the *ram* entries in the SHEEP category, discussed in the following chapter), although it may subsequently have been influenced by this.

[7] One of these is stob n 1825; the *OED* suggests that this is 'partly a variant (sometimes merely graphic), partly a cognate, of STUB'.

[8] This is slightly more complex etymologically. The earliest attested example refers to the part of the body left after a limb is amputated, and a cognate adjective in Middle Dutch is defined in the *OED* as 'mutilated, blunt, dull'; the meaning connected with wood is attested a little later. A number of other entries are connected with body parts in the INTELLIGENCE data, but none of these seem to be comparable and therefore I have not judged this other element of the meaning to be relevant. I have placed the entry in the category WOOD because it appears more likely to be primarily motivated by this later meaning in the context of the rest of the group, and I have also included the label LEFTOVER in the core category field of the data table.

### 3.2.3 EARTH

The twelve entries in this group are derived from only three roots, and again these are predominantly in compounds with a HEAD element. Six items are derived from *clod*, and one of these, clod-skull n 1707 is one of only six entries in the INTELLIGENCE data with the element *skull* for HEAD. There are five entries from *mud*, and the final entry in the group is turf n 1607.

### 3.2.4 FOOD

This is the second largest group in DENSITY, and the 16 entries are mainly related either to meat substances or course-textured grain-type substances. Of the MEAT entries, which total eight, two derive from *meat* itself, four from *beef*, and two from *mutton*. There are also two other entries that do not come from meat but are from a substance closely linked to this subgroup: suet-brained aj 1921 > and suet-headed aj 1937 >.[9] The lexemes in the group I have labelled GRAIN are all from two roots: three entries have *grout* as a root, and two are derived from *pudding* (which is likely to be from the older sense of a dish made from a mixture of ingredients, with a gritty texture).

### 3.2.5 MISCELLANEOUS

This group contains nine entries, although two of these are similar to entries in other DENSITY groups. Clay-brained aj 1596 seems fairly closely aligned to the EARTH entries, and similarly knuckle-head n 1944 > may not be unconnected with the MEAT entries, since it may relate to *knuckle* as a food substance used as the basis of soup etc. Of the other entries, two derive from *bone* and another from *ivory*; there are also two entries from *stone* (one of them from a variant form, stunpoll n a1794 >); and the final two entries in the group derive from *leather*.

### 3.3 DATES

As with the ANIMAL group, there are no entries dating to pre-1500, and this corresponds to the relative lack of early STUPIDITY words in the data as a whole. It is also consistent with the balance of data in the *Thesaurus of Old English*, in which there are far more entries relating to cleverness than stupidity. There are a total of 226 entries in the INTELLIGENCE data for which

---

[9] There are other entries that might also belong to this group, although I have not categorised them as such, which are from *fat*; it is unclear whether these are more closely linked to fat as an edible substance, as suet tends to be, or whether they come from the idea of fat as a part of the body, as I am inclined to assume.

the earliest recorded example is dated to pre-1500 (including those dated a1500, but not 1500 or c1500), compared with 849 entries dated 1500 and later. Within these two time periods, the balance between STUPID and CLEVER entries is quite different: pre-1500, there are 73 signifying stupidity (16 relating to VISION) and 153 signifying cleverness; from 1500 onwards, there are 575 and 274 respectively. As I will go on to discuss in section 4.3, although there are no early ANIMAL entries there is clearly a well-established tradition of ANIMAL-HUMAN thought that made animals an available source concept for the indication of intelligence (and lack of intelligence). For the DENSITY group, it seems far more difficult to determine whether the conceptual link between texture and intelligence had already been widely made by the time there is written evidence of the metaphor. However, it does not seem unlikely that the primary metaphors that underlie the DENSITY mapping were already core to early conceptualisation of the intellect. For example, it is uncontroversial to suggest that the MIND AS CONTAINER metaphor was well established in Old English, where it is common to talk about things being 'in' mind, and in fact one entry in the data attests this: idel aj OE also means 'empty'. A number of cognates suggest that this is the earliest sense of the root (see the *OED* entry for *idle*). This would indicate that even if DENSITY was not commonly associated with stupidity, the building blocks for this link were in place.

## 3.4 MOTIVATION

The motivation for the DENSITY mapping is not immediately obvious, but I would suggest that it is the product of the complex interaction of a number of processes that are variously cognitive, cultural and intralinguistic. Most basically, one aspect of the motivation for the mapping is metonymical, and in this sense it can be compared to the SENSES mapping explored in the previous chapter. However, the group also has parallels with the ANIMAL group in its gestalt-like nature, but the specific 'reasoning' that lies behind the metaphor is quite different from this conceptually.

In their work on blending theory (discussed in more detail in section 3.4.1, this chapter), Fauconnier & Turner discuss the metaphorical sentence *He digested the book*. The way in which they analyse this gives an important insight into the way certain metaphors can be grounded, and the kind of process they describe is integral to the way in which the DENSITY mapping is motivated.

> A fundamental motivating factor of blending is the integration of several events into a single unit ... Even metaphoric mappings that ostensibly look most as if they depend entirely on the construction of metaphoric counterparts can have integration of events as a prin-cipal motivation and product. 'He digested the book' of course has

metaphoric counterparts, such as food and book, but it also projects
an integration of events. In the source, digesting already constitutes
an integration of a number of different events. But its counterpart in
the target is, independent of the metaphor, a series of discreet events
– taking up the book, reading it, parsing its individual sentences,
finishing it, thinking about it, understanding it as a whole, and so on.
The integrity in the source is projected to the blend so that this array
of events in the target acquires a conceptual integration of its events
into a unit. On one hand, the metaphor blends conceptual counterparts in the two spaces – eating and reading. On the other hand,
the metaphor helps us to integrate some distinct event sequences in
the space of reading. (Fauconnier & Turner 1998: 158)

An important distinction is made here between the metaphor at its simplest
level – in which the source concept is mapped to a second, target concept –
and the projected source 'process' that provides a basic motivation for this
mapping. In a similar way to that described here by Fauconnier & Turner
for the metaphor *He digested a book*, the DENSITY mapping has two
metaphoric 'counterparts': a dense substance and intelligence (or rather,
stupidity). But the motivation for the metaphor is rooted in an
"integration" of several factors – it is based on an image, and works
almost like a narrative. As the high number of compounds formed with
HEAD/BRAIN words indicates, the DENSITY mapping is derived from the idea of
the compositionality of the mind, seen as a physical part of the body; there
is a metonymical relationship between the head or brain and the mind,
which are obviously conceptually close. The basic idea is presumably that if
something is dense in its physical texture, it will be difficult to penetrate, so
if a person's mind is dense, ideas and knowledge cannot easily get in or
through. A number of common phrases have the same basis: it is natural
and conventional to talk about *getting something through one's head* or
*skull*, or to say that an idea or theory *won't go in*. Important to this
conceptualisation is the idea of impediment to motion, since the density of
the mind prevents the passage of ideas; and metaphorically this can also
cause a temporary problem, when one has a *mental block*, as opposed to
experiencing a *flow of ideas*.

Although, as with the SENSES mapping, the connection between density
and intelligence is motivated by metonymy, in other ways it appears to
contrast fairly sharply with the motivation for other core category groups
within the data. There does not appear to be any kind of primary metaphor
involved as with the SENSES group, and it is difficult to argue for any kind of
perceived similarity between source and target as with some groups like
ANIMAL (examined in Chapter 4). However, the account I have suggested
does have a number of entailments, dependent on certain other metaphors
that are fundamental to the way the mind is conceptualised. For the mind

to have any sort of texture, it must be a physical, bounded entity, and this is a common and well-documented mapping: ATT-Meta lists MIND AS PHYSICAL ENTITY (Barnden 1997), and the Conceptual Metaphor Homepage includes THE MIND IS A BODY and THE MIND IS A MACHINE, both specific examples of this (Lakoff 1994). For things to get 'through' the mind's boundary and 'inside' it, a container schema must be closely aligned with the mapping. This fits in with other core category groups within the data, including CONTAINER itself, as well as the entries relating to grasping, which I referred to above within the SENSES group – a basic way of accounting for grasp is roughly as a blend of TOUCH and CONTAINER. A common mapping related to the CONTAINER metaphor is IMPORTANT IS CENTRAL (Grady 1997: 284), and this seems relevant as well.

As with the ANIMAL data, an important part of the motivation of the DENSITY group is the negative implication of the mapping. Comparing a human to an animal in terms of intelligence denies them fully human status in that respect, and therefore implies that they are intellectually 'lower'. In a similar way, assigning any physical texture to the head or brain, the crucial centre of intellectual activity, implies that this is not correctly composed, and therefore lacks the capacity for intelligent thought. To a greater extent than the ANIMAL group, a high percentage of these entries are compounds with a *head/brain* element, and this indicates explicitly that terms are concerned with the intellect.

As discussed in section 1.3.5, a huge number of entries in the INTELLIGENCE data as a whole are compounds of *head* or *brain*. Several of those outside the DENSITY group (e.g. those relating to the core categories CONTAINER and HARD/SOFT) provide parallels to those in this group, in that they also conceptualise intelligence in terms of the physical composition of the mind, and presumably also imply that a person is stupid because the mind is composed of the wrong material. In his study of approximately 500 German idiomatic expressions for stupidity, Feyaerts schematizes the conceptual relationships involved in the mapping between stupidity and its various source fields (1999: 323ff.). He argues that the key feature that characterises all the expressions and motivates their mapping to stupidity is that they deal with 'deviant human properties'; he then proposes various sub-categories at different hierarchical levels of his classification. All of the phrases he has found that are associated with the head or brain being constituted from physical objects or substances (other than a properly functioning brain) are subsumed under the heading 'deficient head/brain'. Similarly, Jonathan Charteris-Black's work (2003) comparing English and Malay phraseology, part of which deals with figurative phrases containing English *head* or Malay *kepala*, identifies a number of phrases in each language that link the physical composition of the head with lack of intelligence. As I will go on to discuss in this chapter, there are certainly other considerations that operate alongside this general motivation, and it is noticeable that through time certain substances, and certain types of substance, are repeatedly used in the mapping. These can have additional, secondary motivations that support and strengthen the link with intelligence. However, it is important to recognise that they also fit into a broader framework, and one that is also found in languages other than English.[10]

Some of the mappings in this group are also influenced by an image-based metaphor: there are several entries in the DENSITY data with a first element that comes from an object that is very roughly head-shaped. Much of the WOOD data falls into this category, since a number of entries are drawn from lumps of wood, such as chuckle-headed aj 1764 > and nog-head n c1800 >. It is also true of most of the entries in the FRUIT/VEG category mentioned above, as well as for others including pot-headed aj 1533 (categorised as OBJECT&CONTAINER) and possibly knotty-pated aj 1596 (categorised as LUMP). I would guess that this kind of source is particularly appropriate because associated entities can be mentally 'substituted' for the head very easily in image terms.

The individual motivations for each of the specific substances that occur as sources will be discussed in the sections below; but taking these as a group it is possible to make generalisations about what makes any particular substance successful as a source. Paralleling the ANIMAL group, the subgroups within DENSITY are all very common, everyday entities which would have been familiar to speakers at the time and are still part of daily human experience. None is of particularly high value: though wood and food can be important commodities, they tend not to be costly in their crude, uncrafted state and are certainly not perceived as prestigious items of worth. Furthermore, all of the substances involved are of basic rather than complex structure, with uniform consistency, reflected by the fact that most of them are mass nouns or are constituted from mass noun substances. For example, logs are countable but are units of wood, and in the same way potatoes have a single texture throughout even though they are discrete bounded items.

However, as with all the other core category groups I have presented within this book, this explanation of the motivation of the group does not provide a full explanation for all the DENSITY data. As I have pointed out above, a high proportion of the entries I have assigned to this group are particularly interesting in their specificity. DENSITY is proposed as a core category here because it appears to fit the data, but this is a subjective judgement made only on the strength of a number of clues, which include the general density terms within the group and the *thick as* similes (discussed above). For some entries, density seems the most obviously relevant property of the source substance, but for others this is more

---

[10] Although the ANIMAL data does not fit into this group neatly, it is certainly analogous in the way that it emphasises the connection between stupidity and a less-than-human brain.

questionable, and this group perhaps more than any other highlights the problems of interpreting the motivation for any particular mapping. It should be pointed out that the most important aspect of my approach to the data is that it is corpus-centred, and that the classification that I have imposed results from an analysis of the data, rather than being theory-based. It is for this reason that I would argue for its validity, even where individual entries require further discussion or justification.

I will go on to discuss this matter of motivation in more detail in relation to each of the core category groups in the sections below. In general, though, it seems to me that the idea of cognitive 'cohesion' is helpful here. The DENSITY entries do seem to me to have a basic property in common, but I acknowledge that the source concepts are not suitable to express lack of intelligence only because they are dense substances. Other properties must also be relevant, and perhaps the combination of properties make them more cognitively 'convincing', especially since metaphorical sources are not selected as a result of conscious reasoning about motivation. Furthermore, it may also be the case that even though a particular item is not originally motivated in the same way as some others that appear similar, it may still be influenced by these and this influence may even account for its continued usage, at least in part. As I have already indicated, the importance of folk etymology is by now widely recognised; it seems logical that similar mechanisms might lie behind (conscious or subconscious) reasoning about metaphorical and metonymical mappings.

### 3.4.1 *Blending theory*

Because it allows for a range of different processes and connections like those discussed throughout this chapter whilst also acknowledging the conceptual importance of primary metaphor, I would suggest that in a general way blending theory provides a helpful framework in which to analyse the DENSITY group. This theoretical approach has been most closely associated with 'online' mental processing, but Fauconnier & Turner do point out that it can also be relevant to 'fixed projections', found linguistically in conventionalised metaphorical expressions (or expressions that can be assigned to conventionalised mappings).

> Like other forms of thought and action, blends can be either en-
> trenched or novel. 'Digging your own grave' is a complex blend
> entrenched conceptually and linguistically ... We often recruit
> entrenched projections to help us to do on-line conceptual projec-
> tion. On-line projections and entrenched projections are not differ-
> ent in kind; entrenched projections are on-line projections that have
> become entrenched. Our seemingly fixed projections are highly

entrenched projections of an imaginative sort. (Fauconnier & Turner 1998: 161)

As Grady et al. point out, blending theory and conceptual metaphor theory have been seen as incongruous by some scholars, but are in fact complementary approaches that can combine to form a framework that can be both structured and flexible (Grady et al. 1999: 101).[11] Whilst metaphor study has traditionally focused on the unidirectional relationship between two concepts, the source and target of the mapping, blending theory allows for a more complex interaction of a number of elements that result in a 'blend'. Input is taken from a number of mental 'spaces', each the source of information of a variety of sorts. This information might be of the nature of a particular type of reasoning, such as analogical mapping; it might involve some background knowledge about a particular situation or scenario, i.e. the frame or idealised cognitive model of a particular concept; or it might activate a commonly made link between two particular conceptual entities, including conventional metaphors or metonymies. These pieces of information are then combined selectively to produce a new conceptual unit, which might itself become conventional, and can be one source of input for subsequent blends.

I would argue that blending theory is particularly helpful because it allows for such a wide range of influences on any one mapping. As I have argued above, whilst a metaphor may have one principal motivation, it may be especially successful because it is cognitively cohesive in the way that it can be strengthened by other possible motivations as well. This also allows for the influence of folk etymology on the way a metaphor (or metonymy) is understood, and recognises these kinds of supporting motivation as equally valid elements of the mapping. One of the examples that Fauconnier & Turner analyse illustrates some of the possibilities for inputs that can be involved in any blend.

> Blends can combine non-counterpart elements that come from different inputs. Consider The Grim Reaper, which is a blend with several input spaces, including a space of harvest and a space of

---

[11] This article goes on to point out that blending theory parallels the theory of primary metaphor in the way that it focuses on conceptual 'building blocks' that combine to produce something different and yet meaningful:

> The idea that simple metaphors interact to yield more elaborate conceptualizations has been discussed by researchers working in the CMT framework. (See, for instance, Lakoff & Turner's 1989 discussion of 'composite' metaphors, and Grady's 1997 more explicit analysis of the "unification" or "binding" of metaphors.) The blending framework offers a neat way of representing this complex interaction of concepts and links, since it explicitly allows for multiple spaces and multiple iterations of the integration process (Grady et al. 1999: 109).

In fact, both theories have elements reminiscent of Max Black's interaction theory, in which he argued that the meaning of any metaphor is the result of the interaction between the source and target (or in his terminology, tenor and vehicle), rather than a direct mapping of one onto the other (Black 1962, discussed in section 1.2.1).

particular human death ... elements in a single input space that are metonymically related can be combined in the blend. Priests, monks, mourners, and members of lay brotherhood that are associated with dying, funerals, burial and afterlife are metonymically associated with Death. They are not counterparts of Death, but in the blend, an attire we associate with them – robe and cowl – can be the attire of The Grim Reaper ... The possibility of combining non-counterparts on the basis of metonymic connections – like the connection between Death and a skeleton – gives blending a great power: the blend can combine elements that contribute to the desired effect *even though those elements are not counterparts.* The combined elements 'go together' according to the counterpart connections between the input spaces ... Composition, completion, and elaboration all recruit selectively from our most favored patterns of knowing and thinking. This makes blending a powerful conceptual instrument, but it also makes it highly subject to bias. Composition, completion, and elaboration operate for the most part automatically and below the horizon of conscious observation. This makes the detection of biases difficult. Seepage into the blend can come from defaults, prototypes, category information, conventional scenarios, and any other routine knowledge. (Fauconnier & Turner 1998: 161–2)

The 'seepage' that is mentioned at the end of this passage may be a relevant notion when analysing the DENSITY group, since the specific substances that are involved in particular instances of the density mapping are as relevant to the mapping as the general property of density itself. In a sense, therefore, the motivation for these lexemes is complex, and involves more than one input; this is discussed further in the following section. Blending is also a helpful notion in considering the animal data, since a good deal of anecdotal information tends to be involved in each ANIMAL–HUMAN mapping. This can continue to happen even when the metaphor is conventionalised and has become relatively fixed. At each stage of the fable tradition described in Chapter 4, or at any other point in time, another 'layer' of fact or fiction can affect the folk knowledge about any animal and be integrated into the blended whole.

It should perhaps be noted that some scholars have regarded the way in which blending theory can accommodate such diverse 'inputs' with suspicion; the open-ended nature of the theory has led to criticisms that it is so general as to be meaningless. It is extremely difficult to produce any analysis of a blend which can be considered in any way objective, and the analyses of two scholars might look substantially different depending on their interpretation of data. Despite this, flexibility seems to me to be the strength of blending as an approach, and I think that Ray Gibbs's observation about the usefulness of the theory to psychology is useful here:

it is … important to realise that blending theory is not a single theory that can be studied and potentially falsified within a single experimental test. Instead, blending theory is a broad framework that suggests a variety of localized hypotheses … (Gibbs 2000: 349)

In my opinion, this 'broad framework' can be useful in examining and describing metaphoric and metonymical mappings as well as non-figurative language. Crucially, Fauconnier & Turner have stressed the importance of an interdisciplinary approach: 'Research on meaning … requires analysis of extensive ranges of data, which must be connected theoretically across fields and disciplines by general cognitive principles' (Fauconnier & Turner 1998: 136). Potentially, blending theory sits comfortably alongside established theories from semantics, and I believe that this is particularly important because traditional semantics as a discipline has been overlooked in much of the recent research within cognitive linguistics.

### 3.4.2 *General terms vs. specific substances*

As mentioned in the data section above, entries derived from general terms for density found in the data constitute just under one fifth of the group. This raises the question of why DENSITY should be mapped predominantly through lexemes that denote specific concepts (such as WOOD), rather than through more 'central' vocabulary' related to the source concept such as the term *density* itself. If the motivation for the specific groups is DENSITY, as I suggest here, it is unclear why specific substances are preferred to represent the mapping, since the motivation of these does appear to be relatively opaque. Linking a general concept directly with INTELLIGENCE does not present the problems of interpretation that can arise from referring to this concept indirectly via specific substances with the same general property, so that it would seem more logical for the mapping to be restricted to these.

However, there do seem to be various possible reasons for this. To a certain extent there may be a connection with the point Feyaerts makes about the general mapping between stupidity and a deficient head/brain. Using a specific substance or entity fits into this 'model' far more neatly and naturally, thereby plugging these metaphors into a more established pattern that can support and strengthen the blend. As well as this, the selection of a specific entity rather than a more general property may be connected to the way in which humans tend to process the world around them and relate concepts to known, familiar sources. A number of scholars have observed that abstract notions tend to be conceptualised in terms of concrete objects, and in general this is the direction that metaphorical mappings tend to follow. Mapping INTELLIGENCE to DENSITY draws upon a less abstract source domain, since density is a concept that is used with reference to concrete physical entities; but using a specific, physically apprehensible entity to stand for this concept may be an even better source. It may be relevant that the DENSITY mapping is based (at least in part) on a mental image, i.e. that of something trying to penetrate the mind: in order to form a mental picture of density, some substance that has the property of being dense must be involved.

The issue of cognitive 'cohesion' may also be related to the selection of particular sources. As I suggest above, it may be that the most convincing or 'successful' metaphors are those that potentially relate to a number of motivations, and selecting a particular entity as the source of a mapping allows for greater flexibility in this sense than using a more general property. In other words, it may be the very opaqueness of the motivation for some of these mappings that make them particularly apt. If several motivations are possible and a metaphorical expression can therefore be interpreted in several ways, this may be more effective, even though this process of interpretation is not conscious – and in fact these possible motivations may combine so that each adds an extra 'layer' to the blend. In the following sections I will go on to look in more detail at some of the properties connected with each of the subgroups of the core concept DENSITY.

### 3.4.3 WOOD

This is the largest subgroup in the DENSITY data, and furthermore it has the highest percentage of words still in current use of all the specific substance groups, 12 entries out of 35. (In the GENERAL group nearly half of the entries, 10 out of the total of 18, are marked current.) It is my impression that it is the most recognisable and prominent of the specific groups in its connection with stupidity, although for a number of these words the etymology is probably not generally recognised. For example, *chump* may not be widely known as a term for a piece of wood, and *block* has come to be used of a range of substances, such as manufactured materials including concrete, rather than only with wood (though this may still be its most common collocation). In fact, the way in which *block* has widened semantically may be further proof of the importance of familiar substances in even general terminology, since it seems unlikely that a term connected with a less familiar substance would develop semantically so that it could be used in such a general way. *Nugget* seems to exemplify this. In its earliest use in Standard English it specifically referred to 'a lump of gold', and although the *OED* lists the definition 'A lump of anything' for the term (with two supporting quotations from the end of the nineteenth century), in practice it tends to be used of a very limited number of substances in PDE. Furthermore, the substances which it can denote tend to be perceived as similar to gold either in terms of appearance or value.[12]

The entries in this group are not simply connected with wood, but tend to be from words for wood of particular specifications. Apart from the general terms *wood* and *timber*, a high proportion of the entries are formed from terms denoting pieces of wood – there are entries from *block*, *stock*, *log* and *logger*, *hulver* and *chump* – and almost all of these more specifically connote large chunks of wood. As well as being composed of a dense material, they are also unwieldy, awkwardly sized, heavy lumps that are uncrafted, and all of this makes them more cognitively 'convincing' or 'cohesive' as sources. In fact, in its notes about etymology, the *OED* suggests that *logger* was 'invented as expressing by its sound the notion of something heavy and clumsy'. A few entries in the rest of the INTELLIGENCE data parallel these characteristics; furthermore, largeness and heaviness can correlate with slowness, and SPEED is very important in the way intelligence is conceptualised. Similarly, the idea of formlessness can be found elsewhere in our vocabulary for the mental – we talk about ideas 'taking shape' or 'being shaped by' external influences.

One of the entries in the group, <u>stock n 1594 ></u>, may give a clue to the way in which this mapping became established. *Stock* is from OE *stoc*, 'tree trunk', which has a number of cognates in other Germanic languages. The *OED* lists the later meaning 'a senseless or stupid person' as part of a wider definition, and the supporting quotations illustrate the subtle progression from association between concepts to well-established, conventional mapping.

> As the type of what is lifeless, motionless, or void of sensation. Hence, a senseless or stupid person.
>
> **1303** R. Brunne *Handl. Synne* 940 Dowun he smote hys mattok, And fyl hym self ded as a stok.
>
> **c1330** *Arth. & Merl.* 3855 Arthour on hors sat stef so stok.
>
> **c1407** Lydg. *Reson & Sens.* 6411 As deffe as stok or ston.
>
> **c1440** *Alphabet of Tales* 356 Evur sho talkid vnto hym wurdis to provoce hym to luste of his bodie, and yit be no wyse myght sho induce hym Þerto, ... he was a stokk, sho sayd, & no man.
>
> **1569** T. Underdown *Heliodorus* iv. 59 Yee vnhappy people, howe longe will ye sitte still, dombe like stockes?
>
> **1594** Spenser *Amoretti* xliii, That nether I may speake nor thinke at all, But like a stupid stock in silence die!
>
> **1640** Sir E. Dering *Carmelite* (1641) B ij, I am not so credulous to thinke every Stock a Stoicke.

---

[12] For example, *chicken nuggets* as opposed to *\*beef nuggets*, and *nuggets of wisdom* rather than *\*nuggets of foolishness*.

**1644** Milton *Educ.* 3, I doubt not but ye shall have more adoe to drive our dullest and laziest youth, our stocks and stubbs from the infinite desire of such a happy nurture then we have now [etc.].

These quotations demonstrate that wood can also be metaphorically associated with a lack of feeling, and this draws attention to the fact that wood, like all the sources associated with DENSITY, is inanimate and static. Another set of entries, which I have categorised as ALIVE/ANIMATE,[13] has this as its primary motivation. In the quotations for *stock*, wood is more specifically used as something to exemplify deafness and dumbness (in the *c*.1407 and 1569 quotations respectively), as well a lack of physical or emotional sensitivity (particularly in the *c*.1440 quotation). In this respect the DENSITY group links in with the SENSES data, and again this relates to the idea of cognitive cohesion.

The *c*.1407 and 1569 quotations, in particular, show a possible connection between the physical sense of *stock* and an emergent mental sense, but in both cases the lexeme is found within a simile with the relevant property explicitly stated rather than in a more implicitly understood metaphor. The fact that both kinds of usage of *stock* can be found historically would support the view that metaphors and similes are of the same order, and that it is difficult to draw any precise distinction between the two; there are some cases in which it seems only to be a matter of convention whether one or the other is used. Any distinction between the two other than a purely formal one is particularly unconvincing in cases where metaphor can be seen to develop from simile. As Kay has pointed out, diachronic data indicates that it is possible for similes to become conventionalised to the level that they are still understood when they are condensed in language, for example, when someone is called a *plank* rather than being described as *as thick as two short planks*:

> ...creative literary metaphor [is] where a concept in one area of meaning is expressed and made more vivid by words taken from another domain ... Often such a metaphor may start life as a simile, since the establishment of likeness is implicit in any metaphor, and then progress to full metaphorical status. (Kay 2000: 276)

Though Kay separates creative literary metaphor from conventional metaphor here, it has been pointed out that creative literary metaphor is very often an extension or elaboration of conventional metaphor.

It may be that at the time the similes discussed in section 3.2.1 are recorded, the connections between the source substances and the target concept, STUPIDITY, are not sufficiently conventionalised to be understood

---

[13] This is a symmetrical category, containing both entries like quick aj 1484>, relating to the core category ALIVE/ANIMATE, and a small number of entries that use the opposite quality like dead from the neck up aj 1930>.

clearly in linguistic metaphor. By contrast, substances that are found in a number of entries in the database which are not in the form of similes must have reached a point where they are associated strongly enough with intelligence that they do not present any problems when used metaphorically. The mapping has simply become conventionalised to the extent that any explicit reference to the characteristic selected has been lost in some linguistic expressions.

Three other entries should be mentioned alongside this group, and these are all compounds of *stick*: clever-boots/-sides/-sticks n 1847 > , barm-stick n 1924 > and poop-stick n 1930 > . These do present a question for this group, and in fact have not been classified alongside the WOOD group. Although sticks are obviously constituted from wood, the motivation for these lexemes does not appear to be associated with DENSITY. In these entries, *stick* appears to be an element that simply means 'person'; the *OED* gives this as a definition, with quotations dated from 1682 onwards:

> **12. a.** Applied, with qualifying adj., to a person, orig. with figurative notion of sense 2 or 4, as ***tough stick***; ***crooked*** (*Sc.* ***thrawn***) ***stick***, a perverse, cross-grained person.

Exactly why *stick* should denote a person is unclear, but there are several possibilities. This may be a simple image-based metaphor drawn from the everyday. Sticks are familiar objects that are very roughly human-shaped in that they are long and narrow (attested by the fact that from early times, sticks have been fashioned into human figurines, for ritualistic purposes or as children's toys). Moreover, sticks have traditionally been used for, or made into, a variety of tools and weapons, and as the *OED* entry attests many of these have also been referred to as *sticks*. It is quite common for the equipment that is typically used for a particular purpose to be extended metonymically to mean the individual using it, and this may account for some transferred uses of *stick* to denote people. This is the case in both *OED* senses 4e and 10e, where particular senses of *stick* are associated with particular pursuits or professions. In the first instance the definition given is 'A rod of dignity or office, a baton; also the bearer of such a stick', and in the second, 'The hammer or mallet with which a dulcimer or drum is struck. Hence *pl.*, a nickname for a drummer (*Naval slang*)'. If this kind of motivation accounts for these three entries, they are unrelated to the DENSITY mapping. Nevertheless, it is not impossible that they may have been influenced to some limited extent by the other WOOD entries, and because of this I have included them here for the purposes of comparison.

### 3.4.4 EARTH

As the above figures indicate, the EARTH group is substantially smaller than the WOOD group, and most of the entries in the group have a comparatively short life-span. As well as this, most of the entries are derived from either *clod* and *mud*: 11 out of 14 entries, around 79% of the group, have one of these as an element. Both factors seem to fit in with my own intuition that this is a less central concept for stupidity than wood. Although this group has a less well-established link with intelligence, it is interesting that the substances within it form a reasonably clear group, and that there is so much variation in words with a common source. For this reason it is presented here as a core category.

Earth substances fit all the suggested criteria for sources within the DENSITY group given above. Earth is common, familiar and, at least in its natural state, considered worthless. Additionally, it lacks any definite form, and is commonly found in an unstructured mass or in rough lumps. Like wood, it is an organic substance, and perhaps in a very general way this adds to their commonalities as substances. One entry, turf n 1607, is not central to this group, but has been included because it is conceptually close.

Other factors may affect the individual entries and groups of entries within this subcategory; in particular those derived from the two roots given above, *mud* and *clod*, are likely to have been influenced by associations particular to the substances that they signify. More than other substances in the group, mud has turbidity as one of its salient properties, especially in its liquid form, and this may link it with the idea of lack of clarity. As Chapter 2 attests, this is central to the way intelligence is conceptualised because it is so closely linked with vision. It may not follow logically that lack of ability to perceive visually relates to the opaqueness of a physical substance, but a vague connection still seems possible and cannot be dismissed.[14] It is interesting that the etymology of *muddle* shows the same root as *mud*: according to the *OED muddle* is derived from *mud*, as the equivalents are in Middle Dutch. Again, this may reinforce the link with lack of mental faculty. In a similar way, the fact that a clod is a cohesive body of earth aligns it with entries categorised as LUMP.[15] The *OED*

---

[14] This may be similar to the way in which *mince* is associated with stupidity in Scots. A stupid person can be *thick as mince* or having *mince for brains*, but ideas that are not regarded as sensible or rational can also be described as *mince*. Other substances, such as *excrement*, can be used in the same way (in fact, *shit* can be used in place of *mince* in the expressions *thick as shit* and *shit for brains*, as well as to describe ideas themselves), as can a huge variety of lexical items such as *dumb*, *lame* and even *stupid* itself. This may relate to point made in Ch. 5, section 5.1.1 about the opposite and conflicting general ways intelligence is conceptualised: on one hand, the mind can be the agent, as in the SENSES metaphors and ANIMAL metaphors, but on the other it can be the passive recipient of active ideas, as in the DENSITY metaphors.

[15] It may be that these should be placed alongside the EARTH data as part of the DENSITY group. The reason I have not classified them in this way is that the image element of the concept LUMP which is discussed in this section seems to be equally as important as DENSITY, so that assigning the LUMP entries to a separate core category group whilst acknowledging them alongside DENSITY intuitively seems preferable. For the same reason, the FRUIT/VEG entries have also been categorised separately, but for both cases I would accept that this is questionable, and the entries should perhaps have been placed in both categories.

definition for the most general sense of lump is 'A compact mass of no particular shape; a shapeless piece or mass; often with implication of excessive size, protuberant outline, or clumsiness'. Obviously several elements of this definition tie in with other core categories in INTELLIGENCE. The idea of shapelessness is relevant to the DENSITY group as a whole and may relate to the corresponding small number of SHAPE entries. SIZE also appears in the data, and largeness is correlated with stupidity; closely associated with SIZE, clumsiness is also relevant to a number of other mappings, including some of the ANIMAL entries and most of the WOOD group. The description of a *lump* as a 'compact mass' is also significant, since this suggests that, like the FRUIT/VEG entries, any lump is easily substituted for the head in terms of mental image, since the prototypical shape of a compact mass tends to be very roughly spherical without any sharp distensions, like the head. Again, this relates to Feyaerts' point about the mapping between STUPIDITY and a deficient head/brain, since a lump is perhaps the least complex, most basic conceptual entity relating to physical substances in general (Feyaerts 1999, discussed above in section 3.4).

### 3.4.5 *FOOD*

Like all the substances in the WOOD and EARTH categories, FOOD appears to be appropriate as a source concept for DENSITY because it is so familiar in daily life; furthermore, just as in both of these groups, the entries in FOOD are derived from a small number of specific substances, as section 3.2.4 shows. Eight out of the 19 entries are related to MEAT, and it is noticeable that all the entries derived from specific kinds of meat come from either *beef* or *mutton*. In fact, these can be compared with entries in the ANIMAL data, since BOVINES and SHEEP, the animals from which these meats come, are the two largest subgroups in the category. Presumably this is because cattle and sheep have always been amongst the most common, familiar animals for English people, and logically the types of meat that they yield are equally familiar. Two more entries are compounds of a related substance, *suet*, which the *OED* defines as 'The solid fat round the loins and kidneys of certain animals, *esp.* that of the ox and sheep, which, chopped up, is used in cooking, and, when rendered down, forms tallow. (Occas. applied to the corresponding fat in the human body.)'.

A further three entries come from *grout*. This has various senses, but the *OED* picks out the sense related to grain or meal, and compares the items with another two entries in this group that have a similar source:

> **grout-head** ... [f. grout *n.*, taken as the type of something big and coarse; cf. *pudding-head* ... ]

*Pudding* in these entries seems to retain the older sense of a savoury mixture of minced meat and course grain or oats, held together and boiled in the stomach of an animal (usually a sheep or pig). As well as being similar in texture to *grout*, again puddings are roughly head-shaped, and must have this as an additional part of their motivation.

The final entry in the group is <u>macaroon n a1631–a1633</u>. This is not motivated as clearly by DENSITY as other entries in the group, though in light of the other data it may have this as a motivating factor. *Macaroon* is related to *macaroni*, and appears to have as its earliest sense the paste that is used to make pasta. The extension of the term to signify STUPIDITY seems only to be related to this early sense indirectly. *OED3* suggests that *macaroon* follows the same path as this alternative form *macaroni*, and supplies the following background information about the semantic development of the term:

> **2.** A dandy or fop; *spec.* (in the second half of the 18th cent.) a member of a set of young men who had travelled in Europe and extravagantly imitated Continental tastes and fashions. Also in extended use. Now *hist.* [This use seems to be from the name of the Macaroni Club, a designation probably adopted to indicate the preference of the members for foreign cookery, macaroni being at that time little eaten in England. There appears to be no connection with the extended use of Italian *maccherone* in the senses 'blockhead, fool, mountebank' (compare <u>MACAROON</u> *n.* 3), referred to in 1711 by Addison *Spectator* 24 Apr. 178/2: Those circumforaneous Wits whom every Nation calls by the name of that Dish of Meat which it loves best:..in Italy, *Maccaronies.*]

The change of meaning that *macaroni* has undergone is clearly the result of the specific cultural context in which the lexeme has been used; and this illustrates the importance of taking account of cultural context alongside cognitive factors in examining the motivation for particular mappings.

The FOOD group was perhaps the most challenging to classify, and I think that it highlights the difficulty of interpreting the basic metaphor involved in the transfer of meaning from a highly specific source even more than the other data presented in this chapter. Within the group, the variation in type of source is intuitively much greater than in the WOOD or EARTH groups, and this relates to Rosch et al.'s ideas about basic-level categories (1976). WOOD and EARTH both qualify as basic-level categories: it is not difficult to visualise a prototypical piece of wood, or a prototypical mass of earth. FOOD, on the other hand, is a much broader superordinate category, which includes basic-level entities including some of those found in the group, like MEAT, as well as lower-order substances like particular types of meat and the other sources in the group. Because FOOD is such a broad category, it might be criticised as a less convincing core category for this data. It is certainly true that a substantial proportion of the group is related specifically to MEAT, whilst the rest of the entries come from a variety of other, quite different substances of various kinds.

However, these entries are presented together as part of a single group because they all appear to be principally motivated by DENSITY, and it seems significant that they are all edible substances. This is especially true because there are a number of other groups in the data that contain entries related to edible substances, which appear not to have the same motivation. The first of these is the group mentioned above, FRUIT/VEGETABLE. As I have already suggested, it seems likely that this is largely motivated by image. With the exception of nana n 1965>, all the sources within the group, which are mainly vegetables, are roughly spherical, and like some of the other DENSITY entries these can be mentally 'substituted' for the head very easily. Many of them can also be related to DENSITY – this is true of turnips and potatoes in their raw form, in particular – but I would guess that their shape is more important in the mapping (or at the very least, equally important).

There is also a group that I have labelled LIQUID/SEMI-LIQUID. There are 13 entries in this group, derived from five different specific substances and one more general term.[16] Two entries, dope n 1851> and dopey aj 1896>, are derived from Dutch *doop* 'dipping, sauce' (from *doopen* 'to dip'). Although (in English) *dope* has been used to refer to various substances,[17] it seems to have been most closely associated with food-related substances; the first listed *OED* sense defines *dope* as 'Any thick liquid or semi-fluid used as an article of food, or as a lubricant'. The entries vappe n 1657, whey-brained aj 1660 and barm-stick n 1924> all derive from edible liquids: vappe n 1657 is from Latin *vappa*, flat or sour wine; whey-brained aj 1660 is from PDE *whey*, the watery liquid that separates from curds when milk coagulates; and barm-stick n 1924> is from OE *beorma* (> PDE *beer*), originally the froth that forms on fermenting malt, which is used to cause fermentation in other liquids and as yeast to leaven bread.

### 3.4.6 *MISCELLANEOUS*

The remaining data in the DENSITY group have been classified as MISCELLANEOUS, because the entries do not fit neatly into any of the four

---

[16] This term, mess n 1936>, merits some attention, and as with many other terms its metaphorical link with INTELLIGENCE is related to the semantic changes that the term had already undergone. The earliest recorded meaning is simply a serving or prepared dish of food; with the development of some parallel meanings, this gradually extended to imply food of a particular pulpy or semi-liquid texture, and then to be used with its most common current meaning of a 'muddle or jumble', sometimes with the suggestion of dirtiness. All of these meanings may feed into the meaning 'a stupid person'.

[17] It seems likely that the use of *dope* to mean 'stupid person' is reinforced by the sense listed in *OED* as 'Also (*U.S. slang*), a person under the influence of, or addicted to, some drug'. This comes from *dope* 'drug not specifically named', later becoming 'stupefying drugs and narcotics in general'. There are several other entries in the data connected with intoxication, such as US rummy n 1912> (from *rum*) and sodden aj 1599–1611+1841> (from OE *seopan*, originally connected with heat and boiling, but shifting to mean 'drunk' before being connected with lack of intelligence).

main groups. Having said this, more than one of the eight entries have some possible relationship with either a single entry or one of the other groups in DENSITY. clay-brained aj 1596 could arguably be put into the EARTH category, since clay is a similar type of substance used for many of the same purposes as earth. leather-headed aj a1668 is only a step away from some of the entries connected with meat, since it is also an animal product, though not an edible one; the entry is unusual in the data in that leather is a relatively high value substance, but given that it has a single supporting quotation this may account for its lack of success. knuckle-head n 1944> might also be similar to the MEAT entries in the respect that it is a substance found alongside animal flesh, but it could also be viewed alongside the two entries in this group that are compounds of *bone*, bone-headed aj 1903> and bonehead n 1908>. ivory dome n 1923> also belongs with these entries, which stand out as much harder substances; ivory is high-value and, like leather, seems out of place in this group. The motivation for these items may be slightly different from the others in DENSITY, and may be more closely related to fact that the outside of the head is made of this substance – i.e. the implication may be that the head is bone all the way through, rather than containing a brain.

There are also two entries that are compounds of *stone*, stone n 1598 and stunpoll n a1794>. These are discussed in more detail below.


## 3.5 SEMANTIC 'PATHWAYS'

The fact that there are so many entries from such a small number of sources seems to be evidence of a principle similar to that discussed in section 2.5 in relation to VISION vocabulary. When a link between two concepts has been made that is cognitively 'cohesive' for speakers, this seems to establish a pathway that attracts other mappings between the same general semantic fields (and, more narrowly, from the same lexical root). At least in part, this can account for the productiveness of particular source substances, and for the high number of items that are variant forms from a single root, that can be seen in the DENSITY groups, as well as in the rest of the INTELLIGENCE data.

Interestingly, this kind of attraction to established pathways seems to have an effect even in cases where the mappings between fields have different motivations, or even mutually exclusive motivations. The variety of entries from edible substances seems to bear this out. Some of the relevant entries in FRUIT/VEGETABLES are complementary to those in DENSITY because close texture is one motivating factor in their mapping to STUPIDITY, so these can be compared with the DENSITY-FOOD group. By contrast, the entries in the LIQUID/SEMI-LIQUID group have almost the opposite motivation – the substances discussed above have a completely different consistency, and are loose-textured and insubstantial. Despite this, the group is a further indication that generally, edible substances are subconsciously 'available' to be mapped to STUPIDITY, and that this source field becomes increasingly available by association as it is exploited more and the link between concepts is strengthened. In fact, the remaining seven entries in the LIQUID/SEMI-LIQUID group are also closely related to one of the subgroups in DENSITY: these are all simplexes or compounds of PDE *sap*, the watery fluid found in trees and plants. This means that all of the entries in this core category mirror those in either the WOOD or FOOD subgroups of DENSITY, suggesting strongly that these are particularly appropriate to be selected and linked with STUPIDITY.

The same principle seems to be evident in the ANIMAL group, within the sub-group SHEEP. As I will go on to discuss in section 4.4.1.2, the motivation for the SHEEP group is generally held to relate to female sheep, because of their status as flock members, but in the data this is not always the case and there are a number of entries derived from terms for male sheep. The motivation for these cannot be the same, since rams exhibit entirely different behaviour, but it is credible that the general perceived connection between the species and stupidity strengthens both mappings. In turn, this further increases the availability of male sheep as sources for INTELLIGENCE.

## 3.6 SPECIFICITY AND LACK OF OTHER SUBSTANCES

As I have pointed out, there seem to be constraints on the type of entity that can be the source in a mapping (evident from the ANIMAL group as well), and the substances that appear in the group seem almost without exception to conform to these.[18] One question that presents itself here is why certain other dense substances are less successful as sources. Obviously, some are excluded because of other properties they have, which 'override' their potential to be used; an obvious example would be a precious metal like gold. The high value and rarity of gold (and its generally positive associations) are more salient than its density, and because of these it would be extremely unusual for it to be associated with a negative characteristic like stupidity. However, this does not appear to be the case for all other possible sources, and there are a few that would seem to be equally as available and suitable as those that do appear in the data. Stone and low-value metals such as iron and steel seem ideal to be mapped to STUPIDITY, given that they are also reasonably common, high-density substances that are used by man in a variety of ways, and yet these do not emerge as established sources.

---

[18] There are a very few exceptions, all categorised as MISCELLANEOUS, and more detail about these is given in section 3.4.6. The very fact that these tend not to be productive, or are rare, or fall out of usage very quickly, seems to prove the point that substances conforming to the 'rules' of appropriateness are generally much more cognitively 'convincing'.

*Stone* does appear in the data, but only in two entries (listed within the MISC section): stone n 1598, which has a single supporting quotation, and stunpoll n 1794, which continues into current usage. The *OED* suggests uncertainly that *stunpoll* is derived from a variant of *stone* in compound with *poll*, 'head', but it should be noted that folk etymology would be likely to associate this with the verb *stun*. There are other items in the data connected to the idea of physical impact (classified as HIT/STUNNED) – for example, *stupid* itself can be traced back to Latin *stupere* 'to hit, stun' – so that this explanation for the etymology of *stunpoll* is intuitively satisfying. If someone has suffered physical impact to the head, it is likely that their mental faculties are affected negatively, so it is understandable that this can be used to imply a lack of intelligence. This must be a factor in the continued use of this word, and may be more significant than its actual ethymology. I would speculate that there may be various reasons for the lack of any other *stone* entries. Stone itself may be simply too hard – although substances like wood and lumps of earth are dense, they can be penetrated with effort, whereas stone is a completely different texture, and has no 'give' at all. The same is true of all metals, and also of bone, which yields three very recent entries, bone-headed aj 1903 >, bonehead n 1908 > and US ivory dome n 1923 >. Correspondingly, there is a difference between being able to comprehend something with difficulty (i.e. get it 'into one's brain') and being wholly incapable of this; it is perhaps quite different to imply that someone has limited and underused potential to learn compared to no ability at all.

### 3.7 CONCEPTUAL LINKS AND LIMITS ON REFERENCE

Aside from this, and perhaps more convincingly, there may be an issue about the other properties metaphorically associated with any entity. Little research appears to have been done on whether either lexemes or the source concepts they represent are limited in the number of referents they can support, but this may be a possibility; equally it may be that there are restrictions on the possible number of target domains that a single source domain can map onto.

Assessing the precise range of reference of a particular linguistic item – i.e. the number of discrete meanings it sustains, and the semantic 'distance' between these meanings – is an impossible task. The high level of variation in the number of entries assigned to individual lemmas by different dictionaries gives some idea of the problems involved in coming to any kind of consensus about reference. Robert Allen (1999) discusses the way in which lexicographers vary in their approach to dividing the meanings of words by either 'lumping' or 'splitting', i.e. either giving general definitions and leaving the user to 'extract the nuance of meaning that corresponds to a particular context', or giving a greater number of definitions that 'enumerate differences of meaning in more detail' (p. 61). The approach that a lexicographer adopts tends to be affected by the functions of a particular dictionary edition – e.g. it is considered more helpful for a learner of English to be given a list of 'focused' meanings, where less central meanings are listed as associated subsenses, than to be given a list of several more narrowly demarcated senses – but, as Allen points out, this is only a very general guide. Two dictionaries with very similar aims can vary enormously; similarly, even a particular dictionary can vary from edition to edition through time, and depending on the preferences of editors:

> The Fowler brothers, editors of the first *Concise Oxford Dictionary* (1911), were broadly speaking splitters, but they lumped as well, as they had to if they were going to describe the verb *set* (for example) in one and half pages as against the 60-odd columns of the *OED*. The Fowlers' entry for *make* occupied a little over a column. Their edition didn't number the meanings ... but counting the semicolons gives a sense count of around 70 ... By the ninth edition, this had been reduced to 24 ... and in the new edition, published this year, there are only 10. (Allen 1999: 62)

This sort of variation in approach, which relates clearly to the nature of polysemy itself and the 'fuzziness' of word meaning, means that little or no data has been compiled that gives any indication of the possible number of meanings that a lexeme can sustain. Similarly, related information such as the average number of meanings of any polysemous lexeme, or the comparative multiplicity of meanings amongst different types of lexical item,[19] seems extremely problematic.

Added to this is the special difficulty posed by metaphorical extension of meaning, which tends only to be included in dictionaries when it is highly conventionalised in a particular lexical form, whether this be a single word or a fixed expression. More 'general' mappings between concepts, which may be represented linguistically in a variety of lexical items relating to the source concept, like those in the VISION, ANIMAL and DENSITY groups, are obviously much more difficult to identify and formalise, and therefore (from a cognitive linguistic point of view) these are handled less well. Lakoff & Johnson discuss the limitations of dictionaries in dealing with this sort of phenomenon:

> ...students of meaning and dictionary makers have not found it important to try to give a general account of how people understand normal concepts in terms of systematic metaphors like LOVE IS A JOURNEY, ARGUMENT IS WAR, TIME IS MONEY, etc. For example, if you look

---

[19] 'Different' on all sorts of criteria, e.g. nouns vs. verbs, concrete vs. abstract nouns, adjectives relating to animate vs. adjectives relating to inanimate entities.

in a dictionary under 'love,' you find entries that mention affection, fondness, devotion, infatuation, and even sexual desire, but there is no mention of the way in which we comprehend love by means of metaphors like LOVE IS A JOURNEY, LOVE IS MADNESS, LOVE IS WAR, etc. If we take expressions like 'Look how far we've come' or 'Where are we now?' there would be no way to tell from a standard dictionary or any other standard account of meaning that these expressions are normal ways of talking about the experience of love in our culture. Hints of the existence of such metaphors may be given in the secondary or tertiary senses of other words. For instance, a hint of the LOVE IS MADNESS metaphor may show up in a tertiary sense of the word 'crazy' ( = 'immoderately fond, infatuated'), but this hint shows up as a part of the definition of 'crazy' rather than as part of the definition of 'love'. (Lakoff & Johnson 1980: 115–16)

Conventionalised metaphorical usages tend to be recognised within the definitions for the most central terms associated with particular source concepts. Amongst the terms found in DENSITY, it is standard for general terms like *thick* and *dense* to be defined as 'stupid' (or something similar) by lexicographers. Similarly, any other conventionalised metaphorical usages will also be listed – for example, *thick* as an adjective is also defined as '*colloq.* intimate or very friendly (esp. *thick as thieves*)' in the *Concise Oxford Dictionary* – and by identifying these it might be possible to gain some very rough idea of the comparative level of variability in mappings between source concepts from larger dictionaries. However, this would obviously be an extremely approximate method – any theories based on this kind of research could only be of the most impressionistic and general nature.

Having said this, it is generally accepted that there are constraints on reference, and specifically on the meanings that one lexical item can sustain, both in terms of quantity and semantic 'distance'. Any language system must strike a balance in being both economical and unambiguous. Historically there are examples of over-lexicalisation, where a language is flooded with words for one particular concept, and of the opposite phenomenon, where a single word has two related but distinct meanings and it becomes unclear which one is intended. Either situation can result from some extralinguistic factor (like borrowing or influence from another language), and since language is a system, neither is sustainable. Consequently, intralinguistic pressure will force change, and this is known as 'systemic regulation'. Smith (1996: 126) puts it like this: 'the systematic nature of language means that there are regulatory forces – the extra- and intralinguistic 'blind watchmakers' of linguistic evolution – which constrain the selection of variables.' In his 1972 work, Samuels details some of the specific processes of systemic regulation that have been observed in diachronic semantic change.

I. *Ambiguity and limitation*. If a form has two meanings – whether as the result of polysemy or homonymy – so incompatible that they cause ambiguity, one of the meanings dies out, or, more rarely, the form itself becomes obsolete.

II. *Synonymity and differentiation* ... If, for extralinguistic reasons such as cultural borrowing or foreign conquest, two exact synonyms exist for a time in the spoken chain, *either* one of them will become less and less selected and eventually discarded, *or* a difference of meaning, connotation, nuance or register will arise to distinguish them. (Samuels 1972: 65)

These principles constitute two important points about the lexicon of a language. Firstly, there cannot be a huge number of words with the same meaning, so that true synonymy is rare or nonexistent; secondly, it is unlikely for a word to have two disparate meanings that can be used in the same context and might be confusing for users. The example that Samuels uses to illustrate this second point (see Fig. 3.1) is the adjective *silly* (from OE *gesælig*), which has undergone various shifts in meaning since OE, and was highly polysemous between the thirteenth and sixteenth centuries.

As Fig. 3.1 illustrates, *silly* had both positive and negative meanings from the thirteenth century onwards, but all of the meanings with positive connotations gradually died out in the following six centuries. Samuels accounts for this as follows:

It seems reasonable to suppose that meanings as unlike as "happy' and 'pitiful', if their occurrences overlapped, would give rise to ambiguity, and that that is the main reason for the obsolescence of

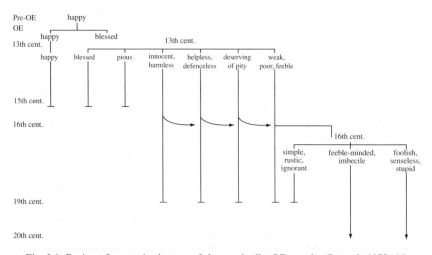

Fig. 3.1. Dating of semantic changes of the word *silly*, OE *gesælig* (Samuels 1972: 66)

the meaning 'happy' in the fourteenth and fifteenth centuries, and of the meaning 'harmless' in the eighteenth and nineteenth centuries. (Samuels 1972: 67)

What is notable about this example is that all of the polysemous meanings of *silly* were concentrated in the same semantic field, human characteristics. The reason that a number of these died out does not seem to be related to the number of meanings that the expression sustained at one time, although this might be a factor. Rather, the obsolescence of these polysemous meanings seems to be directly linked to the fact that they would have been used in the same context, i.e. to describe people. Because this could cause confusion, it could not be sustained.

It does not seem unreasonable to assume that there are similar constraints on metaphorical mapping, or at least on metaphors that are likely to become conventional. Davidson contends that 'there are no unsuccessful metaphors, just as there are no unfunny jokes. There are tasteless metaphors, but these are turns that nevertheless have brought something off, even if it were not worth bringing off, or could have been brought off better' (1996: 415). This may well be the case for creative, novel metaphors, but it does not appear to be the case for at least the bulk of conventional metaphors; research carried out so far by Grady and others (as well as my own research) has indicated that a huge number of these have common primary metaphors as their basis.[20] Trying to make any assertions about whether there are limits on the number of concepts that can conventionally map to a target concept, or from a source concept, seems to be an unsupportable task. Lakoff & Johnson have successfully demonstrated that mappings to a target concept can be numerous,[21] and the evidence they present for this, in the form of lists of mappings for particular target concepts, is in no way claimed to be comprehensive. However, I would contend that it is possible to make claims about constraints on the types of target that source concepts are likely to be mapped to conventionally, and that these can be affected by intralinguistic constraints such as those suggested by semanticists including Samuels, described above.

Because the connection involved in the DENSITY mapping is not simply between a concept and a single linguistic form, or even several lexical items that share an etymology, it is much more difficult to examine the nature of this connection in light of this kind of theory. As I have discussed (and as is demonstrated by some of the many disagreements that pose challenges for metaphor study), deconstructing particular metaphors – including the consideration of such issues as whether or not metonymy is involved, and

---

[20] In fact, this also appears to be the case for many creative and literary metaphors; see e.g. comments made by Lakoff & Johnson (1999: 66ff., 149–50).
[21] See e.g. the lists of possible metaphors Lakoff & Johnson supply for various target concepts including LOVE and LIFE (1980: 46–51).

how to determine what motivates the mapping between source and target – frequently rests on subjective judgement. Even in cases where a basic mapping appears to be relatively straightforward and generally agreed, it is often unclear which lexical expressions can be assigned to this mapping. The DENSITY group exemplifies this difficulty. Not only do most of the items involved relate to specific substances like wood or earth rather than general terms meaning 'dense', but many of these entries are associated with hyponyms of these categories, or with entities that seem intuitively to be closely related but do not slot neatly into any particular group. Examples of these entries, such as wattle-head n 1613, are given in the sections dealing with each of the subgroups in this chapter. It is for the reasons above that any conclusions about constraints on these kinds of mapping must be based on conjecture and made tentatively.

Nevertheless, the observations made by Samuels about limits on word reference may offer clues to the reasons for the lack of certain substances in the DENSITY data. If a concept like WOOD becomes conventionally associated with the human characteristic stupidity, it may be that, with some qualifications,[22] this precludes its mapping to other targets within the field of human characteristics. Conversely, other substances may not be mapped to stupidity if they are already have other conventionalised associations in the same area.

Stone is commonly and widely used as a source concept for other human characteristics besides stupidity. It can be connected with steadiness and constancy, as when someone is described as a *rock* or *brick*, and equally it can be used to connote cruelty and indifference, in phrases such as a *heart of stone* or a *stony expression*. The more common base metals steel and iron, perhaps less familiar substances anyway, seem to have similar constraints. Steel has been used to express the idea of endurance, and this was used by the creators of Superman, who they termed the *man of steel*; it is also the source, like stone, for cruelty or indifference, as in *steely-faced*. Iron tends to be associated with the ability to withstand physical or mental difficulty, as in an *iron stomach* or a *will of iron*. These well-established metaphorical connections appear to preclude the selection of these substances and others as sources for STUPIDITY; in themselves, they fit the motivation that lies behind the DENSITY data, but because language is a system that is rooted in one particular cultural context, they are not available for the mapping.

To an extent, the characteristics that come to be associated earliest with particular entities, and inversely the initial selection of specific entities over others to connote these characteristics, must be arbitrary, even though a

---

[22] There are terms that do seem to be able to sustain incongruent meanings, but there may be certain reasons for this in each case. For example, the adjective *wicked* can be found in current usage with the meaning 'evil', but it is also used as a term of approval. However, the latter meaning tends to be restricted to a particular social group or particular contexts, and for this reason it is unlikely that the two meanings could be confused.

general mapping may be clearly motivated. It seems certain that not all mappings will be able to be accounted for precisely and in detail. However, in general this further demonstrates the way in which the shared associations of a community are crucially important, and must be taken into account in the detailed analysis of any metaphorical mapping.

It may be that further research into the nature of metaphor, carried out with some attention to historical semantics as well as cognitive principles, will yield evidence that allows more insight to this kind of phenomenon. However, because conceptual relationships can be as complex as I hope to have shown, it seems unlikely that it will ever be possible to categorically prove theories of this kind. I believe that it is clear that this certainly cannot be attempted without recourse to corpus study, which seems to offer the most promising method of analysis of large bodies of real data that can be seen in the context, either or both, of individual texts and of similar data. In my opinion, this is a useful and significant area for further research, especially as (in general) a great deal more work has been done with target concepts than source concepts.

3.8 CONCLUSION

In general, this chapter is intended to show the value of case studies in identifying mappings that have a significant input into the way particular target concepts are understood diachronically. DENSITY is not a source concept that is generally recognised to be important in the way intelligence is conceptualised, and is certainly not one that has been discussed at any length. However, it is a source concept that has been productive over a long period and continues to generate new expressions, and furthermore it looks likely that it is not a metaphor that is confined to the vocabulary of intelligence in English. Without a sizeable corpus that includes obsolete items, it is not possible to identify and fully analyse this kind of mapping, or to make any evaluation of its relative contribution to the language of the target concept. By using a corpus, though, it is possible to identify groups of data that may not immediately seem significant or conceptually important, but which can shed light on other recognised mappings, as well as on the mechanics of metaphor and metonymy in general.

As well as this, it is my contention that attempting case studies of this kind that focus on particular mappings, either with a source or target concept as a starting point, gives the opportunity to gain some sense of the complexities involved in metaphor. A diachronic approach can offer a fresh perspective on the background and influences of specific expressions and the general groups to which these relate; it is possible to identify linguistic 'failures' as well as 'successes', and this may lead to a better understanding of what constrains and motivates individual metaphors, as well as of the metaphorical process itself and the relationship between metaphor and metonymy. In terms of the DENSITY data, the explanation that I have posited about the source substances that do not appear in the mapping demonstrates the value and importance of bringing newer, cognitive theories of language together with older and more established theories from semantics and historical linguistics; this seems to me to have been lacking from much of the modern research in this area, and must surely be an important direction for lexical semantics in the future. As well as this, and alongside the ANIMAL data, the DENSITY group is evidence of the way in which mappings are frequently motivated by a combination of factors. I hope to have illustrated a few of the ways these can combine, and especially the way in which cultural and intra-systemic influences can interact with cognitive processes to produce complex and yet cohesive mappings.

## 3.9 DATA TABLES

### 3.9.1 *DENSITY-GENERAL*

Table 1

| Record no. | Meaning | Word | Part of speech | OE? | Plus/ and | a/c1 | Date 1 | +/- | a/c2 | Date 2 | -/+ | a/c3 | Date 3 | Current? | Label | Derivation |
|---|---|---|---|---|---|---|---|---|---|---|---|---|---|---|---|---|
| 241 | stupid | gross | aj | | | | 1526 | – | | 1844 | | | | | | gross |
| 324 | stupid | grosshead | n | | | | 1580 | – | | 1606 | | | | | | gross head |
| 332 | stupid | thick(-)skin | n | | | | 1582 | – | | 1893 | | | | | | thick |
| 390 | stupid | thick | aj | | | | 1597 | | | | | | ^ | | mn cf cq | thick |
| 481 | stupid | thick-brained | aj | | | | 1619 | | | | | | | | | thick brain |
| 511 | stupid | thickwitted | aj | | | | 1634 | | | | | | ^ | | | thick wit < *weid- |
| 548 | stupid | thick-skulled | aj | | | a | 1653 | | | | | | | | | thick skull |
| 671 | stupid | thick-skull | n | | | | 1755 | – | | 1894 | | | | | | thick skull |
| 719 | stupid | thick-headed | aj | | | | 1801 | – | | 1891 | | | | | | thick head |
| 748 | stupid | dense | aj | | | | 1822 | | | | | | ^ | | | dense |
| 756 | stupid | thick-head | n | | | | 1824 | | | | | | ^ | | | thick head |
| 840 | stupid | thick | n | | | | 1857 | | | | | | ^ | | mn cf cq | thick |
| 852 | stupid | crass | aj | | | | 1861 | – | | | | | | | | crass |
| 876 | stupid | thick-head | aj | | | | 1873 | | | 1894 | | | | | | thick head |
| 931 | stupid | thickwit | n | | | | 1904 | | | | | | | | | thick wit < *weid- |
| 1060 | stupid | thickie | n | | | | 1968 | | | | | | ^ | | cq | thick |
| 1071 | stupid | as thick as (two) plank(s) | aj | | | | 1974 | | | | | | ^ | | cq | thick plank |
| 1072 | stupid | thicko | n | | | | 1976 | | | | | | ^ | | cq | thick |

3.9.2 *DENSITY-WOOD*

Table 2

| Record no. | Meaning | Word | Part of speech | OE? | Plus/ and | a/c1 | Date 1 | +/- | a/c2 | Date 2 | -/+ | a/c3 | Date 3 | Current? | Label | Derivation |
|---|---|---|---|---|---|---|---|---|---|---|---|---|---|---|---|---|
| 272 | stupid | blockish | aj | | | | 1548 | - | | 1868 | | | | | | block |
| 275 | stupid | blockheaded | aj | | | | 1549 | - | | 1860 | | | | | | block head |
| 276 | stupid | blockhead | n | | | | 1549 | | | | | | | ^ | | block head |
| 284 | stupid | block | n | | | a | 1553 | - | | 1810 | | | | | | block |
| 310 | stupid | log-headed | aj | | | | 1571 | + | | 1926 | | | | ^ | | log head |
| 342 | stupid | wooden | aj | | | a | 1586 | | | | | | | ^ | | wood |
| 351 | stupid | loggerhead | n | | | | 1588 | | | 1821 | + | | 1892 | ^ | | log head |
| 378 | stupid | stock | n | | | | 1594 | | | | | | | | | stock |
| 381 | stupid | logger-headed | aj | | | | 1596 | - | | 1831 | | | | ^ | | log head |
| 382 | stupid | stockish | aj | | | | 1596 | | | | | | | ^ | | stock |
| 395 | stupid | block-pate | n | | | | 1598 | | | | | | | | | block pate |
| 447 | stupid | blockhead | aj | | | | 1606 | - | | 1719 | | | | ^ | | block head |
| 526 | stupid | stub | n | | | | 1644 | | | | | | | | | stub |
| 529 | stupid | as sad as any mallet | | | | | 1645 | | | | | | | | | sad mallet |
| 567 | stupid | timber-headed | aj | | | | 1666 | | | | | | | | | timber head |
| 581 | stupid | logger | aj | | | | 1675 | - | | 1781 | + | | 1812 | | 1812dl | log |
| 594 | stupid | loggerhead | aj | | | | 1684 | | | | | | | | | log head |
| 602 | stupid | a piece of wood | n | | | | 1691 | | | | | | | | | wood |
| 612 | stupid | hulver-head | n | | | a | 1700 | | | | | | | | | hulver head |
| 678 | stupid | chuckle-headed | aj | | | | 1764 | | | | | | | ^ | | chuckle head |
| 718 | stupid | nog-head | n | | | | 1800 | | | | | | | ^ | dl | nog head |
| 743 | stupid | chuckle-pate | aj | | | c | 1820 | | | | | | | | | chuckle pate |
| 757 | stupid | stob | n | | | | 1825 | | | | | | | ^ | dl | stob < stub |
| 759 | stupid | stump | n | | | | 1825 | | | | | | | ^ | | stump |
| 775 | stupid | log-head | n | | | | 1831 | | | | | | | ^ | | log head |
| 777 | stupid | woodenhead | n | | | | 1831 | | | | | | | ^ | | wood head |
| 782 | stupid | blockheadish | aj | | | | 1833 | + | | 1863 | | | | | | block head |
| 821 | stupid | timber-head | n | | | | 1849 | | | | | | | | sl | timber head |
| 858 | stupid | wooden-headed | aj | | | | 1865 | | | | | | | ^ | | wood head |
| 884 | stupid | off his chump | aj | | | | 1877 | | | | | | | ^ | | chump |
| 894 | stupid | chump | n | | | | 1883 | | | | | | | | | chump |
| 910 | stupid | nog-headed | aj | | | | 1891 | - | | 1893 | | | | | | nog head |
| 1075 | stupid | woodentop | n | | | | 1983 | | | | | | | ^ | sl | wood top |

3.9.3 *DENSITY-EARTH*

Table 3

| Record no. | Meaning | Word | Part of speech | OE? | Plus/and | a/c1 | Date 1 | +/- | a/c2 | Date 2 | -/+ | a/c3 | Date 3 | Current? | Label | Derivation |
|---|---|---|---|---|---|---|---|---|---|---|---|---|---|---|---|---|
| 428 | stupid | clod-poll/clod pole | n | | | | 1601 | | | | | | | > | | clod poll |
| 441 | stupid | clod | n | | | | 1605 | | | | | | | > | | clod |
| 453 | stupid | turf | n | | | | 1607 | | | | | | | | | turf |
| 513 | stupid | clod-pate | n | | | | 1636 | | | | | c | 1690 | | c1690sl | clod pate |
| 518 | stupid | clod-pated | aj | | | | 1638 | − | a | 1679 | + | | | | | clod pate |
| 523 | stupid | muddy-headed | aj | | | | 1642 | − | | 1822 | | | | | | mud head |
| 527 | stupid | clod-head | n | | | | 1644 | − | | 1815 | | | | | | clod head |
| 558 | stupid | muddish | aj | | | | 1658 | + | | 1829 | | | | | | mud |
| 625 | stupid | clod-skull | n | | | | 1707 | | | | | | | | | clod skull |
| 629 | stupid | mud | n | | | | 1708 | + | | 1886 | | | | | sl | mud |
| 700 | stupid | mud-headed | aj | | | | 1793 | | | | | | | | | mud head |
| 889 | stupid | mudhead | n | | | | 1882 | − | | 1886 | | | | | sl | mud head |

### 3.9.4 *DENSITY-FOOD*

Table 4

| Record no. | Meaning | Word | Part of speech | OE? | Plus/ and | a/c1 | Date 1 | +/- | a/c2 | Date 2 | -/+ | a/c3 | Date 3 | Current? | Label | Derivation |
|---|---|---|---|---|---|---|---|---|---|---|---|---|---|---|---|---|
| 278 | stupid | grout-head | n | | | | 1550 | – | | 1649 | | | | | | grout head |
| 318 | stupid | groutnoll | n | | | | 1578 | – | | 1658 | | | | | | grout noll |
| 319 | stupid | grout-headed | aj | | | | 1578 | – | | 1694 | | | 1847/78 | | dl | grout head |
| 444 | stupid | beef-witted | aj | | | | 1606 | | | | + | | | | | beef wit < *weid- |
| 496 | stupid | beef-brained | aj | | | | 1627 | | | | | | | | | beef brain |
| 504 | stupid | macaroon | n | | a | | 1631 | – | a | 1633 | | | | | | macaroni |
| 648 | stupid | pudding-headed | aj | | | | 1726 | – | | 1867 | | | | | | pudding head |
| 680 | stupid | mutton-headed | aj | | | | 1768 | | | | | | | | sl&dl | mutton head |
| 685 | stupid | beef-head | n | | | | 1775 | | | | | | | | | beef head |
| 721 | stupid | mutton-head | n | | | | 1803 | | | | | | | ^ | | mutton head |
| 768 | stupid | beef-headed | aj | | | | 1828 | + | | 1900 | | | | | | beef head |
| 826 | stupid | pudding head | n | | | | 1851 | | | | | | | ^ | | pudding head |
| 959 | stupid | suet-brained | aj | | | | 1921 | | | | | | | ^ | | suet brain |
| 1001 | stupid | suet-headed | aj | | | | 1937 | | | | | | | ^ | | suet head |
| 1022 | stupid | meat-head | n | | | | 1945 | | | | | | | ^ | sl cf us | meat head |
| 1027 | stupid | meat-headed | aj | | | | 1949 | | | | | | | ^ | | meat head |

3.9.5 *DENSITY-MISCELLANEOUS*

Table 5

| Record no. | Meaning | Word | Part of speech | OE? | Plus/ and | a/c1 | Date 1 | +/- | a/c2 | Date 2 | -/+ | a/c3 | Date 3 | Current? | Label | Derivation |
|---|---|---|---|---|---|---|---|---|---|---|---|---|---|---|---|---|
| 379 | stupid | clay-brained | aj | | | | 1596 | | | | | | | | | clay brain |
| 396 | stupid | stone | n | | | | 1598 | | | | | | | | | stone |
| 573 | stupid | leather-headed | aj | | | a | 1668 | | | | | | | | | leather head |
| 614 | stupid | leather-head | n | | | a | 1700 | | | | | | | | sl | leather head |
| 701 | stupid | stunpoll | n | | | a | 1794 | | | | | | | ^ | dl | stone poll |
| 930 | stupid | bone-headed | aj | | | | 1903 | | | | | | | ^ | sl og us | bone head |
| 942 | stupid | bonehead | n | | | | 1908 | | | | | | | ^ | sl og us | bone head |
| 968 | stupid | ivory dome | n | | | | 1923 | | | | | | | ^ | us sl | ivory dome |
| 1021 | stupid | knuckle-head | n | | | | 1944 | | | | | | | ^ | | knuckle head |

# 4

# ANIMALS

## 4.1 Introduction

The final ∈ mapping that is analysed here differs substantially from those examined in the preceding chapters. In terms of a metaphor–metonymy continuum, the ANIMAL group appears to be a fairly unproblematic example of prototypical metaphor; what is interesting is the complexity that this mapping exhibits in other respects, and the fact that the metaphor is rooted in common conceptual processes but is also clearly culturally informed.

Animals, in the widest sense of the term, are one of the richest metaphorical sources in English (and other languages), not only in the vocabulary of intelligence but in a huge number of semantic fields. At every level of society, people are described as animals of all kinds: one can encounter *cows, dogs, sharks, worms, rats, weasels* and *lambs* in everyday experience, and there are few animals that cannot be related to humans in some meaningful way.

Although many of the early studies of metaphor focused on 'A is B' type expressions and animals were often used as examples of sources (e.g. *John is a lion*), relatively little research into animal metaphor appears to have been done, and there are few large-scale studies based on empirical data. Within cognitive linguistics it has not been a central topic of interest, although there are several studies that examine ANIMAL metaphors in English and other languages. For example, Lakoff & Turner give a general account of the mapping from animal to person, though this does not go into any detail about the associations of specific animals (1989: 166ff.), and Grady also offers some insight into the motivation of the mapping within his study of primary metaphor (1997: 219ff.). Various cross-linguistic studies which compare animal metaphors in different languages have also been done: for example, Talebinejad & Dastjerdi (2005) compare examples from English and Persian; Hsieh compares expressions in Mandarin Chinese and German (2006); Dobrovol'skij & Piirainen (2005: 323–52) consider data from ten languages including Japanese and Lithuanian as part of their comparative study of figurative language.

## 4.2 Data

The core category group ANIMAL accounts for 100 entries in total, making up just over 8% of the total data. I have split the entries into four subcategories: MAMMAL, BIRD, INSECT[1] and FISH. Almost all of the data is used to signify stupidity – 93 entries compared with only seven signifying cleverness. Strikingly, of these seven, one is used in a derogatory way, and all of the others bar one are pre-classified as SHARP or SHREWD. The exception is eagle-wit n 1665, which is labelled GENIUS; this has only one supporting quotation in the *OED*. Clearly, then, in the rare cases where intelligence is associated with animals, it is a particular type of intelligence; sharpness and shrewdness seem to indicate a worldly, practically applied cleverness, and perhaps also a certain lack of trustworthiness. There is an implication that, in terms of mental faculties, it is not natural for animals to be associated with humans, so that when they are it cannot be entirely positive.

One of the noticeable features of the data is the high proportion of basic-level category terms.[2] Of superordinate level terms like those used to label the groups, *mammal, bird, insect* and *fish*, only *bird* can be found, in the entry bird-brain n 1943 >. This demonstrates the importance of the specific within this general concept group, and the importance of the qualities and behaviours attributed to particular animals in a culture. This will be discussed in detail below.

### 4.2.1 MAMMALS

This is narrowly the biggest group in the data, comprising 39 entries in total (i.e. around two fifths of the ANIMAL group, and just under 4% of the total data). Almost three quarters of these entries are related to three ANIMAL groups, the largest of which is DONKEY, made up of 13 entries. Seven entries are derived from *ass*, two from *donkey*, and one from *mule*; there are two entries that denote donkeys less directly, long-eared aj 1605 > and long-ears n 1845, and one that comes from a personal name used commonly of the donkey family, neddy n 1823 >.[3] The other large groups contain eight entries each, from expressions for BOVINES and SHEEP. In the first, one entry is from a general term for animals of this family, bovine aj 1855 + 1879, and there are also two entries from expressions associated with male cows, bullhead n 1624 + 1840 and ox-head n a1634 + 1806, and two from *calf*, as

---

[1] This group includes entries relating to snails, which are not insects in the technical sense but more correctly gastropods. I would contend that for most people these belong in the same working category and, for the purposes of simplification, are best seen as part of the same group.

[2] This is perhaps unsurprising, given the privileged status of basic level categories, but it should be noted that the findings of Rosch et al. (1976) suggest that biological taxonomies do not correspond to unscientific categorisation for all groups. The term *mammal* denotes a superordinate category for both traditional and current biology and folk classification of animals, and terms like *cat* and *dog* (as well as many of the animal names in the INTELLIGENCE data) are at the basic level. However, rather than being equivalent to *animal* in the hierarchy, *bird* and *fish* appear to be used as basic rather than superordinate level terms.

[3] Both stages are noted in the core category field in the database, which is labelled PERSONAL NAME > ANIMAL-MAMMAL-DONKEY.

well as three entries derived from *buffle* (a variant form of *buffalo* which came into English through French).

Alongside these, there are three entries that the *OED* suggests are related to *shrew*, and which all signify CLEVERNESS (shrewd aj 1589>, shrode aj 1594–1606 and shrewdish aj 1823>). Another entry, varment aj 1829>, from *vermin*,[4] has a similar meaning. The rest of the entries are all STUPID expressions: two are derived from terms for young dogs, puppy-headed aj 1610 and dunderwhelp n 1621 + a1625 (from *whelp*); two are compounds of *squirrel*; and there is one entry has been placed in this group with the label ANIMAL-MAMMAL-BODY PART, soft-horn n 1837> (discussed below in section 4.4.1.4). Finally, the earliest attested entry in the ANIMAL data, ape n c1390–1741, is also in this group.

## 4.2.2 BIRDS

There are 36 entries in the BIRD category, making this the second largest subgroup of ANIMAL. As mentioned above, one of these is from the term *bird* itself (bird-brain n 1943>). The largest of the species-specific groups is GOOSE, which contains ten entries, seven derived from *goose* itself, one from the term used for a male goose, gander n 1553–1816, and two related to *anserine* (from Latin *anser*, 'goose'). There are also five entries derived from *buzzard*, and a further five from *cock*, which has the earliest meaning of 'domestic fowl', but later came to be used to mean the male of a variety of birds. Four entries are labelled DAW (a small bird of the crow family, now more commonly known as a *jackdaw*), three derived from *daw* itself, and alongside these jay n 1884> (see section 4.4.2 for explanation). Two entries are from *sparrow*, and there are seven single entries that come from a variety of birds: dotterel n c1440–1681, owl n 1508>, cuckoo n 1596>, widgeon n 1612–1741, eagle-wit n 1665, dove n 1771, and as crazy as a loon aj 1845>. Finally, there are three entries in the group ANIMAL-BIRD-BODY PART, and all of these are derived from *comb*, the red crest that is found on the head of the domestic fowl, particularly pronounced on males.

## 4.2.3 INSECTS

This is a significantly smaller group, containing 15 entries. Two of these have not been labelled in a more specific group, since they derive from *dor*, which has been used differently at different times to mean various insects. Five more entries are derived from *beetle*, and the *OED* suggests that the first element of bottlehead n 1654 + 1815, is a variant form of the same lexical item. A further

---

[4] *Vermin* is a general term that can be applied to various small mammals, but also some insects or birds; varment aj 1829> has been categorised in the group ANIMAL-MAMMAL-OTHER ANIMALS because this seems to reflect its most general and central meaning, but it could equally have been placed in either the INSECT or BIRD categories.

four have been labelled SNAIL, and are derived from *hoddy*, which seems to have come to be associated with the snail indirectly: the *OED* notes:

> The element *dod* is evidently the same as in DODMAN a shell-snail; *hoddy-dod*, *hoddy-doddy*, *hodman-dod*, are perhaps in origin nursery reduplications; but the element *hoddy-* appears itself to have come to be associated with or to mean 'snail' (or ? horned), as in several words that follow.

The other three entries in the group are derived from *nit*, i.e. the egg or young of a louse.

### 4.2.4 *FISH*

The FISH group contains the fewest entries in the ANIMAL data, a total of nine, and these relate to five different types of fish. Three entries each derive from *cod* and *mullet*, and there are two entries from other fish, <u>smelt n 1599–a1625</u> and <u>loach n 1605–c1620</u>. One other entry in this group is not connected with a species of fish, <u>gubbins n 1916></u>; this term originally meant 'fish parings', the fragments of scales etc. that are discarded when a fish is prepared to be eaten. It is classified in the core category VALUE as well as in FISH, since its connenction with stupidity appears to result from the fact that it is something inherently worthless.

### 4.3 MOTIVATION

Perhaps more than any other within the INTELLIGENCE data, the ANIMAL group illustrates the complexity that can be involved in a seemingly simple mapping. It is possible to generalise about the motivation for the group as a whole, and this is a valuable and necessary starting point in examining the data. The connection between intelligence and animals in general can only itself be accounted for by reference to a number of mechanisms and principles, and these are discussed below. However, like the DENSITY group, beyond this it is necessary to look beyond this at the particular sources found in the data for this core concept, which appear to be culturally selected.

### 4.3.1 *Nature and nurture, the brain, and cognitive fluidity*

It appears to be generally agreed by anthropologists and psychologists that our compulsion to see animals as humans, and humans as animals, is just that – a compulsion, which is the inevitable result of nature and nurture combined. In a discussion criticising the way in which anthropomorphism has hindered study of animal behaviour, Kennedy recognises that it is difficult to avoid because of its implicitness:

... anthropomorphic thinking about animal behaviour is built into us. We could not abandon it even if we wished to. Besides, we do not wish to. It is dinned into us culturally from earliest childhood. It has presumably also been 'pre-programmed' into our hereditary make-up by natural selection, perhaps because it proved to be useful for predicting and controlling the behaviour of animals. (Kennedy 1992: 5)

It is easy to identify examples of the crossover between animals and humans in culture, because this occurs so pervasively. Literature and the media overflow with anthropomorphic images: animal characters are a staple of children's fiction in books, TV and film, and adults are also encouraged to think of animals as semi-human, for example in the way that pet food and services are advertised. As some scholars have pointed out, language itself is anthropomorphic, since it is designed by and for humans – it 'derives from human experience and, as a result, it inevitably presupposes consciousness. There simply is no "neutral" language in which to describe the behaviour of animals that does not prejudge the issue' (Dunbar 1984: 45).[5] Even though some scientists argue that they are using particular language metaphorically (e.g. Krebs & Davies 1981: 256; McFarland 1989), others, like Kennedy, believe that it is difficult to maintain awareness of this and ensure that observations about animal behaviour are always 'translated' by readers (Kennedy 1992: 14–15). Furthermore, anthropomorphism in culture does not seem to be a recent tendency. Evidence of anthropomorphism in art dates as early as 40,000 years ago to the Palaeolithic era, for example in cave paintings depicting half-man, half-animal beings.

It is more difficult to explain the 'nature' element of our identification of animals with humans, that which gives rise to the emergence of this aspect of culture. One convincing account is given in Mithen's exploration of the development of the imagination (1996), where he suggests that anthropomorphic and zoomorphic (by which I mean the opposite of anthropomorphic) thought are a by-product of the way the brain has developed. Mithen argues (pp. 132ff.) that for early humans, the brain was essentially modular: different kinds of intelligence – technical intelligence, natural history intelligence and social intelligence – were isolated from one another by cognitive 'barriers' that kept each kind of intelligence essentially separate from the others. When these barriers were broken down, the brain became

[5] Crist appears to disagree with this, suggesting that a distinction can be made between 'ordinary' and 'technical' language used to describe animals. Even if this is the case, though, it is the ordinary language that is significant for wider usage and that will therefore affect perceptions of animals, and of this she says the following: 'The ordinary language of action is largely the everyday language of human affairs ... In virtue of its affiliation with everyday reasoning about human action, the use of the ordinary language of action reflects a regard for animals as acting *subjects*; the immanent, experiential perspective of animals is treated as real, recoverable, and invaluable in the understanding of their actions and lives' (Crist 1999: 2).

'cognitively fluid', so that the types of knowledge relating to each of the modules were able to be combined, and this was the trigger for the 'cultural explosion' that took place during Upper Palaeolithic times. Aside from the early art mentioned above, one particularly interesting piece of evidence for this change can be found in the gradual evolution of hunting practices from the time of Early to Modern Humans. Early Humans relied on 'opportunistic' hunting, targeting individual animals of any species available at the time; by contrast, the methods of the first Modern Humans involved much more organisation and planning:

> Although they continued to kill individual animals, or at most small groups, they began to specialize on specific animals at specific sites ... Indeed certain sites seem to have been selected for ambush hunting, indicating that Modern Humans were much better at predicting the movements of animals than Early Humans. (Mithen 1996: 191)

Mithen contends that this ability to predict movements only develops when animals are ascribed thoughts and intentions – in other words, the basis of anthropomorphism – and this is only possible if natural history intelligence and social intelligence are not separate, so that humans consider and predict the ways animals are likely to think and act. Crucially, if these two modules are integrated, anthropomorphic and zoomorphic thought seem inevitable.

### 4.3.2 *Cultural influences: the medieval tradition and beyond*

Aside from cognitive factors, there are also cultural influences that are equally important and should be taken into account in exploring mappings between humans and animals. The cultural tradition of the Middle Ages is particularly rich in anthropomorphic images and symbols. Its inheritance from Antiquity embraces, amongst other influences, both the beast fable traditions epitomised by Aesop and the rich animal imagery found in the Bible and absorbed into subsequent Christian writings. These fed into the popular medieval bestiaries, about which Hassig makes the following comments:

> ... is it really surprising that imaginative thinking about animals became a medieval preoccupation? With a gradually accumulated and rich store of symbolic associations, animals were excellent, fig-urative vehicles for religious allegory, political satire, and moral instruction. The medieval bestiary was the culmination and apogee of allegorical functions for animals, assembling stories and pictures of beasts and birds for the purposes of moral instruction and courtly entertainment. It is indisputable that the bestiaries were an im-portant medieval contribution to didactic religious literature. But far from comprising an isolated, specialist's genre available only to the

religious and literate elite, bestiaries also addressed concerns central to virtually all walks of Christian life. That is, familiarity with the bestiary stories did not necessarily require direct access to the bestiary manuscripts, as the stories were available from a multitude of sources, some textual, some visual, some word of mouth. (Hassig 1999: xi)

Hassig points out that bestiaries were central to religious teaching, and whilst this is certainly the case, it is important to remember the influence of the Bible itself. The Old and New Testaments are both permeated with animal imagery, and particular animals are found again and again. For example, a range of animals including sheep, goats, snakes, wolves and asses (donkeys) are central to biblical narrative,[6] and came to be used fairly conventionally in later allegorical art and literature (and in bestiaries) to represent specific human characteristics.

Perhaps the earliest and most important of all the sources of the medieval bestiary tradition were Aesop's *Fables*. These had been well known and popular in classical times and were pervasive in Greek and Roman culture; the earliest evidence for them is found in Herodotus, writing in the fifth century BCE, but it is clear from this that familiarity with the *Fables* was widespread by the time he committed them to the page. Laura Gibbs discusses a reference to them in Aristophanes' *The Birds* (late fifth century BCE), which gives a sense of their significance:

What exactly does Aristophanes mean by someone 'going over' their Aesop? The Greek verb he uses is *pepatekas*, which literally means to 'have walked through' or 'gone over' Aesop. Citing precisely this passage in Aristophanes, the Liddell-Scott dictionary of Greek suggests that the verb should also mean 'to thumb through', or 'to be always thumbing Aesop'. Such a translation, however, misses the mark. To 'thumb through' Aesop implies that there was a text of Aesop to read, like the book you are holding in your hands right now and which you can certainly 'thumb through' at your leisure. In fifth-century Athens, however, there were no books of Aesop to be thumbed through, since the first written collections of Aesop did not yet exist. It is very hard for us as modern readers to appreciate the fact that Aesop could still be an authority whom you had to consult, even if he were not an author of books to be kept on the shelf. To 'go over' or 'run through' Aesop meant to bring to mind all the many occasions on which you had heard the stories of Aesop told at public assemblies, at dinner parties, and in private conversation. Aesop's

---

[6] A huge amount of information about what these animals came to symbolise is available in various dictionaries of the Bible; see e.g. Achtemeier 1985; Douglas 1982; Metzger & Coogan 1993.

fables and the anecdotes about Aesop's famous exploits were clearly a familiar way of speaking in classical Greece, a body of popular knowledge that was meant to be regularly 'gone over' and brought to mind as needed. (Gibbs 2002: x–xi)

In the Middle Ages, when there was renewed interest in Antiquity, Aesop's *Fables* enjoyed a resurgence in popularity, and seem to have been disseminated by similar means. Medieval audiences, or at least readers, would certainly have been aware of classical retellings such as the Latin verse fables of Phaedrus and the Greek verse fables of Babrius, and later versions like Odo's Christianised medieval Latin texts (thirteenth century). However, it was not until much later that any of the *Fables* were translated into English on the page. The first English print edition was translated by Caxton, and it is telling that this was one of the earliest texts to become available in print (in 1484), only eight years after the printing press had been brought to Britain. It may not be true that Aesop's *Fables* were core to the bestiaries in themselves, but the way in which they established a tradition of animal allegory bound together with morality was central to the way in which bestiaries were written, and to their didactic and social function.

One account of the way in which these sources and others are related, and form a tradition of animal narrative, is given by T. H. White in a family tree of the bestiary (Fig. 4.1 below). With such a strong tradition established so early, it is unsurprising that anthropomorphic and zoomorphic thought continues to be an important and central part of western culture and specifically English language texts of all kinds.

It is only in medieval Europe that a more elaborate narrative form begins to emerge with the medieval 'beast epic' stories of Reynard the fox, inveterate rival of Ysengrimus, the wolf. In the beast epics, the animals become self-aware individuals, endowed with memory, motivation and – perhaps more importantly – personal names. It is but a slight jump from this tradition to the horse named Boxer in Orwell's *Animal Farm*, the famous pigs named Wilbur or Babe or Porky, not to mention Bugs Bunny, Mickey Mouse, and innumerable other cartoon animals, along with the extraordinary comic-book animals in Spiegelman's *Maus*. (Gibbs 2002: xx)

There may be other factors worth considering as well. The way in which animals are viewed in general depends on how familiar people are with them, and this seems to have changed during and after the Middle Ages. Obviously animals had always been important, and were familiar in everyday life, but for the majority of people (and especially the lower classes), real-life experience of animals was restricted to a fairly limited group of mainly semi-domesticated farm animals and indigenous wild animals. Animal ownership was governed by necessity rather than choice, and animals had practical purposes, for the survival and benefit of humans. Other animals that were not encountered daily would have undoubtedly been well known, but in a much more remote way; these were unfamiliar and exotic creatures found in literature and tradition.[7] However, with the advancement of science and technology, and greatly improved opportunities to travel, better-informed knowledge about a wide range of animals became much more widespread. There was a huge surge of interest in animal behaviour during the Renaissance, reflected in and perpetuated by the appearance of zoology books. According to the *Encyclopaedia Britannica*:

> **Zoology** continued in the Aristotelian tradition for many centuries in the Mediterranean region and by the Middle Ages, in Europe, it had accumulated considerable folklore, superstition, and moral symbolisms, which were added to otherwise objective information about animals. Gradually, much of this misinformation was sifted out: naturalists became more critical as they compared directly observed animal life in Europe with that described in ancient texts. The use of the printing press in the 15th century made possible an accurate transmission of information.

It seems certain that this increased attention had an indirect impact on the extent to which people thought of animals and humans as similar. As Mithen points out (discussed above), it is when people begin to consider the motivation for the behaviour of animals that they begin to anthropomorphise, since the obvious reference point for any kind of mental process is the human mind. If there is greater focus on animal behaviour, presumably people will be more susceptible to anthropomorphic thought. This is likely to be further perpetuated by sentimentality about animals, and this also appears to have surfaced around the time of the Renaissance, as the status of animals in society began to be different. As living conditions and practices changed, animals began to be kept for pleasure rather than practical purposes, and were domesticated to a greater extent. In the Middle Ages, some animals and birds were kept by the aristocracy; very gradually, over the following centuries, pet ownership became less uncommon and spread to the middle classes.

---

[7] The extent to which some animals were unfamiliar is demonstrated by their representations in illustrations and sculpture – there are many examples of elephants, lions and other animals portrayed quite inaccurately in medieval art. The lion sculptures on a column of Modena Cathedral from *c*.1100 have body shapes similar to that of a horse, short defined fringes of hair on the forehead and thick 'moustaches', and bird-like talons (pictured in Salvini 1969: fig. 51). The elephant portrayed some 400 years later in the *Bestiary of Ann Walsh* (Kongelige Bibliotek, Gl. kgl. S. 1633 4o), fo. 6v, is no more accurate: it has cloven hoofs, a long bushy tail and short, dog-like ears (digital facsimile online at http://base.kb.dk/pls/hsk_web/hsk_vis. side?p_hs_loebenr = 3&p_sidenr = 14&p_illnr = 0&p_frem = 10&p_tilbage = 12&p_navtype = rel&p_lang = dan).

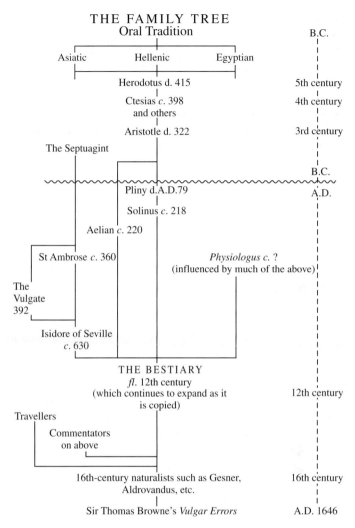

Fig. 4.1. The bestiary 'family tree' (White 1954: 233)

### 4.3.3 *Dating issues: a problem?*

In an analysis of the role and importance of animals in the Middle Ages, Salisbury claims:

> ...animals of the imagination shaped people's views of animals so much that if you wanted to insult someone, you would call him a dog; whereas if you wanted to praise someone, you would call her a lion. (Salisbury 1996: 49–50)

However, evidence from the INTELLIGENCE data does not reflect this claim. A noticeable feature of the ANIMAL group is the fact that the entries are dated surprisingly late, most of them significantly later than the medieval period. Only six entries (i.e. just under 6% of the total data) date to pre-1500, and the earliest entry dates to *c.*1330 (ape n c1330–1741). Without extensive research, it is difficult to say conclusively whether this is the case for all animal terms applied to humans or whether it is only a feature of intelligence lexis. It seems likely that some of the earliest transferred animal names might be those of animals found in Bible narratives, and that an investigation of these might be a helpful starting point in gauging this. Biblical material was hugely influential in the Middle Ages, and there are numerous references to animals throughout the Bible, used allegorically to portray human characteristics; a few representative animals, which are considered below, are sheep, wolves, pigs and dogs.[8]

Sheep are perhaps the most commonly found animals – one web-based online study Bible which runs searches in the full text of different Bible editions picks up 179 verses in the King James Version that contain the word *sheep*,[9] though obviously many of these are references to the animals themselves. When used in a transferred or symbolic sense, *sheep* stands for the followers of God, who are unable to look after themselves and get lost very easily.[10] The *OED* entry makes it clear that there are early examples of *sheep* used with a transferred sense (and draws attention to biblical influence), but the possible definitions and supporting quotations seem to indicate that straightforward metaphorical usage, where *sheep* is used directly to mean 'person', is attested relatively late. The numbered sense definition which acts as a heading for the lettered subsenses calls this group 'Similative (often passing into figurative) uses', and the next level subheading uses the term 'allusions' to describe the way the lexeme is used:

> **a.** In allusions to: **(a)** The sheep's timidity, defencelessness, inoffensiveness, tendency to stray and get lost: chiefly in echoes of biblical passages, and sometimes with allusion to sense 4. **(b)** The fabled assumption by a wolf (or other beast of prey) of the skin of a slaughtered sheep. **(c)** The division into 'sheep' and 'goats' (saved

---

[8] I have selected these fairly randomly, although they are all mentioned in Bible dictionaries as examples of animals that are used figuratively of humans. The *Oxford Companion to the Bible* specifically mentions sheep, wolves and dogs in its 'Animal Imagery' section (Metzger & Coogan 1993: 29–30); in its entry for *swine*, *Harper's Bible Dictionary* says: 'The low estate to which the prodigal son fell is signified by his occupation as a swineherd' (Achtemeier 1985: 1002). Both volumes have more extensive sections on animals in the Bible; see also Douglas (1982: 38ff.).

[9] www.crosswalk.com, accessed Apr. 2008.

[10] I refer here to adult sheep. Lambs are also very common in the Bible, but have quite different and far more positive connotations; the most recurring use of *lamb* is to refer to the Christ, who is seen as the innocent sacrifice for the sins of humankind.

and lost) at the Last Judgement. Also *attrib.*, as **sheep-and-goat**. **(d)** The infection of the whole flock by one sheep. **(e)** The shearing of sheep; with suggestion of 'fleecing' or robbing.

The wolf is also found in both the Old and New Testaments, and is the representative of vicious people, often those attacking the followers and doctrines of the church: 'its habits of tearing its prey and stealing upon it at night-time are ... symbolical of dishonest persons, oppressors and extortioners' (Bolton 1901: 19). As with *sheep*, *wolf* is applied to people very early – the *OED* dates it as far back as 900 – in metaphorical senses strongly influenced by the Bible. But again, the quotations in the *OED* indicate that it is not used more generally for people until the fifteenth and sixteenth centuries, and the relevant definitions use the same phrase, 'in allusion to', to describe some usages. Metaphorical uses applied to people fall into the following two senses. The first of these is not confined to humans in its application:

> **1b.** In comparisons, with allusion to the fierceness or rapacity of the beast; often in contrast with the meekness of the sheep or lamb.

The second displays a more direct connection with the human:

> **5a.** A person or being having the character of a wolf; one of a cruel, ferocious, or rapacious disposition. In early use applied esp. to the Devil or his agents (**wolf of hell**); later most freq., in allusion to certain biblical passages (e.g. Matt. vii. 15, Acts xx. 29), to enemies or persecutors attacking the 'flocks' of the faithful.

Pigs (or *swine*) and dogs were both seen as unclean animals in the Jewish tradition, and are therefore used a symbols of filthy, subhuman creatures, 'standing for what is despicable and hated' (Douglas 1982: 41). The *OED* entry for *swine* refers to this symbolism within the definition of the first sense of the word, which also deals with the literal meaning itself.

> An animal of the genus *Sus* or family *Suidæ*, comprising bristle-bearing non-ruminant hoofed mammals, of which the full-grown male is called a *boar*, the full-grown female a *sow*; esp. the common species *Sus scrofa*, domesticated from early times by Gentile nations for its flesh, and regarded as a type of greediness and uncleanness.

The quotations supporting this definition date from as early as 725. There is also an entry for the word 'In proverbial and allusive expressions, and in fig. context', with supporting quotations dating from 1000 onwards. The more direct metaphorical sense is separated into a later sense, attested from *c*.1380 onwards:

> **2.** *fig.* Applied opprobriously to a sensual, degraded, or coarse person; also (in mod. use) as a mere term of contempt or abuse.

*Dog* is the only one of the four animals for which no intermediate 'allusive' stage of usage is listed, and a single relevant definition is given that connects the term directly with humans.

> Applied to a person; a. in reproach, abuse, or contempt: A worthless, despicable, surly, or cowardly fellow. (Cf. cur 1 b.)

The supporting quotations date from *c*.1325, i.e. relatively early, though a good deal later than the OE period; it should be pointed out that the earliest quotation for the term used literally of the animal only dates to *c*.1050, i.e. relatively late.[11] In all of quotations given with the definition above, *dog* is used as a direct term for a person, in some cases as a term of address.

Without any larger-scale study into the transfer of animal terms, it does not seem impossible that the INTELLIGENCE data might reflect a general trend in animal metaphors that apply to humans. However, some evidence appears to contradict these findings, and for this reason any suggestions offered here are made tentatively. Thornton's (1988) study of animal names used in noun phrases for GOOD and EVIL, based on 164 items, found 31 items (just under 19% of the total data) dating to pre-1500. Although this total may not be directly comparable to my own,[12] this figure must still be taken into account.

On balance, it seems likely that, for at least some animals, straight metaphorical transfer does not occur even though the connotations and symbolism from which this draws may be in place, and this is the case for the lexical items within my data. Almost without exception, it is possible to find some reference or tradition relating to each of the animals in the data (discussed below) which makes it available as a source concept for INTELLIGENCE; in all cases, this shared folk knowledge pre-dates the emergence of the animal metaphor that reflects it. However, if it is the case that the 'architecture' of the brain gives rise to human-animal thought, one would expect to find evidence of this in the lexicon very early indeed; and it seems

---

[11] This may be because the term *hund* was also found in OE, and seems to have been more common than *dog*.

[12] Thornton's analysis differs from mine in its approach. First, it preserves the classification of *HTE* more faithfully. Apart from general intelligence types assigned in pre-classification, I have used data without retaining precise labelling; by contrast, Thornton presents entries with their sub-heading 'definitions'. This means that two terms are repeated in different sub-heading groups (*shrew* and *whelp*). In addition to this, some items would be classed as variants of the same entry in my own data: *shrew*, *sherew* and *shrow*, which are only identified as variant spellings in the *OED*, are all found within the same sub-heading group, OE *docga* and its reflex *dog* both appear, and *hellehund* and *hellhound* are listed as separate entries. Taking account of this differing methodology to bring it in line with my own would reduce the number of entries in the group to 25; without examining all the rest of the data in the same way it is not clear whether this would affect the percentage total.

surprising that there is such a long delay between the evidence of folk traditions relating to these animals and the straight metaphorical usage of their names as terms for humans.

One possibility is that the dates recorded for these entries are inaccurate. As is discussed in Chapter 1, section 1.2, current revisions in the *OED* suggests that redating will apply to a significant number of entries, and it may be that the ANIMAL group will be affected to an unusually large extent. There are also other factors of a similar nature that must also be taken into account. It is only written language that is used as evidence for earlier periods in the *OED*, and this can vary substantially from spoken language in terms of both timescale and register. Revised and expanded editions of synchronic dictionaries demonstrate that at best there is a substantial delay between the emergence of spoken language and the time at which it is written down, even for well-established spoken forms, and in earlier periods this transfer may not have occurred at all for some vocabulary. As well as this, early evidence of the vocabulary linked to a particular semantic field is dependent on surviving texts, and to a certain degree these demonstrate the nature of written sources in any period. The majority of early medieval texts appear to have been fairly formal in register, and many dealt with biblical material; presumably, even if there was other material dealing with 'lower' matters it may not have been considered as respectable or important, and its lower status may have made it less likely to survive. In this respect it is unsurprising that few metaphorical animal terms are found within these early texts; these items are more associated with spoken language and are very often considered to be slang, and therefore it would be uncommon for them to be used in written texts. This is especially true given that almost all of the terms in the data presented here denote stupidity and are therefore derogatory. It seems that this concept is much more likely to be associated with colloquial and informal language than, for example, GOOD/EVIL, and this might account in part for the imbalance between the number of metaphorical animals dating to pre-EModE in the INTELLIGENCE data compared to that included in Thornton's study.

In general though, colloquial language tends to be written down much more from EModE onwards, when the type of material available begins to be far more varied. This is exemplified in the work of Shakespeare, whose plays include dialogue full of colloquialisms as well as more 'high-flown' rhetoric in which one is unlikely to find abusive terms. Even more simply, it is significant that during the Renaissance period there was simply much more literature available in English, and also that the English lexicon underwent enormous expansion. The emergence of more animal terms must in part reflect a tendency throughout the lexicon (and indeed within the data included in this study).

### 4.3.4 *Derogatory terms and the Great Chain metaphor*

The association of people with animals in general tends to be derogatory, and often indicates some quality perceived as 'less than human'.[13] To call someone an *animal* is to imply that some element of their humanness is lacking; one *OED* definition for *animal* is

> Contemptuously or humorously for: a human being who is no better than a brute, or whose animal nature has the ascendancy over his reason; a mere animal. (Cf. similar use of *creature*.)

Similarly *beast* can mean 'A human being under the sway of animal propensities' or, worse,

> 'A brutal, savage man; a man acting in any manner unworthy of a reasonable creature.' J. In earlier usage, often connoting stupidity or folly (cf. Fr. *bête*); in modern phraseology opprobriously employed to express disgust or merely aversion. Now freq. in weaker sense.

The definition presented here makes indirect reference to the traditional view of the division between man and animal, resting on man's possession of reason, which animals lack. This links up with the way in which reason and emotion have been seen as almost opposites, with emotion more closely associated with animals. It also goes some way to explaining the fact that, in general, animal terms that are transferred to humans become derogatory. Anecdotal evidence and general observation bears this out; Leach comments 'Most of the monosyllables denoting familiar animals may be stretched to describe the qualities of human beings. Such usage is often abusive but not always so' (1964:47). However, there is also some corpus-based evidence for the bias. In Thornton's study of animal names used to signify good and evil, the bias is even more marked than in the INTELLIGENCE data, with 157 out of 164 items (95.7%) signifying evil (Thornton 1988: 411). Moreover, this does not seem to be the case only in English. In an analysis of 2,980 Mandarin Chinese and 2,630 German animal fixed expressions, Hsieh comments: 'The present corpora demonstrate that about 80% of AEs [animal expressions] are used to scorn or warn people. Thus, we can say AEs are a vocabulary of peoples' values. They convey values from different cultures and societies' (Hsieh 2003: 5–6).

This division between the human and non-human fits into a broad schema, a sort of 'order of being', that has existed since medieval times.

---

[13] Interestingly, there is one entry in the data that seems to carry the opposite idea, and is classified as HUMAN. cretin n 1884 + 1930 > was used earliest in English as a term for a class of people who lived in certain valleys in the Alps, who were (as defined in the *OED*) 'dwarfed and specially deformed idiots'. Amongst the etymological information given for this term, the *OED* suggests that *cretin* came through French and Swiss from Latin *Christiānum*, 'human creature', and was used as a term for these individuals, 'the sense being here that these beings are really human, though so deformed physically and mentally'.

This is discussed and formalised by Lakoff & Turner, who refer to it as a 'cultural model' which they believe is an important factor in the way in which humans understand the world and relate it to themselves.

> The Great Chain of Being is a cultural model that concerns kinds of being and their properties and places them on a vertical scale with 'higher' beings and properties above 'lower' beings and properties. When we talk about man's 'higher' faculties, we mean his aesthetic and moral sense and rational capacity, not his physical characteristics, his animal desires, or his raw emotions. We speak of higher and lower forms of life. The Great Chain is a scale of forms of being – human, animal, plant and inanimate object – and consequently a scale of the properties that characterize forms of being – reason, instinctual behaviour, biological function, physical attributes, and so on ...
>
> In the cultural model comprising the basic Great Chain, part of any being's nature is shared with lower beings. For example, it is not our instincts that separate us from beasts, because beasts also have instincts. It is the basic Great Chain that makes it sensible for us to speak of *our* 'bestial instincts' and *our* 'animal drives'. Though we are not beasts, we share these properties with beasts and not with trees or algae. They are called 'bestial instincts' because such instincts are a property that beasts and beings above them have while lower order beings don't.
>
> At any level in the basic Great Chain, the highest properties of beings at that level characterize that being. For example, the highest level properties of animals are their instincts ... Similarly, the mental, the moral, and the aesthetic are generic-level parameters of human beings; though different people have different mental capacities and different moral and aesthetic sensibilities, all human beings nonetheless have some of these or other. Thus, there is a generic-level characterization of our implicit unconscious cultural model of the basic Great Chain, a characterization that does not distinguish among kinds of humans, among kinds of higher animals, among kinds of lower animals, among kinds of plants, and so on. What defines a level are the attributes distinguishing it from the next level below. (Lakoff & Turner 1989: 167–8)

The crucial point about this is that the Great Chain underlies all ANIMAL metaphors, regardless of the particular animal, bird, fish or insect involved. In one sense, employing any animal metaphor (or at least any derogatory one) has as its foundation the denial of human status – in other words, the emphasis is on subhumanity rather than actual animality (i.e. [–human] rather than [+animal]). This is particularly true for metaphors using basic-level category terms, represented by the dictionary entries above.

This also goes some way to explaining the high percentage of entries (around a quarter of the total ANIMAL group) that are compounds formed with a HEAD/BRAIN element. This element appears simply to act as a marker, making it clear that the 'similarity' to animals is being made with the mind and mental faculties. As with the other *head/brain* groups, there is a clear implication that a stupid person does not have the kind of mind proper to humans, but has something in its place that is different and inappropriate. This is discussed more fully in the previous chapter (section 3.4).

## 4.3.5 *An analysis of animal metaphorisation*

Although I would not argue that it is a conscious linear process, the basic principle of animal metaphorisation can be broken down into several key elements, which combine to form an intuitive, gestalt-like source of description of people as animals.

The first of these stages involves some of the most general of human tendencies in dealing with non-human entities, the most important being personification, i.e. the way in which humans ascribe human qualities to non-human entities (more or less deliberately). Personification is very common, and is evident in the way we deal with all sorts of entities; some specific examples can be found in mappings identified in metaphor corpora, for example IDEAS AS PERSONS OR OTHER ANIMATE BEINGS (Barnden 1997), MACHINES ARE PEOPLE, and THEORIES ARE PEOPLE (Lakoff 1994). As I have mentioned already, several scholars have pointed out (with reference to anthropomorphism) that the language we use is designed to deal with human issues and therefore 'presupposes consciousness' (Dunbar 1984: 45); whether this is the result of the personification tendency or something that causes it is a moot point.

In the case of animals specifically, the term 'anthropomorphism' tends to be used. Although the basic principle is the same, in that the non-human is attributed human mentality, controversy about the nature of animal consciousness renders the connection somewhat more complex. Many (and probably most) people would argue that at least some animals do have mental facilities close to those of humans, whereas inanimate objects are an entirely different proposition; however, there still appears to be an almost total lack of consensus amongst the scientific community about how much animals and humans can be said to be comparable mentally. Anthropomorphic thought is attacked by some scholars, who contend that it hinders the study of animal behaviour because it is unconducive to theoretically sound evaluation. Kennedy goes as far as to say: 'our penchant for anthropomorphic interpretations of animal behaviour is a drag on the scientific study of the causal mechanisms of it ... If the study of animal behaviour is to mature as a science, the process of liberation from the delusions of anthropomorphism must go on' (1992: 5). As Mitchell et al. point out (1997: 7), much of the most persuasive evidence for strong similarity between humans and animals is anecdotal in nature, and is often criticised for this reason – Dennet dismisses anecdotes as 'officially unusable' in contemporary science (Dennet 1987: 250). But even the extensive investigations into individual species that have been carried out do not seem to have gone any distance towards resolving the debate about the mental capacities of animals, since any findings are subject to interpretation. In some cases even the experimenters themselves have changed their opinions on the conclusions that can be drawn from their own studies. For example, Kennedy cites one investigation into language learning by chimpanzees, where the researcher, Terrace, first concluded that his subject had mastered some grammatical rules, but later withdrew this claim after re-examining material he himself had collected (Kennedy 1992: 42). Clearly, then, the extent to which animals and humans can be compared mentally is an issue that looks unlikely to be resolved in the near future. The important point in relation to this study is that anthropomorphic thought is unquestionably powerful, whether it is based on fact, folk theory or a combination of the two. If it is a powerful conceptual tool within scientific communities, where it is regarded suspiciously at best, it is certainly even more pervasive in non-scientific discourse and thought.

Coupled with this tendency to anthropomorphise is another process that is common to human conceptualisation: our propensity to see entities in terms of a single defining feature, which is selected on the basis of what appears most typical or distinguishing. Lakoff & Turner refer to this as the 'quintessential property', and give a few examples: piety is often viewed as quintessential to saints, filthiness as quintessential to pigs, and courage as quintessential to lions (Lakoff & Turner 1989: 196). The selection of a quintessential property is fundamental to a huge number of metaphors; many explicit examples can be found in formulaic similes (of the form *as — as a —* ), where a single property is picked out and implied as the defining characteristic of an entity, very often an animal. This seems to me to be related to a similar phenomenon which occurs with inanimate objects, and is connected with prototypicality. Within an analysis of metaphorical vehicles, Glucksberg & Keysar discuss this:

> Parts of objects vary in 'goodness' (Tversky & Hemenway, 1984). Good parts are those that are functionally significant and often perceptually salient. The *wing* of an airplane is a good part, the floor of an airplane is not. This concept of part goodness is theoretically analogous to the concept of prototypicality or goodness of a category member, and so the goodness of a part may, for this purpose, be analogous to the prototypicality of a metaphor vehicle in simple nominative metaphors. (Glucksberg & Keysar 1993: 420)

For animals, it is characteristics that 'vary in goodness'. Crucially, the selection of these characteristics is rooted in human perception: what is quintessential about any animal is dependent solely on the status of this animal in relation to people.

### 4.3.6 *Similarity theory*

Similarity (or comparison) theory has often been associated with a classical view of metaphor, which sees metaphor as a matter of language rather than thought. Because this view has been so much criticised within the past 20 years, especially within cognitive linguistics, similarity theory in its oldest form was for a time considered to be irrelevant and outdated; much attention shifted away from the kind of examples that had been easily explained by a comparison between source and target. Many older studies tended to discuss metaphors expressed linguistically in the form *A is B*, such as *Jimmy is a monkey*, and it is reasonably easy to identify some kind of perceived similarity between source and target in this example. By contrast, recent work in the Lakoffian tradition has shifted focus to highly conventional conceptual metaphors, which appear to be motivated by everyday physical experiences rather than by any inherent similar between source and target. The SENSES group exemplifies this kind of mapping: it would be very difficult to argue for an objective similarity between *seeing* and *understanding*, but it seems more acceptable to suggest the mapping is motivated by the way knowledge is first gained.[14] If this mapping is regarded as purely metaphorical, then it suggests that similarity is not an adequate property by which to identify and describe metaphor. However, growing interest in metonymy has led some scholars to propose that examples like this, along with many others generally classed as metaphor, are most accurately described as metonymical in nature, since they are motivated by a experiential connection between source and target. If this is the case, similarity may offer a helpful criterion that can be used to distinguish between prototypical examples of metaphor and metonymy. In accounting for the ANIMAL mapping, some version of similarity theory seems to be an unavoidable and crucial factor, especially in light of the other processes discussed in this chapter, and this seems significant in light of recent ideas about a metaphor–metonymy continuum (discussed in Chapter 1, section 1.1).

One of the earliest criticisms of similarity theory was that made in the 1960s by Max Black, within his influential account of interaction theory. Black argued that any explanation of metaphor based on comparison between source and target was essentially inadequate and failed to describe the fundamental nature of metaphor.

---

[14] Although, as discussed in Ch. 2, it has been suggested that the mapping might be more accurately described as metonymy, since the two processes are linked in experience.

The main objection against a comparison view is that it suffers from a vagueness that borders upon vacuity. We are supposed to be puzzled as to how some expression ($M$), used metaphorically, can function in place of some literal expression ($L$) that is held to be an approximate synonym; and the answer offered is that what $M$ stands for (in its literal use) is *similar* to what $L$ stands for. But how informative is this? There is some temptation to think of similarities as 'objectively given,' so that a question of the form, 'Is $A$ like $B$ in respect of $P$? has a definite and predetermined answer. If this were so, similes might be governed by rules as strict as those controlling the statements of physics... We need the metaphors in just the cases when there can be no question as yet of the precision of scientific statement. Metaphorical statement is not a substitute for a formal comparison or any other kind of literal statement, but has its own distinctive capacities and achievements... It would be more illuminating in some of these cases to say that the metaphor creates the similarity than to say that it formulates some similarity antecedently existing. (Black 1962: 36–7)

This idea that metaphor can create similarity, rather than simply reflect it, has been taken up by scholars arguing against an objectivist philosophical stance according to which entities are believed to have inherent properties. Lakoff & Johnson reason that our conceptual system relies so heavily on basic, conventional metaphors – what they later term 'primary metaphors' – that many of the similarities between sources and targets that appear to be obvious and self-supporting are themselves rooted in metaphor.

Since we see similarities in terms of the categories of our conceptual system and in terms of the natural kinds of experiences we have (both of which may be metaphorical), it follows that many of the similarities that we perceive are a result of the conventional metaphors that are part of our conceptual system. (Lakoff & Johnson 1980: 147)

In other words, many of the metaphors that seem natural follow on from primary metaphors, and themselves create the impression that particular sources and targets are similar.

One interesting hypothesis that has received attention recently is the idea that many or even all metaphors are motivated by metonymy (Barcelona 2000a). This is significant because it suggests that any perceived similarity between the source and target of a metonymically motivated metaphor is ultimately rooted in a relationship of contiguity between the source and the target, rather than in any inherent similarity. This does not seem to me to conflict with Lakoff & Johnson's comments above, since it preserves the idea that the two concepts involved in a mapping (more or less metaphorical or metonymical) are linked for speakers in a natural and obvious way.

However, it seems to me that while this kind of explanation, which qualifies the idea of similarity between source and target, holds for many metaphors, different kinds of metaphor work in quite different ways. I would agree with John Taylor when he comments, 'It is tempting to see all metaphorical associations as being grounded in metonymy ... There are, however, numerous instances of metaphor which cannot reasonably reduced to contiguity... [and] the theoretical puzzle of similarity remains' (2002: 342–3). In the case of the ANIMAL metaphors, the mapping does depend on basic common processes of conceptualisation, but these are not metonymical in nature. Whilst there is obviously no direct and objective similarity between animals and people, it also seems misleading to say either that there is any creation of similarity, or that the relationship is grounded in metonymy in the way that, for example, the SENSES group appears to be. In my opinion, the simplest and most logical way to account for the mapping is to say that there is a subjective but shared interpretation of animals that equates particular types of behaviour or characteristic with those of humans; in other words, the similarity may not relate to any scientific or factual reality or be in any way objective, but it is no less real for those observing it. In his consideration of animal terms used for humans, Richards comes to the same conclusion, making a brief reference to metaphors 'which work through some common attitude which we may (often through accidental and extraneous reasons) take up towards them both [the tenor and the vehicle]' (1936: 117). Grady gives a much fuller explanation in his discussion of non-primary metaphors:

> Why do we project human bravery onto aspects of lions' instinctive behavior, and vice versa? I propose that the simplest explanation is that we do perceive something in common between the behavior of certain lions and the behavior of courageous people (or some influential person once did, and created a stereotypic image of leonine behavior which still shapes our naive schemas of lions). Lions and courageous people both (appear to) confront dangerous opponents without fear. Let me make it as clear as possible that I am not advocating the 'similarity theory' which Lakoff & Turner (as well as Lakoff & Johnson and others) have successfully discredited. My proposal does not imply that there is any literal similarity whatsoever between brave people and lions. It is helpful, though, to recognize that the metaphorical association between them – involving projection in whichever direction – is most likely based on the *perception* of common aspects in their behavior. I will call this proposition the 'resemblance hypothesis,' in order to distinguish it from the 'similarity theory,' and to highlight the role of

our perceptions, as opposed to facts about the world. (Grady 1997: 222)

It is at this stage that folk theories, mythology and cultural values also influence the process, since they tend to become part of the shared folk knowledge of a community, and are thus involved in the stereotyping that influences the later perceptions of particular animals.

In terms of the metaphor–metonymy continuum that Radden (2000), Dirven (2002a; 2002b) and others propose, mappings like those in the ANIMAL group, which are motivated by a relationship of similarity (real or perceived), appear to be at the extreme metaphorical 'end' of the continuum. The animal mappings explored here are more prototypical examples of metaphor than the other mappings described in this study, which have a closer relationship to metonymy in their motivation. In other words, it becomes less problematic to claim similarity as a central feature of metaphor in the context of a metaphor–metonymy continuum where mappings can be located anywhere along this continuum.


4.4 PARTICULAR ANIMALS FOUND

As well as examining the general background to the metaphorical mapping between animals and intelligence, it is crucial to consider each of the core category groups within ANIMAL individually, and more specifically, to look at the data within each group. This must be done in context of a wide range of sources that inform folk beliefs, since these are often more influential than 'real world' knowledge in determining the metaphors associated with particular animals and the ways in which these can be motivated. Black makes this point in his brief consideration of animal metaphors:

> Consider the statement, 'Man is a wolf. ... What is needed is not so much that the reader shall know the standard dictionary meaning of 'wolf' – or be able to use that word in literal senses – as that he shall know what I will call the system of associated commonplaces. Imagine some layman required to say, without taking special thought, those things he held to be true about wolves; the set of statements resulting would approximate to what I am here calling the system of commonplaces associated with the word 'wolf.' ... From the expert's standpoint, the system of commonplaces may include half-truths or downright lies ... but the important thing for the metaphor's effectiveness is not that the commonplaces shall be true, but that they should be readily and freely evoked. (Black 1962: 39–40)

I would agree that it is not possible to reach an adequate account of any group of entries without examining cultural beliefs, symbolism and folklore, both contemporary and historical. The sources I have discussed above give a valuable insight into the way in which particular animals were regarded, and the characteristics they came to represent. For example, in the bestiaries and the *Fables*, animals tended to be portrayed not as individuals so much as 'generic representatives of their species' (Gibbs 2002: xx). In the following section I have tried to give a brief account of each of the groups in the data, which draws from these sources whilst also considering the rationale that might lead to their characterisations of animals. My approach is intended to follow on from comments made by Spence in his article 'The human bestiary':

> The original inspiration for the associations has to be sought mainly in human psychology and its varying perceptions of points of similarity between particular animals and particular types of human or types of human behaviour, but one would have to distinguish different layers, both chronological and cultural, given that some parallels are not only ancient but have religious, symbolic, or literary origins, whereas others, humorous, cynical, or affectionate, are more popular, in the sense of belonging to popular culture, and often more transitory in nature. (Spence 2001: 913)

There is a single entry in the ANIMAL group that I have not placed into any specific category, and this is <u>plant-animal n 1673–1706</u>. In its source sense this refers to a zoophyte, and can therefore be applied to either the very lowest level animals, i.e. as 'A general name for various animals of low organisation, formerly classed as intermediate between animals and plants', or to the highest level plants, i.e. 'certain plants having or supposed to have some qualities of animals' (*OED*). I assume in this case that the transfer of meaning of this item is motivated simply by the Great Chain, since this is an uncommon organism which would probably have been unknown to most speakers. However, the term is formed from two familiar and basic elements so that its meaning is not opaque, and this perhaps makes it more readily 'available' to speakers (though they may not be using it in a technically correct way). This idea is supported by the fact that the more specialised and technical synonym *zoophyte* does not undergo the same metaphorical extension.

## 4.4.1 MAMMALS

The bias towards mammals in the data seems entirely understandable if it is true that the most 'successful' metaphors of this kind are those for which the source and target are not perceived to be too dissimilar, as various scholars have contended. For example, Katz states: 'There is a wealth of evidence that a strong predictor of perceived metaphor goodness is the number and saliency of features shared in common by the concepts' (1989: 487).[15] Furthermore, it is consistent with Thornton's findings in her investigation of animal-related terminology for good and evil:

> The greatest number [of items] belongs to the mammals – the class which is most familiar and similar to mankind (and to which mankind also belongs). The smallest number is in the class which is probably least similar to mankind – the Crustaceans. The pattern is roughly, but not entirely, borne out by the numbers in between. Insects, birds and mammals are all familiar to man and are well-represented. (Thornton 1988: 443)

Whilst it seems logical that it should be more insulting to metaphorise a person in terms of a fish or insect, and that this should signify lesser intelligence, in reality this kind of source may be cognitively less convincing. Lakoff & Turner point out that, in relation to the Great Chain, this group is further classified by criteria like 'functional structure' and 'interior state'.

> We think of humans as higher-order beings than animals, animals as higher than plants, and plants as higher than inanimate substances. Within each of these levels, there are higher and lower sublevels, so that dogs are higher-order beings than insects, and trees higher than algae. This scale of beings embodies a scale of properties. While a rock is mere substance, a chair additionally has a part-whole functional structure, that is, it has a seat, a back, and legs, each of which serves some function. A tree has both substance and part–whole functional structure, and in addition it has life. An insect has all of these properties – substance, a complex functional structure, life – and in addition animal behaviour such as self-propulsion. According to our commonplace knowledge, higher animals like dogs have all of these properties plus interior states such as desires, (like wanting to play), emotions (like fear), limited cognitive abilities (like memory), and so on. Humans have all these properties plus capacity for abstract reasoning, aesthetics, morality, communication, highly developed consciousness, and so on. Thus, where a being falls in the scale of beings depends strictly on its highest property. (Lakoff & Turner 1989: 167–8)

This places individual animals in direct comparison to humans, since, by implication, to call a human an animal is to draw attention to exactly those 'functions' they lack. It may be that a less exaggerated comparison, with an animal that is only one or two 'levels' lower than humans, is a more convincing insult in terms of intelligence. As I will discuss below in section

---

[15] There is perhaps also a parallel here with the DENSITY data. In the same way that very dense substances (e. g. stone, metals) are not exploited to the same extent as substances that can be penetrated with difficulty, creatures that are 'closer' to humans seem to be more suitable as sources than those that are further removed in the Great Chain.

4.4.3, levels too far below that of humans may be more usefully employed with reference to characteristics other than intelligence, since organisms on lower levels are perceived as significantly less 'human'. Insect terms tend to be used most commonly to indicate a particular kind of disgust. Mammals, by contrast, have more obvious similarities to humans in terms of intelligence (and, of course, physical structure), which is why they are more commonly anthropomorphised, and why issues about their treatment tend to be seen as having moral implications. The very fact of their greater similarity seems to render them more suitable as metaphorical sources in this semantic field.

In his investigation of animal terms used for verbal abuse, Leach theorises that taboo entities always belong to the interstices between clearly separate things: 'it is the ambiguous categories that attract the maximum interest and the most intense feelings of taboo ... taboo applies to categories which are anomalous with respect to clear-cut category oppositions' (Leach 1964: 39). He goes on to set out a hierarchy of animals in relation to their status as food for humans, and draws up four categories:

1. Those who are very close –'pets,' always strongly inedible.
2. Those who are tame but not very close – 'farm animals,' mostly edible but only if immature or castrated. We seldom eat a sexually intact, mature farm beast.
3. Field animals, 'game' – a category toward which we alternate friendship and hostility. Game animals live under human protection but they are not tame. They are edible in sexually intact form, but are killed only at set seasons of the year in accordance with set hunting rituals.
4. Remote wild animals – not subject to human control, inedible. (Leach 1964: 44)

He concludes that it is the animals in categories 2 and 3 that are potentially most taboo; pets are so close to humans that they can be viewed as themselves semi-human, whilst wild animals are completely separate and therefore 'irrelevant'.[16]

Whilst I am unsure about Leach's 'edibility' criteria, his categories correspond to the animals found in this data remarkably closely, and a more general point that comes out of his analysis is fundamental to understanding ANIMAL metaphor: for metaphorisation purposes, the most important feature of any animal or animal group is its status in relation to humans. Regardless of whether or not their members can be eaten, the

---

[16] Thornton makes a similar point whilst considering the lack of primate terms in her data: 'perhaps names of primates are just too familiar, and too close to man, to be freely applied to people in a derogatory fashion' (1988: 444). This is plausible, but it should be noted that in another sense, primates are not at all familiar; most of the animal terms that become conventionalised figuratively, and that tend to fall into long-term usage, seem to be those of well-known, usually indigenous animals.

categories 'pet', 'farm animal', 'field animal' and 'wild animal' all relate to the human-defined purposes that animals serve, and the relationship between each 'level' of animal is often the result of human intervention. Which animals are domesticated or used in farming is a matter of human judgement about their suitability; this is informed by the varying temperaments of different animals, and the potential products that can be acquired from them, and to some extent it can also be arbitrary, but it results solely from human perspective. The same is true of the Great Chain; its hierarchical structure is based on the complexity and sophistication of the organisms involved, but this is by no means objectively determined, depending instead on how the creature is popularly perceived. In terms of cognitive abilities, there may be no significant theoretical difference between the animals Lakoff & Turner identify as higher on the scale, like dogs, and lower ones within the same group, for example cows or goats, but there is a marked difference in the roles they are assigned by people, equating to the 'properties' Lakoff & Turner discuss above.

### 4.4.1.1 DONKEYS/MULES

This is the largest of the MAMMAL sub-groups, and represents a long-established mapping. Donkeys are probably the animals most character-istically used as a symbol of stupidity, and there are a number of well-known examples in literature. In Aesop's *Fables*, donkeys are portrayed as senseless, fairly passive creatures that often bring about their own downfalls through lack of judgement. In one *Fable*, for example, a donkey admires a cricket so much that it imitates its diet of fresh air and dew, eventually starving to death (Gibbs 2002: 163); in another, discontented with its own lot, it dresses up in a lion skin to fool others but is clubbed to death when the disguise is unsuccessful (p. 155). In *A Midsummer Night's Dream*, it is a donkey's head that Puck attaches to Bottom to 'make an ass of' him or, in other words, make him look foolish. Spence has pointed out that donkey metaphors are common in a number of languages:

> ...the names of the donkey are used in all the languages to designate a fool, on their own or in phrasal combinations: compare the English *donkey*, *ass*, and *jackass*, the French *âne*, *un âne bâté*, 'a complete ass' (literally 'a donkey wearing a packsaddle'), *un âne rouge*, 'a stupid and malicious person', *une bourrique*, 'a stubborn or stupid person', the German *ein alter Esel*, the Spanish *burro* (feminine, *burra*, 'stupid woman'), *un burro cargado de letras*, 'a pompous ass' (literally 'a donkey loaded with book-learning'), and the Italian *asino*, *un pezzo d'asino* 'a fool', *somaro*, and *ciuco*. (Spence 2001: 916)

Amongst the adages collected by Erasmus, there are a huge number featuring donkeys, and again these focus on the animal's reputation for stupidity. One of the most direct is 'Ονος ἐν μελίτταις, 'A donkey among bees', which Erasmus explains by saying: 'This occurs when a person finds himself among satirical and insolent people, himself being a dull fellow whom they mock with impunity' (Phillips & Mynors 1982: 421).

Donkeys have always had a specific and limited purpose for humans – like oxen, they are traditionally designated as 'beasts of burden', farm animals that are kept to do heavy jobs like lifting, carrying and pulling. These are menial, routine tasks, and it is significant that *donkey work* has come to mean 'hard, boring, monotonous, "no-brain" work ... [requiring] little intelligence' (Palmatier 1995: 119). For this reason donkeys have quite a different status from horses, which are not found in the data at all, though both are equines. Horses have high value and high prestige, and have tended to be used to carry people, whereas donkeys are far less desirable and have been used more to carry loads, and are associated more with the lower classes. Palmatier makes the point: 'When the horse came along, with its speed and ability to carry knights in shining armour, the donkey, although also an equine, lost even more status by comparison' (Palmatier 1995: 119). In the biblical story commemorated on Palm Sunday, Christ rides into Jerusalem on a donkey, and this story had such resonance and power precisely because the donkey was not considered a worthy or dignified mode of transport for the nobility or royalty. In the gospels this is said to fulfil the prophesy in Zechariah 9:9, where the donkey represents the humbleness of Christ:

> Rejoice greatly, O daughter of Zion!
> Shout aloud, O daughter of Jerusalem!
> Lo, your king comes to you;
> triumphant and victorious is he,
> humble and riding on an ass,
> on a colt the foal of an ass.[17]

The contrast between the way horses and donkeys have always been perceived is illustrated by one of the Greek proverbs found in Erasmus, Ἀφ' ἵππων ἐπ'ὄνους, 'From horses to asses', which was used 'When a man turns aside from an honourable vocation to something less reputable ... [or] when someone has sunk from affluence to a humbler station' (Mynors 1989: 83). Interestingly, one entry in the data is <u>mule n c1470</u>. A mule is the sterile offspring of a female horse and a male donkey, but has negative associations, since the negative associations of the donkey seem to have entirely cancelled out the positive ones of the horse. This is the subject of one of the *Fables*, 'The boastful mule':

> Feeling his oats, so to speak, he burst into a run, whinnying and
> shaking his head to and fro. 'My mother is a horse,' he shouted, 'and

---

[17] All biblical passages are quoted from the *Revised Standard Version*.

I am no worse at racing than she is!' But suddenly he drew to a halt and hung his head in shame, remembering that his father was only a donkey. (Gibbs 2002: 104)

As the data analysis above shows, most of the words in this group are compounds of *ass*. Despite the fact that *ass* has been largely superseded by the term *donkey*, several of these compounds continue into current usage. One reason for this may be that they have become conventionalised to the extent that they are now fixed expressions, but it also seems likely that they have been influenced by British *arse* and American *ass*, both meaning 'buttocks'; in fact the phonological overlap with these terms may be largely responsible for both the decline of *ass* used as an animal name and concurrently its success as a term for a 'stupid person'. According to some research, the process of sound change that accounts for the confusion between the British forms appears to have happened over a long period, and had its beginnings as early as the seventeenth century.

Another instance of the avoidance of unpleasant associations is the case of *ass* ... The reasons which account for the substitution of *ass* with *donkey* are both phonetic and semantic. By 1600 the /r/ in syllable final position, when followed by another consonant, stopped being pronounced with the subsequent lengthening of the previous vowel (see Dobson 1968: 724ff). Thus, *arse* came to be pronounced with a long *a*. By the end of the 17th century there was also a lengthening of short *a* followed by the voiceless alveolar fricative, which made *ass* homophone of *arse*. Fairman refers to the process (1994: 31–34) and dates the avoidance strategies between the years 1760–1730. He explains that the first strategy was to employ *jackass*, but failed soon, because it ceased to mean the male of animals and 'became a lexical determiner', in such a way that speakers continued using *ass*. Several substitutes took its place in different parts of the country ... According to Fairman (1994:32), the first instance of *donkey* is in a list in Robert Nares' grammar (1784); the *OED* gives his second reference Francis Grose (1785) as the first record of the word. Gradually, *donkey* was gaining ground and favoured the decline of *ass*. However, he admits that there are still unclear aspects and the topic is open to discussion. Barber assures that *ass* underwent a modification in its pronunciation in order to avoid such an objectionable merger and the variant with / æ/ became standardized, although the long vowel can still be heard occasionally in expressions like *silly ass* (1976: 312–313). (de la Cruz Cabanillas & Tejedor Martínez 2002: 239)

Both *arse* and *ass* appear in the data listed under BODY PART-SEXUAL, which contains a total of ten items, and because this is a well-known and commonly used source field it is natural that it might be understood to motivate the *ass* entries, even though this might not be the actual etymological root. A similar phenomenon can be seen in other entries in the INTELLIGENCE data, notably stunpoll n a1794 >, which is listed in the core category group DENSITY and discussed in Chapter 3.

### 4.4.1.2 *SHEEP*

In his discussion of sheep metaphors, Palmatier concludes that the sheep's reputation for stupidity comes from the behaviour of female and young animals, rather than that of the ram, which has an entirely different character.

> The sheep is, at the same time, both the most forceful mammal (the ram) and the most defenseless mammal (the ewe), and the lamb is the most defenseless of all sheep. A person who is a *sheep* is vulnerable, gullible, impressionable, and easily influenced by others. The analogy is to the ewe or lamb, not to the ram. (Palmatier 1995: 341)

From the sources I have examined, it seems as though sheep are not seen as stupid in quite the same way that some other animals are. They are perceived primarily as being passive and lacking any independent thought, presumably because they belong to flocks rather than living individually. Their association with stupidity is the indirect result of this, and is the theme of Aesop's *Fables* such as 'The butcher and the flock':

> Some castrated sheep had been gathered together in a flock with the rams. Although the sheep realized that the butcher had come into the flock they pretended not to see him ... In the end there was only one sheep left. This is what he reportedly said to the butcher when he saw that he too was about to be taken away: 'We deserve to be slaughtered one after another since we didn't realize what was happening until it was too late ...' (Gibbs 2002: 31)

This is consistent with the way in which sheep are portrayed in the Bible. Throughout both the Old and New Testaments, sheep are used allegorically to stand for people. They are not represented in a particularly negative light, but the impression given is that they have no ability to act individually or safeguard their own survival. In Isaiah 53:6, humanity is described as being 'like sheep [that] have gone astray ...every one to his own way'; later on, in the gospels, Jesus sees a large crowd and 'he had compassion on them, because they were like sheep without a shepherd' (Mark 6:34). A more modern example of this can be found in the 'Far Side' cartoons drawn by Gary Larson, many of which feature sheep (which, like all the animals in his cartoons, tend to be 'humanised'). One picture shows a flock of sheep at a party, one of whom is obviously the host, and the caption reads: 'Henry! Our party's total chaos! No one knows when to eat, where to stand, what to ... Oh, thank God! Here comes a border collie!'

Also central to the mapping is the fact that sheep, like donkeys, have a particular and limited use for humans. Whilst donkeys can be used for labour, sheep are bred and kept specifically for the products that they yield, mainly food and wool. In one medieval bestiary, this usefulness to man is listed as part of the qualification for herd animals: 'Properly speaking, the word "herd" is applied to those animals which are bred for food (like sheep) or which are otherwise suitable for the use of man (like horses and cows)' (White 1954: 71).

Although Palmatier's notion that rams are associated with completely different human characteristics than sheep seems logical, it is not borne out by my data in relation to intelligence. Half of the entries in the group relate to male sheep, deriving from the root *ram* or *tup* or from *wether*, a castrated male sheep. It may be that this is simply a case of the term being used in an over-general way because it is a hyponym of *sheep*. However, it is also possible that the motivation for these entries is slightly different, and is not based on the same characteristic of passiveness and dependence. One feature of all these entries is that they are compounds with *head/brain* elements; in general, sheep seem to be systematically linked with lack of intelligence, but this does not seem to be the case with rams. In other contexts *ram* has associations with force or violence (as in to *ram*, or *ram* as defined in the *OED*, 'a sexually aggressive man; a lecher'), presumably as a result of the ram's tendency to react violently, butting other animals to assert dominance and defend territory and status. It seems likely that it is this behaviour that accounts for the fact that Latin *aries* could mean either 'ram' or the military device used to demolish walls, translated directly as 'battering ram' in English. As the *OED* points out, the wood and iron element of this device that would strike the wall first was sometimes in the form of a ram's head. This imagery, and the term *battering ram* itself, are also likely to have further highlighted this particular aspect of rams' behaviour. Rams are also commonly used in the names and logos of wrestling clubs (e.g. the Lafayette Rams and the Wyalusing Rams) and this may be related to the fact that in the Middle Ages a ram was the usual prize in a wrestling match (see Kirkpatrick 1992: 847). In Chaucer's portrait of the Miller, in the 'General prologue' to *The Canterbury Tales*, one of the Miller's features is that 'At wrastlinge he wolde have alwey the ram' (Benson 1987: 32, l. 548).[18] For these reasons, it seems plausible that the quintessential property attributed to male sheep may be rooted in this

---

[18] In this passage, the narrator goes on to say of the Miller, 'Ther was no dore that he nolde heve of harre, / Or breke it at a renning with his heed' (Benson 1987: 32 ll. 550–51). It is clear from Chaucer's descriptions of the Miller that he is not regarded as a clever man, and this is a subtle comment that is part of this, since it amounts to the most positive characteristic attributed to the Miller. This provides a parallel to the *ram* entries in the way that it portrays stupidity and connects it to this particular physical behaviour of knocking against things with the head.

behaviour pattern, rather than in the herd mentality most associated with sheep in general. If this is the case, perhaps the association with stupidity is a metaphorical reference to 'charging in' to solve problems, rather than to lack of independent thought. The fact that the specific source for this mapping comes from the same species as another one with the same target is presumably advantageous, since it increases the familiarity and conventionality of the metaphor.

Other entries in the data that can helpfully be viewed alongside the RAM group, and may be helpful in understanding the mapping. Three entries have *hammer* as an element, hammer-head n 1532–1628 + 1947, hammer-headed aj 1552 > and ninny-hammer n 1592–1853. It seems likely that these are motivated by the same idea, the practice of blindly and pointlessly knocking against things instead of directing one's efforts to negotiating them more effectively. If this is the case, one corollary of the mapping is that the mind is a physical, active agent, rather than the passive receiver or container of ideas,[19] and this aligns it with a number of other core categories. One of these is SHARP/PIERCING, one of the larger groups in the data which accounts for 42 entries, and I would suggest that this is a roughly opposite group that provides a symmetrical counterpart to the *ram* and *hammer* entries. If the role of the mind is to penetrate or 'get into' physical ideas (which are themselves similar to containers, in that knowledge is 'enclosed' inside), then it is logical that an individual with a sharp or piercing mind will possess intelligence since they are able to do this with precision and ease. By contrast, the mind of a stupid person must be unable to do this. This is consistent with the data in SHARP/PIERCING, in which there are entries like obtuse aj 1509> and unpenetrating aj 1748 that signify stupidity, as well as a large number of entries related to the notion of sharpness that signify cleverness. The *hammer* entries are an extension of this idea, with the added element of force: instead of being able to pierce an idea, a *hammer-head* strikes it clumsily, in the same way that a ram reacts to situations by butting with its head rather than responding in a more logical and constructive way.

The mapping between SHEEP and STUPIDITY is not restricted to English. Spence points out that 'the names of the adult sheep are often associated with timidity and stupidity: compare the English *sheep*, "stupid, poor-spirited person", and German *Schaf* and *Schafskopf*, "dolt, ninny"' (2001: 918). If it is the case that there is some biblical influence in the way that sheep are perceived, one would expect to find similar terms in other languages found in countries where the Bible has also been central to culture. Since the biblical portrayal of sheep comes from Hebrew culture, it is likely that this is also the case for other Afroasiatic languages, but further research is required before any definitive statement about this can be made.

---

[19] This is discussed in Ch. 5, section 5.3.1.

## 4.4.1.3 *BOVINES*

The connection between the bovine family and stupidity is not immediately obvious, but it appears to be similar to that of the sheep group in that it results from an indirect link between characteristics, types of behaviour and lack of intelligence. Rather than being motivated by a single (real or perceived) characteristic of bovines, or even one that stands out as the most salient, there are several strands that might be significant in this mapping, and these combine to create a cognitively cohesive source that is intuitively convincing. Moreover, each one is paralleled elsewhere in the data, and this is an important indication that these low-level metaphorical connections are 'real' for speakers even if they exist entirely unconsciously.

Like sheep, bovines tend to be kept as farm animals, and again the fact that they are herd animals can be perceived as indicating a lack of independent thought. Unlike the sheep group, however, there are no entries in this group that relate specifically to female bovines, and in fact half of the entries are connected specifically with either the males of the species (or animals more commonly thought of as male) or young animals. One possible reason for this is the role of females: cows are kept for milk, rather than simply to be eaten, and this is a role that may be perceived differently from that of other herd animals, and be seen as more sophisticated or even more individualistic. By contrast, male bovines tend to be reared specifically for food, or, like donkeys, as 'beasts of burden' that carry out heavy work requiring strength, like pulling ploughs. The *OED* entry for *ox* draws attention to these functions, commonly associated with cattle:

> The domestic bovine quadruped (sexually distinguished as *bull* and *cow*); in common use, applied to the male castrated and used for draught purposes, or reared to serve as food.

Additionally, the entry bullhead n 1624+1840 may share some of the connotations that motivate the male sheep entries discussed above. Rams are famous for violent behaviour including butting, and similarly bulls are known for reckless destruction and charging, as in the phrase *like a bull in a china shop*.

The entries that derive from young bovines are both from *calf*: calf n a1553–1711 and calvish aj 1570–1834 are the earliest dated entries in the group. As with all six entries in the core category AGE, age is taken as equating to experience and intelligence, and is therefore symbolic of intelligence; youth therefore stands for inexperience and so lack of intelligence. The only two entries in the ANIMAL group that relate to dogs, puppy-headed aj 1610 and dunderwhelp n 1621+a1625, can be explained by the same reasoning, as can green goose n 1768+1877. Green is the colour of plants and often of unripe fruit, and this has led to its identification with immaturity and lack of development; in this case it has undergone the same semantic shift to signify stupidity.

Three of the entries in the group derive from *buffalo*: these are <u>buffle n 1655 + 1710</u>, <u>bufflehead n 1659></u> and <u>buffle-headed aj 1675 + 1871</u>. The *OED* definition shows that the term *buffalo* (and its variant *buffle*) has been used with reference to various bovine species, though none of these is indigenous to Britain. This lack of familiarity would seem to render buffalo a less appropriate metaphorical source, but it is clear from the etymology of the term that the English form *buffle* has come from vulgar Latin through French, in which the metaphor already existed, so that it could be 'imported' directly. However, the term was also borrowed with its animal meaning in English, and presumably the general identification of bovines with stupidity further reinforced the metaphorical meaning in English. The feature that seems to make buffalo suitable for the mapping in either language is size. Bovines tend to be large, bulky animals, and this is particularly true of buffalo (as well as, to a lesser extent, bulls). Similarly, large size is an element common to a number of other groups and entries in the data. For example, the wood group contains sources that are large blocks (see discussion in Chapter 3, section 3.4.3), and there is a group in the data that appears to centre on LUMP, which carries this idea of bulkiness or unwieldiness. SIZE is most commonly correlated with status metaphorically, as in the mapping IMPORTANCE IS SIZE, listed as a primary metaphor by Grady with the motivation 'The correlation between size/volume of objects and the value, threat, difficulty etc. they represent as we interact with them' (Grady 1997: 291). This may explain one entry with no parallels in the data that signifies cleverness, <u>large aj 1535–1667</u>. In this case, however, where *large* correlates with STUPID, the motivation must be different, and it seems most likely that it relates to SPEED. Entities that are large, like buffalo and large chunks of wood, tend to be constrained by size so that they can only move (or be moved) slowly. SPEED is an important concept in the way that intelligence is perceived, both historically and currently. From the core category group SPEED, it is evident that many lexical items that can be seen etymologically to have come from other semantic fields (such as ALIVE/ ANIMATE, the earliest meaning of *quick*) develop to be more closely associated with speed, and it seems likely that this might be the folk etymological explanation for these items. As well as this, SPEED is an important element of various other mappings. Lack of speed is certainly associated with cattle, so this does not seem unlikely as a factor in the mapping.

### 4.4.1.4 Other animals

The remaining ten entries in the MAMMAL group relate to a variety of different animals. As the smaller number of entries for each animal indicates, these are not found so pervasively in English, and correspondingly the motivation for these groups is less clear and supported by a smaller amount of secondary literature. The remarks that I offer here by way of explanation for each group are therefore made tentatively, and are not intended to form a complete commentary on the metaphorical links discussed.

The most general term that yields any data is *vermin*, the root of varment aj 1829>. Historically, *vermin* has had a wide range of reference, and it has been applied to animals 'of a noxious or objectionable kind' (*OED*) that are parasitic or infest, including insects, rodents and certain birds. varment aj 1829> is one of the few entries in the ANIMAL group meaning CLEVER, and this seems unusual given the negative connotations of the source. However, as mentioned above, the *HTE* pre-classification associates this with sharpness, and although this denotes intelligence its connotations are not always flattering. I would conjecture that the salient characteristic of all vermin is the fact that they are difficult to catch, control and remove, and in human terms this is interpreted as conscious, crafty behaviour. This may account for the use of the lexeme to signify cleverness. It may be telling that *vermin* can also be applied to humans with a more straightforwardly derogatory meaning, which the *OED* defines as being 'Applied to persons of a noxious, vile, objectionable, or offensive character or type. Freq. used as a term of abuse or opprobrium; in mod. dial. sometimes without serious implication of bad qualities'.[20] Three other entries that come from *shrew*,[21] shrewd aj 1589>, shrode aj 1594–1606 and shrewdish aj 1823>, may have a similar motivation, and these also signify cleverness (specifically sharpness/ shrewdness). Again, *shrew* can be applied to humans with a number of meanings ranging from 'A wicked, evil-disposed, or malignant man; a mischievous or vexatious person; a rascal, villain' to 'A person, *esp.* (now only) a woman given to railing or scolding or other perverse or malignant behaviour; freq. a scolding or turbulent wife'. All of these are negative, and they denote and connote a variety of characteristics including untrust- worthiness, viciousness, evilness and wretchedness; clearly, a *shrewd* person may be crafty, but they are regarded as having a worldly kind of intelligence that may be regarded with suspicion and regarded with discomfort.

There are two more entries from an animal that is a rodent and may therefore qualify as vermin: squirrel-headed aj 1637 + 1953> and squirrel- minded aj 1837, both meaning 'stupid'. However, it is my impression that, in current usage at least, squirrels are not seen as noxious in the same way

[20] This might be further evidence that it is unusual for a term to be metaphorically transferred to mean two different and completely separate and different human characteristics, but more likely for it to be used to mean two slightly but connected characteristics.

[21] The connection between *shrew* meaning 'animal' and 'person' is unclear, since there are several etymological possibilities that might account for the derivation of these lexemes (see the *OED* for a full discussion). However, the ANIMAL sense is evidenced earlier, and it is undisputed that they are closely related and from a common source.

that many other rodents are, and some of the quotations in the *OED* also seem to indicate that this was the case historically. For example, one supporting quotation from c.1381 is Chaucer's reference, in the *Parliament of Fowls*, to 'Squyrelis & bestes smale of gentil kynde' (Benson 1987: 388 l. 196). Squirrels were formerly eaten as game animals, and this may be relevant, but equally this group may be motivated by the way that squirrels behave. One action commonly associated with squirrels is their agility in scurrying about, which gives rise to the verb *squirrel*, meaning 'To go round in circles like a caged squirrel; to run or scurry (round) like a squirrel' (*OED*). Both SQUIRREL entries are compounds with *head/brain* elements, suggesting that the squirrel-like behaviour is being directly compared with human thought processes, which are similarly energy-wasteful and irrational; in other words it may be that this indirectly implies a lack of logical thought. On the other hand, squirrels are also known for hoarding, and this may be the characteristic being mapped with the implication that the individual is indiscriminate in the way they collect knowledge (drawing heavily on the CONTAINER metaphor).

The entries relating to DOGS have already been referred to in section 4.2.1 above – it seems likely that both of these relate specifically to young animals, i.e. puppies, so that this is more of a reference to AGE and the behaviour of young animals than to dogs themselves. This idea seems to be strengthened by the fact that, although most strongly associated with dogs, *whelp* could be used more generally with reference to the young of various wild animals, and by the fifteenth century it was used to mean 'child' as well. The same phenomenon is found in Thornton's data, and she makes the same point.

> The fact that the animal name is applied to a young animal may be the reason why it is used contemptuously of a person. Contempt is more easily shown for something which is obviously inferior or insignificant in some way ... and any young creature, simply by virtue of being young, can be regarded as possessing both these qualities ... (Thornton 1988: 447).

It should be pointed out that <u>puppy-headed aj 1610</u> is not unproblematic. The quotation to support the mapping to STUPID is from Shakespeare's *The Tempest*; from the evidence available, including Shakespeare's other uses of the term *puppy* and other compounds in which *puppy* is an element, this does seem to be related to ANIMAL and also specifically to AGE. However, the etymology of the term is confused and it is defined in several different ways in the *OED*, so that this is not the only possibility that might motivate the entry. The earliest meaning of *puppy* in English is 'A small dog used as a lady's pet or plaything; a toy dog' (*OED*), and this reflects the origins of the term, which is thought to have come from French *poupée*, meaning 'doll' which has various related senses. It is not implausible that this connotation of lack of practical value might affect the mapping, especially in light of another entry in the data, <u>dolly n 1865–(1922)</u>, which may be motivated in a very similar way. This also incorporates the idea of inanimacy, which is represented in the data in the section ALIVE/ANIMATE.

The entry that stands out in the group because of its lack of similarity to others in the group is also the earliest in the ANIMAL data, and this is <u>ape n c1330–1741</u>. Obviously primates were never native to Britain, so although apes were relatively well known in theory and through hearsay, the metaphorical use of this term cannot result from familiarity of the kind that is possessed by farm or woodland animals. However, the *OED* definition for *ape* seems to offer a clue to the motivation behind this transfer of meaning.

> An animal of the monkey tribe (*Simiadæ*); before the introduction of 'monkey' (16th c.), the generic name, and still (since 1700) sometimes so used poetically or rhetorically, or when their uncouth resemblance to men and mimicry of human action is the main idea (due to reaction of the vb. *ape* upon the n. whence it was formed).

To *ape* something is to mimic it, coming from the idea that apes characteristically try to imitate humans. As this definition shows, although the verb was formed from the noun, in turn it had an important influence on the possible meaning of the noun. It seems likely that, although the 'primate' sense is at the root of the metaphor, it is this verb sense that has had a more immediate bearing on the use of ape to mean 'a stupid person'.

There is also one entry that I have classified as ANIMAL-MAMMAL-BODY PART, <u>soft-horn n 1837></u>. This sits a little uncomfortably in this group, and presumably its main motivation relates to its first element, which fits in with the other data in HARD/SOFT. Having said that, there are a number of entries that are compounds with one element that is a human body part, and considering the quantity of animal data this may not be particularly remarkable. There are several possibilities about the development of *horn*. One possibility is that since it is located on an animal's head, *horn* is simply used to signify the human head, paralleling the roughly similar use of *cap* (as in <u>goose-cap n 1589–(1828)</u>). Although *horn* is not found with this sense in the *OED*, there are three entries in BIRD that contain the element *comb* (discussed below) which might support this idea. Equally, it could be used like an elided form to mean 'a horned animal', and in this case it is possible that the entry could be linked to AGE, since young animals' horns are relatively soft when they are very young.[22]

---

[22] It is also possible that the source concept involved in <u>soft-horn n 1837></u> is sexual, although the *OED* does not suggest this; even though its aim was descriptive, several scholars have suggested that the *OED* is generally less thorough to record sexually suggestive terms, and this might account for the absence of this possible meaning of *soft-horn* before the term is transferred to mean 'stupid person'.

## 4.4.2 *BIRDS*

Birds, like mammals, have always been a familiar and everyday part of life in the UK; as with the other animals, it is natural that they should be drawn upon to denote a particular level of intelligence. Metaphor dictionaries testify to the huge number of bird metaphors that are found in current English, and there are many examples of anthropomorphised birds in culture, ranging from the characters in *The Owl and the Nightingale* and Chaucer's *Parliament of Fowls* to twentieth-century cartoon characters Donald Duck and Tweety Pie. In line with the ANIMAL group as a whole, all but three of the entries in this section denote stupidity. This seems to be consistent with bird metaphors in general: 'In the main, the associations with humans do not flatter birds, with a preponderance of terms evoking stupidity, eccentricity, cowardice, and ugliness: the vulture and the crow share more sinister auras' (Spence 2001: 294). The only entry in this section from the general term *bird* is bird-brain n 1943>. This is negative, and it is interesting that the phrase *(strictly) for the birds* also reflects this generally negative connotation (the *OED* defines this phrase as 'trivial, worthless; appealing only to gullible people'). The only other items in the data that are potentially species-nonspecific are four compounds ending with the element *cock*, which can be used to mean the male of any bird, but this can also mean specifically the male domestic fowl, which is possible given that farm animals are common in expressions signifying stupidity. It is perhaps surprising that there are so few entries in the data relating to general terms, given that 'bird' is a basic-level category and that the majority of the MAMMAL data is connected with categories of this kind. The most likely explanation for this is that although BIRD is a basic-level category on one level, in terms of biological taxonomy it is at the superordinate level.[23] Accordingly, different species of bird seem to have quite different associations, and can be mapped metaphorically to a divergent range of properties; by using a species name instead of a general term this extra 'layer' of associations can be exploited. Obviously, in this group of data there are few high-status birds, and this is consistent with the lack of CLEVERNESS entries.

There are various possible reasons why, predominantly, birds tend to be metaphorically associated with stupidity, and the entries in the group exhibit a number of parallels with other groups of the ANIMAL data. As with most of these, 'herd mentality' seems to be a key characteristic in the mapping,[24] and is especially relevant to some of the bird species that appear.

---

[23] This is evidenced by the study conducted by Rosch et al. (1976), in which the authors concluded that although they initially expected general use to reflect the biological taxonomy, this was not reflected in their data. They suggest that species names of birds indicate that at one time these were categories at the basic level, but that changing society, with its general move towards urban lifestyle, has affected the level at which this category operates. The same appears to have occurred in relation to fish.

[24] This is also alluded to in phrases like *birds of a feather flock together*.

Ten of the entries relate to geese, which have long been farmed in groups, and it is to this that Palmatier attributes their perceived stupidity.

> *Silly goose*, or just plain *goose*, is a polite appellation for someone who has done or said something foolish but is assumed to have known better. The goose has been regarded as a stupid bird for centuries, perhaps because of its tendency to follow the leader in a flock. (Palmatier 1995: 347)

The BIRD entries are also similar to many of the MAMMAL entries, as well as those in the FISH group, because birds have a restricted role in relation to humans. Farmed birds are kept to produce eggs and to be killed for food; wild birds are caught for the latter reason. It is noticeable that birds that are kept for other reasons, such as those used in falconry, not mapped for stupidity – presumably this is because the tasks that they carry out are perceived to be more 'intelligent', requiring more sophisticated behaviour. There is one bird of prey in the data, the buzzard, from which five entries are derived, and this seems to support this idea. Although buzzards are falcons, the *OED* notes that 'The buzzard was an inferior kind of hawk, useless for falconry', and attributes the connection with stupidity to this characteristic.

Several of the birds in the data are indigenous wild birds that are common in the UK, and their mapping to stupidity may be connected with this. There is another core concept group in the data, HUMBLE/ORDINARY, containing 14 entries derived from *simple*. In its earliest use *simple* does not appear to be derogatory, or is at least unmarked; but like other words in the same semantic field such as *common*, *ordinary* and *usual* it has pejorated quickly to mean 'inferior'. Something of the same semantic shift seems to underlie the entries connected with sparrows, and possibly other common birds including crows. *Daw*, an element in three entries, is the term for one of the small birds in the crow family; jay n 1884> was also used to mean 'jackdaw', which later became the more common form of this word, and so it is possible that this fits into the same group. In the gospels, both sparrows and crows are used as examples of creatures of low worth, specifically in contrast to humans. In Matthew 10:29–31, Christ says the following about sparrows:

> Are not two sparrows sold for a penny? Yet not one of them will fall to the ground without your Father's will ... Fear not, therefore; you are of more value than many sparrows.

Luke 12:24 contains a similar reference to birds (translated as 'ravens' in the *Revised Standard Version*, but as 'crows' in some other editions of the Bible, e.g. the *Good News Bible*):

> Consider the ravens: they neither sow nor reap, they have neither storehouse nor barn, and yet God feeds them. Of how much more value are you than the birds!

One unusual feature of the BIRD group is the fact that there are two entries from *sparrow* with different meanings. The later of these is <u>sparrow-brain aj 1930></u>, and this has the motivation discussed above and signifies stupidity, but the other, earlier entry <u>sparrow n 1861></u> signifies cleverness (specifically sharpness). The *OED* entry for this meaning draws attention to the fact that this is associated with a particular group of people, and is commonly found in a collocation: 'A chirpy, quick-witted person; used *spec.* of a Londoner, in **cockney sparrow**, etc.' Various factors might be considered to explain the way in which *sparrow* appears on both sides of the data. The first important point about this concerns the forms of each of the lexemes. The lexeme which means 'stupid' is a compound with the element *-brain*, and as with many other entries, the use of this element seems to make explicit the particular respect in which a stupid person is similar to a sparrow; rather than having an appropriate human brain, he/she has an inappropriate, non-human brain with lesser capability. Moreover, it is significant that the other lexeme has a restricted usage, with a narrow range of reference. Presumably its meaning is much more culturally informed: it is connected with a particular place, London, and depends on the fact that in the UK sparrows can be found in this city, and must adapt to survive by becoming resourceful in a way that they would not have to be in a countryside environment. This seems to be the characteristic that is referred to in the *OED* definition. Without this very specific association, it seems less likely that the two *sparrow* terms could co-exist, but as it is they are motivated quite differently.

Perhaps the most surprising entry amongst those denoting stupidity is <u>dove n 1771</u>. In general, doves are regarded as high-status birds with positive associations; in the Old Testament book of Genesis, the dove becomes a symbol of hope when Noah uses it to find out whether the Great Flood has subsided (Gen. 8:8–12). In modern times, through the influence of the Bible, the dove has become a common symbol for peace. Spence discusses the way in which this has influenced lexis:

> In spite of the importance of the dove as a symbol of peace, it has not featured very much in associations, other than the recent lex-icalizations of the terms for 'dove' and 'hawk' (or, more frequently, 'falcon') to denote, on the one hand, pacifically inclined leaders, and on the other, those who adopt an aggressive stance: *dove ∼ hawk, colombe ∼ faucon, Taube ∼ Habicht, paloma ∼ halcón, colomba ∼ falco*. As far from gentle birds, the hawk and the falcon provide an obvious contrast. (Spence 2001: 294)

The use of *dove* to mean 'stupid person' seems to me to be indirectly linked to these comments. Related to the association of doves with peace, the *OED* definition of *dove* includes the fact that 'The dove has been, from the institution of Christianity, the type of gentleness and harmlessness'. It can therefore also connote innocence, and this is another meaning listed in the *OED* (alongside its use as a term of affection, especially for women). The term *innocent* itself extends semantically to mean 'stupid', and *silly* (labelled HAPPINESS > INNOCENCE in the database) goes through a similar stage before shifting to its current sense; it looks likely that this particular use of *dove* can also be understood with reference to the same semantic development. It is noticeable that there is only a single supporting quotation for this meaning in the *OED*; in all probability this is because the generally positive connotations of the dove are stronger and have 'overridden' this meaning.

One entry that might be influenced by folk etymology is as crazy as a loon aj 1845>. According to the *OED*, *loon* in 'as crazy as a loon' is said to come from the bird meaning, but *loon* has also been used to mean 'worthless person' etc, having come through a different etymological route. In practice, it is not unlikely that both meanings may have informed the connection with stupidity, even if one of these is the sole source of the expression.

Aside from sparrow n 1861>, discussed above, two other entries denote cleverness: owl n 1508> and eagle-wit n 1665. The first of these is not actually used in a positive way; the *OED* gives the following definition:

> Applied to a person in allusion ... to appearance of gravity and wisdom (often with implication of underlying stupidity), etc. Hence = wiseacre, solemn dullard.

In Erasmus, the following adage featuring both an eagle and an owl is listed, and the explanation supplied for this seems to give a clue to why owl n 1508 is derogatory.

> Ἀετὸν γλαυκὶ συγκρίνεις, You match eagle and owl... The eagle has exceptionally keen sight, so much so that it can gaze straight at the sun without winking; and some aver that the bird uses this as a test to decide whether its offspring are legitimate or not. The owl, on the other hand, shuns the sun's light by every means in its power. (Mynors 1989: 190)

Owls are nocturnal animals, and their daytime vision is very poor despite their large eyes. As the SENSES data shows, vision is closely connected with intelligence; the fact that owls have large eyes means that outwardly they appear to be clever, but in fact this is not true. This may be the reason that *owl* can be extended to mean a person who appears or believes themself to be wise, but who is actually lacking in intelligence. The only entry that represents an unqualified positive metaphor for an intelligent person is eagle-wit n 1665. Eagles have long been regarded very positively in western culture, and this is borne out in Aesop as well as by Erasmus. In a number of the *Fables*, the eagle is portrayed as the strongest and most powerful bird, recognised to be superior by other animals. In classical mythology, the eagle is the favourite bird of the Jupiter, the king of the gods, and in modern times it has been used in the names and logos of a huge number of groups and products, including boy scouts, cars, communications companies and sports associations, as well as by America itself as a symbol of freedom. The positive connotations evoked by *eagle* are not found only in English.

> The eagle, an even more redoubtable bird of prey than the hawk and the falcon ... has long enjoyed favourable associations as a symbol of strength and power. Rather curiously, it is intelligence rather than strength that has been highlighted in expressions like *ce n'est pas un aigle*, meaning 'he's not very bright'; *ser un águila*, 'to be a genius'; *aquila*, 'genius', and *non è un aquila*, 'he's no genius'. English and German do not seem to have direct identifications of humans with eagles, and expressions like *eagle-eyed* relate to the bird's sight, not to its strength or intelligence. (Spence 2001: 924)

Because of its consistently positive associations, it is surprising that there are no other entries that have *eagle* as a source. However, it may be that it is not associated with intelligence so much as with other positive qualities of character, and is often used as a very general shorthand for the positive. In compound with *wit* it is successful as a modifier, but on its own it is not clearly linked to cleverness; if there were a conventional association between eagles and intelligence, it seems likely that there would be other linguistic items to evidence this. Spence's comments above support this, and suggest that English (and German) contrasts with French in this respect.

Paralleling the entry in MAMMAL discussed above, there are three entries in this group that I have categorised as BIRD-BODY PART, and these all contain the element *comb*, as in *cock's comb*, the crest on the head of a cock. The earliest of these entries is coxcomb n 1577–1604, and this has undergone an intermediate semantic stage (as well as changing spelling) before mapping to STUPIDITY. It is this stage that seems to make clear the motivation for this particular mapping, and by analogy this may also explain the use of *comb* in other compounds signifying stupidity (the *OED* makes this connection for duncecomb n 1630 but not for nodgecomb n 1593–1596). In the sixteenth century the coloured cap that became part of the standard costume worn by professional fools was known as a *coxcomb*, and this association explains the indirect link with fools in general and with STUPIDITY.

### 4.4.3 *INSECTS*

The final two groups, INSECT and BIRD, have far fewer entries than those discussed above, fitting in with Thornton's findings and perhaps with the idea that animals further from man in the Great Chain may be less suitable as sources. Intuitively, there do seem to be a good number of INSECT metaphors for humans, though many of these seem to be generally derogatory labels expressing disapprobation or disgust. Terms like *worm*, *maggot*, *louse*, *grub* and *slug*[25] can be used to describe individuals regarded with contempt, and at the most basic level these may simply imply a 'lower' form of life than humanity, as also indicated by general terms like *animal* and *beast*. One reason for this, and one that might account in part for the attitude of contempt that is often displayed towards insects (or at least for the rationalisation of this attitude), is suggested by one of the *Fables*, 'The bees and the beetles':

> Once upon a time, the bees invited the beetles to dinner. The beetles arrived, and when dinner was served the bees offered the beetles some honey and honeycomb. The beetles barely ate anything and then flew away. Next the beetles invited the bees, and when dinner was served, they offered the bees a plate full of dung. The bees wouldn't eat even a single bite and instead they flew straight back home. (Gibbs 2002: 187)

In Erasmus there is evidence that in Greek the term for 'beetle' was also used of people in a derogatory way (Mynors 1992: 131), and the explanation for one of the adages makes the same connection with unclean food:

> Αἶρ', αἶρε μᾶζαν ὥς τάχιστα κανθάριῳ, A dung-cake, quick quick for the dung-beetle... It may be used whenever filthy food is set before an unclean guest. (Mynors 1992: 130)

This suggests that part of the idea that insects are a 'lower' form of life may be their eating habits, and this is a certainly a common taboo in many cultures.

One important feature of all insects in relation to humans is size, and this may be relevant here. SIZE is not a symmetrical core category group in the data, since both LARGE and SMALL can be mapped to stupidity with particular motivations. Largeness and bulkiness can be associated with clumsiness and lack of speed, so that they are negative and denote stupidity; but equally, smallness or slightness can be mapped to lack of importance and inferiority and therefore carry a negative sense. Given that many of the entries in this group are compounds with HEAD or BRAIN words, in the INSECT group SIZE is directly linked with the physical size of the mind, and, in line with the MIND AS A CONTAINER metaphor, smallness indicates lack of mental capacity. This seems particularly relevant to the NIT group, since *nit* usually refers to the egg of a louse or similar animal (although it can also mean the young of the insect), which is well known for its tiny size and the difficulty this creates for its detection. It is also interesting that the source of the mapping for the

---

[25] The etymology of this term is discussed below.

BEETLE words, discussed below, may be connected with either SMALL or LARGE – either of these is convincing, and can function successfully.

In the case of the SNAIL words, another core category is also significant. As phrases like *snail's pace* or *snail-paced*, *snail-slow* and *snail-like* attest, the snail has long been viewed as characteristically slow; in the *OED* entry one definition is 'Used with reference or allusion to the exceptionally slow motion of the snail', and from the evidence listed this dates back earlier than the ninth century. SPEED is central to the way intelligence is conceptualised, even though the SPEED group in the data is relatively small at fifteen entries. Unlike SIZE, as a source concept SPEED is symmetrical, and slowness is always equated with stupidity.

As described earlier in section 4.2.3, there is a high level of repetition of forms within the INSECT group. Twelve of the 14 entries relate to BEETLE, SNAIL and NIT, and the other two are from *dor*. As well as this, eight entries in the group are compounds with a HEAD/BRAIN element,[26] and as with many of the entries in the ANIMAL group this may be a more direct way of indicating that the connection that is being made between insects and humans specifically relates to mental abilities. It may be that, as in the case of eagle-wit n 1665 (discussed above), there is not a strong conventionalised link between INSECT and INTELLIGENCE, so that in most cases an insect name is used as a modifier for another element which is specifically connected with the intellect.

From the information given in the *OED*, *dor*, which yields dorhead n 1577 and dor n 1599, has a less specific meaning than the other insect terms in the data, and is used generally in reference to flying insects (including, variously, bees, hornets, flies and beetles). The relevant characteristic involved in the mapping seems to be the noise these insects make when flying, and this would fit with some of the entries in the core concept group SOUND such as dunderwhelp n 1621–a1625, the first element of which appears to be an onomatopoeic nonsense word. These entries seem to share the motivation of the core category group SPEECH (discussed briefly in Chapter 2), and this is the idea that a person's intelligence correlates with their ability to speak, and to speak clearly or sensibly. A person who simply makes unintelligible noise that sounds like the drone of an insect is held to be stupid. For the entry dorhead n 1577, the *OED* also suggests that there is a parallel with *beetle* that may influence the formation.

There are two groups of entries for which the *OED* suggests a more likely etymological source than an 'insect' meaning, and these are the entries from *beetle* and *nit*. Five entries have BEETLE as a source: three of these are compounds with a HEAD/BRAIN element, and one is the phrase deaf/dumb as a beetle aj 1566>. The *OED* does make reference to the parallel meaning

---

[26] One more entry, hoddypeak n 1500–1589, may also relate indirectly to the head, since the sense of *peak* seems most likely to be that of a garment worn on the head. Like *cap*, which appears in several other compounded entries, this may simply have transferred metonymically to mean 'head'.

'insect' in the entries for these items, but etymologically it links them to the other meaning of *beetle*, which is defined with the following earliest attested meaning:

> **1.** An implement consisting of a heavy weight or 'head,' usually of wood, with a handle or stock, used for driving wedges or pegs, ramming down paving stones, or for crushing, bruising, beating, flattening, or smoothing, in various industrial and domestic operations, and having various shapes according to the purpose for which it is used; a mall. ***three-man beetle***: one that requires three men to lift it, used in ramming paving-stones, etc.

This meaning would align these entries with those derived from *hammer* (discussed in section 4.4.1.2) and possibly link them with the wood data rather than with the INSECT group. There is a similar problem with nitwit aj 1922>, nitwit n 1922> and nitwitted 1931>. Though the *OED* does not make any definite claim about the etymology of these terms, it suggests that they may ultimately derive from *nix*, which has itself come into English from 'colloquial Du. and G. *nix*, for (*nichs*) *nichts*', meaning 'nothing' or 'no'. In other words, if this suggestion is correct then these entries are similar to many in the core category COMPLETION, which contains entries such as lackwit n 1667> which suggest either a lack or entire absence of mind or mental facility.

Although it is less dubious in terms of its connection with INTELLIGENCE, the etymology of another lexeme, classified as SNAIL, is also somewhat indistinct. According to the *OED*, *hoddy* came to mean 'snail shell' after it became part of a compound, *hoddy-dod*, and was influenced by the meaning of the other element. Its meaning appears to have shifted slightly after this.

> The element *dod* is evidently the same as in DODMAN a shell-snail; *hoddy-dod*, *hoddy-doddy*, *hodman-dod*, are perhaps in origin nursery reduplications; but the element *hoddy*- appears itself to have come to be associated with or to mean 'snail' (or ? horned), as in several words that follow.

As all of the above information indicates, the evidence for this group is problematic, and it may be that the connection between insects and intelligence owes much to folk etymology. For most of the entries in this group, the etymological information supplied by the *OED* is suggested tentatively, since there is more than one homonymous form that might account for the transferred INTELLIGENCE sense. The INSECT entries fit in to four groups: entries derived from *beetle*, from *hoddy* (which is associated with the snail), from *nit*, and from *dor*. With the exception of the SNAIL group, which is discussed below, for each of the INSECT entries another etymological root is proposed by the *OED* as the more likely origin of the '*stupid*' sense of the item. However, the connection with INSECT is also supplied, and this is an indication that folk etymology is likely to have been an influence, even though it makes an erroneous assumption. A further piece of evidence for the possible important of folk etymology can be found in an entry that has not been included in the INSECT group, but which is found elsewhere in the data. Sluggard aj c1450> is in the core category group SPEED; according to the *OED*, the earliest sense of the term is 'One who is naturally or habitually slow, lazy, or idle; one who is disinclined for work or exertion of any kind; a slothful or indolent person'. The earliest quotation to support *slug* as a noun dates to *c*.1425, and the definition listed for this is 'A slow, lazy fellow; a sluggard. †Also personified, slothfulness'. These terms seem to be derived from a Scandinavian root, which cognates suggest meant something like 'slow' or 'sluggish'. *Slug* meaning 'gastropod' comes from this, but is not attested until significantly later in 1704. Despite this, an informal investigation into the folk etymology of *sluggish* indicates that, for most people, the meaning 'gastropod' is assumed to be the earliest, and other senses relating to slowness or laziness must be transferred metaphorically from this. It seems likely that the psychological credibility of this kind of connection between INSECT and human abilities is not new. Even for the obsolete BEETLE words, the homonymous 'insect' meaning may have been perceived as the relevant source for the metaphor despite the fact that this is etymologically false. By the seventeenth century, when the BEETLE group is first attested with a connection to INTELLIGENCE, animal metaphors were common, so a mapping from insect to human would not have been unusual or unlikely. For this reason I have presented this data in a group, whilst attempting to be clear about other possibilities of source field.

### 4.4.4 *FISH*

This is the smallest group in ANIMAL, and my impression is that this is in line with the overall balance in animal-related vocabulary in English. Spence, whose observations are based on the *Shorter Oxford English Dictionary*, describes around six FISH metaphors and then comments: 'Unlike French, English is otherwise not rich in fish associations' (Spence 2001: 926). All of the entries in this group signify STUPIDITY, and in general it would seem that fish carry negative connotations when associated with humans. The *OED* describes the usage of *fish* to mean 'person' as 'unceremonious', while *Brewer's Concise Dictionary of Phrase and Fable* observes: 'Fish as applied to a human being is mildly derogatory' (Kirkpatrick 1992: 388).

It seems probable that this generally negative implication, and specifically the association of fish with stupidity, again relates mainly to the Great Chain, since fish are considered to be a fairly 'low' life form that is further down the scale of beings than mammals. However, there are other factors worth considering, and these offer parallels with other groups in the data. Like most of the other animals functioning as sources, fish tend to be found in groups; in one Latin bestiary from the twelfth century, the author refers to this to explain the etymology of their name: 'Fish (pisces), like cattle (pecus), get their name because they browse in flocks (a pascendo)' (White 1954: 195). Again, as with the farmyard animals, this may be interpreted as demonstrating lack of independent thought. Even more important than this, until very recently when they have been kept for ornamental purposes, fish have always been used solely for food, and this means they do not tend to be thought of as sentient beings. This is borne out by the way they are portrayed in literature, for example in the *Fables*. Fish do not appear in many of these, and where they do feature they tend to be drawn as passive creatures that are aware and accepting of their fate. *Fable* 190 is a rare example of a fable in which fish are the protagonists, and tells the story of two fish, one saltwater and the other freshwater. The freshwater fish boasts that he has more prestige, and the saltwater fish retorts by saying that, if they are both caught, 'I will be able to prove to you just who is more highly regarded by the crowd of onlookers; you will see that I am bought by the connoisseur at a very high price indeed, while you will be sold to an undiscriminating commoner for a mere penny or two!' (Gibbs 2002: 97).

Another possible factor in the mapping is the fact that, unlike any of the other animals except the INSECT group, fish are unable to make any vocal sound. One of the proverbs listed and discussed by Erasmus is *Magis mutus quam pisces*, 'As dumb as the fishes', and in his description of the reasoning behind this he presents a relatively lengthy commentary citing the beliefs of Pliny, Aristotle and several other Greek scholars and writers on why fish are unable to produce sounds. Although the proverb appears to be associated more with inarticulacy than stupidity, his comments about its usage perhaps suggest that it can also connote a lack of mental efficacy.

> Ἀφωνότερος τῶν ἰχθύων, As dumb as the very fishes; a proverbial metaphor about quite inarticulate people, who have no gift of speech. It will also suit a man of extraordinary taciturnity. Horace in the *Odes*: 'Thou that couldst lend the swan's song to dumb fish / If it pleased thee.' For fish make no sound, except for a very few, among them the dog-fish. Lucian *Against An Ignoramus*: 'Truly you are as dumb as a fish.' Again in *Gallus*: 'I shall be much more silent than fish.' ... their silence [is] a thing peculiar to fish among all living creatures. All the rest have their own voices... Fish alone have no voice. (Phillips & Mynors 1982: 408–9)

Most of the entries in the group relate to varieties of fish that are well known as food – cod (three entries) and mullet (three entries). One of the *mullet* entries is the adjective phrase like a stunned mullet 1953>, referring to the way that fish are knocked on the head after they have been caught to stop them moving. This correlates with the core category group HIT/STUN, as well as relating to the ALIVE/ANIMATE data. Loaches and smelts (with one entry each) were also eaten, and are both small fish, which also seems particularly important in their mapping to stupidity. As discussed above in section 4.4.1.3, smallness is generally associated with low status; there are parallel phrases like *small fry* which allude to lack of importance or inferiority.

There is one entry in the data that stands out because unlike all the other items it does not relate to the edible, and this is <u>gubbins n 1916></u>. The *OED* defines this as 'Fragments, esp. of fish; fish-parings. In later use (also const. *sing.*), trash; anything of little value; a gadget, thingummy'. Although this is unlike the other entries, it seems reasonable to assume that it is motivated by the idea of worthlessness and lack of value. As well as this, one of the most curious entries in the data is the noun phrase <u>cod's head and shoulders 1886</u>. Although there are a huge number of other *head* compounds in the data, there is no comparable entry with *shoulder* as an element. This perhaps accounts for the non-survival of this term, but the reason for its emergence is entirely unclear.

4.5 CONCLUSION

In this chapter I have attempted to give some impression of the complexity of some types of metaphorical mapping, and the subtlety that can be involved when both cognitive and cultural factors are taken into account. Although the information that I have presented is not by any means comprehensive, I hope to have touched upon many of the issues that should be considered in any attempt to give a full account of any metaphor. The ANIMAL group is one that is not generally viewed as presenting any particular problems, and yet it offers an excellent example of the widely varying processes and mechanisms that influence a transfer of meaning from one domain to another. In order to account for the complexity that can be involved, it is important to go beyond the straightforward mapping from one entity to another, and consider wider issues that might influence the connection between source and target. One recent theory that seems especially helpful in the way it deals with this range of influences is blending theory, proposed recently by Fauconnier & Turner; this appears to offer a helpful framework in which to analyse some of the INTELLIGENCE data, and is discussed in relation to the DENSITY group in the preceding chapter (section 3.4.1).

One issue that I have touched on only briefly in this chapter is the similarities and differences that exist between ANIMAL metaphors cross-culturally. There are a number of relatively small-scale projects comparing animal metaphors in two or more languages (some of which deal with large quantities of data , like the study by Hsieh cited in this chapter), but as yet no study with a more comprehensive approach has been attempted. In my opinion this would be an interesting and valuable line of research. Although it would be a particularly difficult and challenging undertaking, a starting point would be to link and expand existing studies, and this would have the advantage of involving a high number of native speakers of different languages whose intuitions would be crucial for the accuracy of the research.

## 4.6 DATA TABLES

### 4.6.1 ANIMAL-MAMMAL

#### 4.6.1.1 ANIMAL-MAMMAL-DONKEY/MULE

Table 1

| Record no. | Meaning | Word | Part of speech | OE? | Plus/and | a/c1 | Date 1 | +/- | a/c2 | Date 2 | -/+ | a/c3 | Date 3 | Current? | Label | Derivation |
|---|---|---|---|---|---|---|---|---|---|---|---|---|---|---|---|---|
| 216 | stupid | mule | n | | | c | 1470 | | | | | | | | | mule |
| 253 | stupid | ass-headed | aj | | | | 1532 | + | | 1609 | | | | | | ass head |
| 277 | stupid | ass-head | n | | | | 1550 | – | | 1601 | | | | | | ass head |
| 304 | stupid | ass-like | aj | | | | 1567 | – | | 1581 | | | | | | ass |
| 333 | stupid | assy | aj | | | | 1583 | | | | | | | | | ass |
| 346 | stupid | assish | aj | | | | 1587 | | | | | | | | | ass |
| 442 | stupid | long-eared | aj | | | | 1605 | | | | | | | ^ | | long ear |
| 446 | stupid | asinego | n | | | | 1606 | + | | 1714 | | | | | | ass |
| 460 | stupid | asinine | aj | | | c | 1610 | | | | | | | ^ | dl | ass |
| 751 | stupid | neddy | n | | | | 1823 | | | | | | | ^ | | ned |
| 774 | stupid | donkeyish | aj | | | | 1831 | | | | | | | | | donkey |
| 799 | stupid | donkey | n | | | | 1840 | | | | | | | ^ | | donkey |
| 806 | stupid | long-ears | n | | | | 1845 | | | | | | | ^ | | long ear |

*4.6.1.2* ANIMAL-MAMMAL-SHEEP

Table 2

| Record no. | Meaning | Word | Part of speech | OE? | Plus/ and | a/c1 | Date 1 | +/- | a/c2 | Date 2 | -/+ | a/c3 | Date 3 | Current? | Label | Derivation |
|---|---|---|---|---|---|---|---|---|---|---|---|---|---|---|---|---|
| 164 | stupid | sheepish | aj | | | c | 1380 | – | | | | | | | | sheep |
| 266 | stupid | sheep's head | n | | | | 1542 | | | 1692 | | | | ∧ | | sheep head |
| 267 | stupid | sheep | n | | | | 1542 | | | | | | | ∧ | | sheep |
| 440 | stupid | ram-head | n | | | | 1605 | – | | 1630 | | | | | | ram head |
| 489 | stupid | sheep's head | aj | | | | 1624 | | | | | | | | | sheep head |
| 734 | stupid | ram-headed | aj | | | | 1813 | | | | | | | | | ram head |
| 737 | stupid | tup-headed | aj | | | | 1816 | | | | | | | | | tup head |
| 867 | stupid | wether head | n | | | | 1869 | | | | | | | | | head |

*4.6.1.3* ANIMAL–MAMMAL–BOVINE

Table 3

| Record no. | Meaning | Word | Part of speech | OE? | Plus/ and | a/c1 | Date 1 | +/– | a/c2 | Date 2 | –/+ | a/c3 | Date 3 | Current? | Label | Derivation |
|---|---|---|---|---|---|---|---|---|---|---|---|---|---|---|---|---|
| 283 | stupid | calf | n | | | a | 1553 | – | | 1711 | | | | | | calf |
| 308 | stupid | calvish | aj | | | | 1570 | – | | 1834 | | | | | | calf |
| 491 | stupid | bullhead | n | | | | 1624 | + | | 1840 | | | | | | bull head |
| 510 | stupid | ox-head | n | | | a | 1634 | + | | 1806 | | | | | | ox head |
| 554 | stupid | buffle | n | | | | 1655 | + | | 1710 | | | | | | buffalo |
| 560 | stupid | bufflehead | n | | | | 1659 | | | | | | | | | buffalo head |
| 582 | stupid | buffle-headed | aj | | | | 1675 | + | | 1871 | | | | > | | buffalo head |
| 835 | stupid | bovine | aj | | | | 1855 | + | | 1879 | | | | | | bovine |

*4.6.1.4* ANIMAL-MAMMAL-OTHER ANIMALS

Table 4

| Record no. | Meaning | Word | Part of speech | OE? | Plus/ and | a/c1 | Date 1 | +/- | a/c2 | Date 2 | -/+ | a/c3 | Date 3 | Current? | Label | Derivation |
|---|---|---|---|---|---|---|---|---|---|---|---|---|---|---|---|---|
| 151 | stupid | ape | n | | | c | 1330 | – | | 1741 | | | | | | ape |
| 356 | clever-sharp and shrewd | shrewd | aj | | | | 1589 | | | | | | | > | | shrew |
| 376 | clever-sharp and shrewd | shrode | aj | | | | 1594 | – | | 1606 | | | | | | shrew |
| 459 | stupid | puppy-headed | aj | | | | 1610 | | | | | | | | | puppy head |
| 483 | stupid | dunderwhelp | n | | | | 1621 | + | a | 1625 | | | | | | ?dun dunder < *(s)tenʇ- whelp |
| 515 | stupid | squirrel-headed | aj | | | | 1637 | + | | 1953 | | | | > | | squirrel head |
| 750 | clever-shrewd | shrewdish | aj | | | | 1823 | | | | | | | > | | shrew |
| 772 | clever-sharp | varment | aj | | | | 1829 | | | | | | | > | nn dl | vermin |
| 791 | stupid | squirrel-minded | aj | | | | 1837 | | | | | | | | | squirrel mind < *men- |
| 795 | stupid | soft-horn | n | | | | 1837 | | | | | | | > | sl | soft horn < *ker- |

4.6.2 *ANIMAL-MAMMAL-BIRD*

Table 5

| Record no | Meaning | Word | Part of speech | OE? | Plus/and | a/c1 | Date 1 | +/- | a/c2 | Date 2 | -/+ | a/c3 | Date 3 | Current? | Label | Derivation |
|---|---|---|---|---|---|---|---|---|---|---|---|---|---|---|---|---|
| 157 | stupid | goosish | aj | | | c | 1374 | + | | 1863 | | | | | | goose |
| 163 | stupid | (blind) buzzard | n | | | | 1377 | | | | | | | ∧ | | blind < *bhlendh- buzzard -ard |
| 208 | stupid | dotterel | n | | | c | 1440 | – | | 1681 | | | | | | dote -rel |
| 229 | stupid | daw | n | | | c | 1500 | – | | 1608 | | | | | | daw |
| 232 | clever-wise derog | owl | n | | | | 1508 | | | | | | | ∧ | | owl |
| 240 | stupid | saddle-goose | n | | | | 1526 | | | | | | | | | goose |
| 245 | stupid | daw pate/dawpate | n | | | a | 1529 | – | | | | | | | | daw pate |
| 249 | stupid | noddy | n | | | a | 1530 | | | 1562 | | | | ∧ | | noddy nod |
| 271 | stupid | goose | n | | | | 1547 | | | | | | | ∧ | | goose |
| 285 | stupid | gander | n | | | | 1553 | – | | 1816 | | | | | | gander |
| 291 | stupid | dawcock | n | | | | 1556 | – | | 1681 | | | | | | daw cock |
| 293 | stupid | buzzardly | aj | | | | 1561 | – | | 1654 | | | | | | buzzard -ard |
| 298 | stupid | nodgecock | n | | | | 1566 | | | | | | | | | noddy cock |
| 306 | stupid | peak-goose/ pea-goose | n | | | a | 1568 | – | | 1825 | | | | | | goose |
| 315 | stupid | coxcomb | n | | | | 1577 | – | | 1604 | | | | | | comb |
| 327 | stupid | buzzard-like | aj | | | | 1581 | – | | 1590 | | | | | | buzzard -ard |
| 340 | stupid | niddicock | n | | | | 1586 | – | | 1654 | | | | | | noddy cock |
| 355 | stupid | goose-cap | n | | | | 1589 | – | | 1828 | | | 1844 | | | goose cap |
| 366 | stupid | buzzard | aj | | | | 1592 | – | | 1649 | + | | | | | buzzard -ard |

Table 5 (contd.)

| Record no | Meaning | Word | Part of speech | OE? | Plus/and a/c1 | Date 1 | +/- a/c2 | Date 2 | -/+ a/c3 | Date 3 | Current? | Label | Derivation |
|---|---|---|---|---|---|---|---|---|---|---|---|---|---|
| 373 | stupid | nodgecomb | n | | | 1593 | − | 1596 | | | | | noddy comb |
| 385 | stupid | cuckoo | n | | | 1596 | | | | | > | nn sl | cuckoo |
| 450 | stupid | hichcock | n | | | 1607 | | | | | | | hick cock |
| 466 | stupid | widgeon | n | | | 1612 | − | 1741 | | | | | widgeon |
| 480 | stupid | buzzard-blind | aj | | | 1619 | | | | | | | buzzard -ard blind < *bhlendh- |
| 502 | stupid | duncecomb | n | | | 1630 | | | | | | | dunce |
| 565 | clever-genius | eagle-wit | n | | | 1665 | + | 1877 | | | | | eagle wit < *weid- |
| 681 | stupid | green goose | n | | | 1768 | | | | | | | goose |
| 683 | stupid | dove | n | | | 1771 | | | | | | | dove |
| 733 | stupid | goosy | aj | | | 1811 | | | | | > | | goose |
| 762 | stupid | anserous | aj | | | 1826 | | | | | > | | anserine |
| 808 | stupid | as crazy as a loon | aj | | | 1845 | | | | | > | | crazy < crassen loon |
| 841 | stupid | anserine | aj | | | 1858 | | | | | | | anserine |
| 850 | clever-sharp | sparrow | n | | | 1861 | | | | | > | 498 833 | sparrow |
| 898 | stupid | jay | n | | | 1884 | | | | | > | | jay |
| 989 | stupid | sparrow-brain | n | | | 1930 | | | | | > | cq | brain |
| 1018 | stupid | bird-brain | n | | | 1943 | | | | | > | | brain |

4.6.3 *ANIMAL-INSECT*

Table 6

| Record no. | Meaning | Word | Part of speech | OE? | Plus/ and | a/c1 | Date 1 | +/- | a/c2 | Date 2 | -/+ | a/c3 | Date 3 | Current? | Label | Derivation |
|---|---|---|---|---|---|---|---|---|---|---|---|---|---|---|---|---|
| 227 | stupid | hoddypeak | n | | | | 1500 | – | | 1589 | | | | | | hoddy peak |
| 239 | stupid | hoddypoll | n | | | | 1522 | – | | 1589 | | | | | | hoddy poll |
| 287 | stupid | beetle-headed | aj | | | | 1553/87 | – | | 1596 | + | | 1870 | | | beetle head |
| 299 | stupid | beetle | aj | | | | 1566 | | | | | | | | fg | beetle |
| 302 | stupid | deaf/dumb as a beetle | aj | | | | 1566 | | | | | | | ^ | | deaf dumb beetle |
| 313 | stupid | dorhead | n | | | | 1577 | | | | | | | | | dor head |
| 316 | stupid | beetle-head | n | | | | 1577 | – | | 1656 | | | | | | beetle head |
| 399 | stupid | hoddy-doddy | n | | | | 1598 | – | | 1656 | | | | | | hoddy dod |
| 405 | stupid | dor | n | | | | 1599 | | | | | | | | | dor |
| 417 | stupid | hoddy-noddy | n | | | | 1600 | + | | 1951 | | | | ^ | | hoddy noddy |
| 436 | stupid | beetle-brain | n | | a | | 1604 | + | | | | | | | | beetle brain |
| 553 | stupid | bottlehead | n | | | | 1654 | + | | 1815 | | | | | | beetle head |
| 963 | stupid | nitwit | aj | | | | 1922 | | | | | | | ^ | cq | nit wit < *weid- |
| 965 | stupid | nitwit | n | | | | 1922 | | | | | | | ^ | cq | wit < *weid- |
| 991 | stupid | nitwitted | aj | | | | 1931 | | | | | | | ^ | | nit wit < *weid-? |

4.6.4 *ANIMAL-FISH*

Table 7

| Record no. | Meaning | Word | Part of speech | OE? | Plus/ and | a/c1 | Date 1 | +/- | a/c2 | Date 2 | -/+ | a/c3 | Date 3 | Current? | Label | Derivation |
|---|---|---|---|---|---|---|---|---|---|---|---|---|---|---|---|---|
| 300 | stupid | cod's-head | n | | | | 1566 | – | | 1708 | | | | | | cod head |
| 408 | stupid | smelt | n | | | | 1599 | – | a | 1625 | | | | | | smelt |
| 439 | stupid | loach | n | | | | 1605 | – | c | 1620 | | | | | | loach |
| 626 | stupid | cod's-headed | aj | | | | 1708 | | | | | | | | | cod head |
| 839 | stupid | mullet-headed | aj | | | | 1857 | | | | | | | ^ | us | mullet head |
| 903 | stupid | cod's-head-and-shoulders | n | | | | 1886 | | | | | | | | | cod head |
| 951 | stupid | gubbins | n | | | | 1916 | | | | | | | ^ | cq | gubbins |
| 952 | stupid | mullet-head | n | | | | 1916 | | | | | | | ^ | us | head |
| 1034 | stupid | like a stunned mullet | aj | | | | 1953 | | | | | | | ^ | | stun < * (s)tenƒ- mullet |

4.6.5 *ANIMAL-GENERAL*

Table 8

| Record no. | Meaning | Word | Part of speech | OE? | Plus/ and | a/c1 | Date 1 | +/- | a/c2 | Date 2 | -/+ | a/c3 | Date 3 | Current? | Label | Derivation |
|---|---|---|---|---|---|---|---|---|---|---|---|---|---|---|---|---|
| 576 | stupid | plant-animal | n | | | | 1673 | – | | 1706 | | | | | | plant animal |

# 5

# CONCLUSION

## 5.1 SUMMARY

In this study, I have given an account of some of the factors that can be involved in the motivation for mappings of different kinds of metaphor and metonymy, and used this as a starting point for a wider discussion about the nature of metaphor and metonymy. The connections between INTELLIGENCE and each of the source concepts that are analysed in Chapters 2–4 demonstrate diverse motivations, which illustrate the variety of factors that can be involved in conventional mappings from different time periods.

The SENSES mapping shows clearly how embodiment is central to the way some basic abstract concepts (such as knowing and understanding) are conceptualised. The physical senses are our key means of access to information about the world, and because of this we think and talk about mental perception in terms of physical perception, in other words mapping a concrete process onto an abstract one. The fact that this mapping is evidenced in several different language families suggests that the connection between physical perception and mental perception may be universal, and this supports the theory that connecting these concepts may be 'natural' to the extent that it is inevitable. Furthermore, it is plausible that, etymologically, there are several lexemes in this semantic field that have always had both physical and mental senses; the meanings of these lexemes do not show the kind of clear mapping from an earlier physical sense to a later mental sense that is often assumed for metaphorical 'transfer' of meaning. This appears to have a parallel in the way children learn the meanings of some perception lexemes (or at least frequent vision verbs like *see*). Studies have shown that rather than learning a 'primary' physical sense and then extending this to a secondary mental sense later, in early experience children learn a conflated sense that covers both physical and mental perception. The difficulty of proving a clear $A > B$ mapping historically and developmentally therefore supports the theory that the polysemy exhibited by perception lexemes is evidence for the embodied nature of language, and is motivated by a 'natural' association between concepts related in experience that is shared across languages and cultures. However, this kind of motivation is problematic for traditional theories of metaphor, since it calls into question the idea of a clearly separate source and target which are linked because of some perceived similarity. It seems more accurate to acknowledge the metonymical nature of the connection between physical and mental perception; if the SENSES data can be classed as metaphorical, then the metaphor is metonymically motivated.

The DENSITY data examined in Chapter 3 also seems to provide evidence for metonymical motivation, since the connection between density and intelligence is contingent on a mapping between the abstract mind and the physical head, i.e. the location of the brain. In itself, though, this explanation does not explain the data adequately, and several motivating factors seem to be involved in the mapping, which can be understood as a blend with several inputs including the ontological metaphor IDEAS ARE PHYSICAL OBJECTS, the HEAD AS A CONTAINER metaphor, and an image-based metaphor where a roughly head-shaped OBJECT can stand for the HEAD. Crucially, though, in a significant proportion of the data specific dense substances are mapped to STUPIDITY, and the particular substances that are found are selected on the basis of their value, familiarity and properties within a particular culture. Their selection or non-selection also appears to be dependent on other intralinguistic factors. It is plausible that connections between concepts can establish semantic 'pathways' between lexemes in the same semantic fields which 'attract' further mappings. Conversely, the fact that some theoretically 'suitable' sources are not mapped to a particular target suggests that already established mappings to closely related targets (in this case, other human characteristics) may 'block' mappings. This shows the importance of an onomasiological approach in any consideration of motivation. By considering a number of lexemes in the same semantic field, it is possible to gain a different perspective on the mappings evidenced by individual lexemes, and to explore both intra- and extralinguistic factors that might motivate these mappings.

The ANIMAL mappings explored in Chapter 4 provide a useful contrast to the SENSES and DENSITY mappings, since these are much more prototypical examples of metaphor: particular animals are perceived to be similar to humans in terms of specific characteristics or behaviours. In general, mapping humans to animals is highly conventional, and there is evidence of ANIMAL metaphor in a large number of languages. The general connection between animals and humans appears to be cognitively motivated, and can be broken down into two elements. First, a personification metaphor is involved: humans tend to 'project' human qualities onto non-human entities, and it is particularly natural to do this to animals since they are also animate beings; for example, the behaviour of foxes is interpreted as sly. Secondly, a personified animal is mapped back onto a person; for example, a sly person is metaphorised as a fox. While this process is common across cultures, the animals that can denote particular character-istics vary widely cross-culturally depending on shared values and traditions, and to some extent also depending on the animals that are familiar in given cultures. This demonstrates clearly the way in which both cognitive and cultural factors can interact to motivate particular metaphorical and metonymical lexemes. This is evident in each of the chapters in this study, but the extent to which either culture or cognition is involved is different for each mapping.


## 5.2 THE METAPHOR–METONYMY CONTINUUM

In the introduction to this book, I argued that the terms 'metaphor' and 'metonymy' are both problematic within cognitive linguistics because neither have generally agreed definitions and both are used differently by scholars in the field. In the light of the data I have studied, I would suggest that the simplest and most practical way to resolve this difficulty is not to impose limits on the meaning of the terms that cannot be sustained in practice, but to take the opposite approach. It seems to me that 'metaphor' is most practically useful if employed as a relatively broad, inclusive term, and that, as several scholars have suggested, the relationship between metaphor and metonymy is best viewed as a continuum which accommodates uncontroversial cases of either metaphor or metonymy at either end, and 'messier', less prototypical cases which involve a greater degree of subjective judgement somewhere between the two. This kind of account highlights the fact that there can be huge diversity between the mappings that are generally subsumed in either the category metaphor or metonymy (cf. comments about the difference between referential and propositional metonymy in Warren 2002), but a very close relationship between some instances of metaphor and metonymy. The SENSES group provides a case in point; the mapping involved is very different in nature from that evidenced by the ANIMAL group, but seems very closely related to metonymy. A possible way of dealing with this is to reanalyse many of the mappings that have traditionally been understood as metaphor, but this does not seem to me to offer an unproblematic solution either. The potential danger with this approach is that it can become a way of simply reclassifying and relabelling existing phenomena from a different perspective. The aim of the present study was to try to engage with particular mappings in detail and to go beyond simply describing mappings as either examples of metaphor and metonymy, and I would echo Radden's comments in his discussion of the relationship between literal language, metaphor and metonymy:

> The discussion tried to be open to different possibilities of inter-preting a given expression as metonymic or metaphor. This approach recognises the fact that people may conceptualise things differently. It may also contribute to reconciling the conflicting views laymen and experts, i.e. cognitive linguists, have about metonymy and metaphor. Anybody who ever taught a course on metaphor, or talked to colleagues about metaphor, has in all likelihood come into

a situation where their students, or colleagues, expressed strong
disbelief at accepting something as an instance of metaphor, insisting
that this is literal speech. Both are right in their way ... (Radden
2002: 431)

Any simple reclassification of particular mappings does not address the
central point that Radden makes here: a truly useful account of metaphor
and metonymy must be flexible enough to accommodate real examples that
do not fit neatly into categories, and to have a way of accounting for
examples that might be classified differently depending on perspective. The
idea of a metaphor–metonymy continuum appears promising in this
respect, as Dirven comments in the introduction to the volume in which
Radden's essay appears:

> The originally envisaged title for this volume [*Metaphor and Meto-
> nymy in Comparison and Contrast*] was 'The Metonymy–Metaphor
> Continuum.' It soon turned out, however, that this ambition was
> still premature. Hopefully, this Jakobsonian idea may become the
> research target for a new decade ... only one third [of the papers in
> this volume] embarked upon research in the area of a continuum
> between metonymy and metaphor... we do hope that many more
> will follow in the future. (Dirven 2002a: 37)

## 5.3 A CORPUS-BASED APPROACH

It is essential that any view of metaphor or metonymy is informed by real
data rather than ad hoc examples only; though a theory-based approach
can initially be useful because it lends itself to narrowly focused study on
a single, specific feature of language, if it is to be practically useful it must
be designed to take account of authentic examples of usage rather than
discarding these as 'deviant'. Until recently, metaphor studies have tended
to focus more often on a theory-based approach; but with new techniques
for data collection, and technology that allows larger corpora to be
created and processed relatively easily, scholars are in an ideal position to
explore both metaphor and metonymy from the opposite perspective and
start with data. This has been an important part of my approach in this
study. I chose the three groups of data on which the research would focus
after I had reviewed the whole corpus, and as a result I have been able to
examine three different kinds of mapping. In the SENSES chapter, I
examined a group of metonymically motivated metaphors that have been
studied extensively, which are prototypical examples for current theories
in cognitive linguistics focusing on embodiment and the experiential basis
of metaphor. By contrast, the DENSITY mapping has been all but

overlooked, and has not been recognised as central to INTELLIGENCE. From the evidence of my corpus this has been productive diachronically, and is an important element of the way intelligence is conceptualised; there are parallels between the motivation for the SENSES group and the DENSITY group in that both appear to lie somewhere in the middle of a metaphor–metonymy continuum. ANIMAL metaphors, which are widely recognized but have reveived perhaps less attention or analysis than might be expected, seem much closer to prototypical metaphor in terms of the continuum.

### 5.3.1 Incongruity in conceptualisations of INTELLIGENCE

By studying a corpus centred on a single target concept like INTELLIGENCE in this way, it is possible to gain an overview of the way in which a concept is understood and the aspects of this concept that can be perspectivised differently. One interesting point that the data seems to suggest is that intelligence is conceptualised in two alternative and somewhat incongruous ways, which frame the process of gaining knowledge (and condition of being intelligent, which enables the acquisition of further knowledge) quite differently.[1] For the CONTAINER metaphor and other mappings consistent with this, including the DENSITY group, the mind is seen as an inanimate object that is passive in the way that it interacts with ideas, and the ideas themselves are the active agents involved in the process. This is more explicitly evident in related verb phrases, for example in describing the way that an idea can, or more often cannot, penetrate or go into the head; this suggests that the mind has no control in the action. In some related phrases, it is not the ideas themselves that are active participants, but the individual involved in the thought process: this is the case in phrases like *I can't get that into my head* or *No matter what I do, the theory won't go in*. Despite this change in agency, the mind is still a passive receptor, seen as an entity separate from the individual, and although the ideas/knowledge are not causing their own 'motion' into the mind, they are still 'moving', whereas the mind is 'static'. In fact, this is consistent with one of the most historically influential theories of intelligence, the theory of IQ, which is based on the notion that a person's mental 'capacity' is fixed and limited.

On the other hand, in the alternative conceptualisation of intelligence, the roles of the mind and ideas/knowledge are reversed, so that the mind has agency and ideas are without control. In relation to the SENSES group, an

---

[1] A similar situation can be seen with regard to spatio-temporal metaphors. Boroditsky describes the way in which time can be conceptualised in terms of the 'ego-moving metaphor, in which the "ego" or the observer's context progressed along the time-line towards the future' or alternatively in terms of the 'time-moving metaphor, in which a time-line is conceived as a river or conveyor belt on which events are moving from the future to the past' (2000: 5).

intelligent mind is able to interact with an idea by using the senses: depending on the physical sense involved in the metaphor, this means being able to perceive it visually,[2] aurally, or by taste, or to control it with the hands by touch. Obviously the corollary of this is that the ideas are passive objects that are able to be apprehended or manipulated in these ways. If the mind is SHARP, it is able to *penetrate* ideas or concepts (rather than the other way round), and *get to the bottom of* them, or get *to the core of* problems.[3]

I would contend that this is an issue that could profitably be explored further, and which might benefit from an analysis of the verbs in this semantic field. In particular, it might be helpful to consider transitivity in different verb constructions. My own research has focused almost exclusively on nouns and adjectives, and I have given little attention to verbs except in occasional references to expressions that support the evidence within the INTELLIGENCE corpus and my interpretation of this (for example, in the SENSES chapter). However, a more comprehensive corpus-based study of verb expressions including phrases, carried out with attention to etymology, would undoubtedly be both valuable in itself and complementary to any consideration of other parts of speech in the same semantic field.

## 5.4 A DIACHRONIC APPROACH

A diachronic approach is key to the research I have undertaken; from the evidence I have considered I believe that the importance of including historical data in metaphor research cannot be overestimated. From the present work and evidence from other studies, there emerge a number of examples of the way in which historical data can offer insight into mappings that could not be uncovered by a purely synchronic approach. In many cases these show that the origins of an expression that might be assumed instinctively are not those that are evidenced etymologically. For example, *sluggish* meaning 'slow' (either literally or metaphorically) is generally assumed to come from the name of the gastropod, but in reality the opposite is true; the term *slug* is not recorded as a species name until nearly three centuries after it is used of people. (The *OED* lists the meaning 'A slow, lazy fellow; a sluggard. †Also personified, slothfulness' with supporting quotations from *c*.1425, and the meaning 'A slow-moving slimy

---

[2] The LIGHT metaphors are an extension of this: if someone is *bright*, they are able to *shed light on* an idea, thereby making it easier to *see*.

[3] In general, the ANIMAL metaphors also seem to suggest that the mind has agency rather than ideas, since it is the animate participant in the process (with more or less ability), though taken as a group, these display more complexity that other core concepts. The wide range of factors involved in the mappings involving particular animals means that it is more difficult to generalise with regard to this aspect of motivation.

gasteropod or land-snail ... in which the shell is rudimentary or entirely absent' with supporting quotations from 1704. The noun is probably ultimately a conversion from a verb of Scandinavian origin with the meaning 'to be slow or sluggish'.) In fact, the INSECT group as a whole clearly demonstrates the power of folk etymology, as discussed in section 4.4.3. Although few of the expressions in the group exhibit a straightforward semantic transfer from insect to stupidity senses, and most of the entries are etymologically connected to roots that are not connected to insect terms, the link between the two concepts is sufficiently convincing to attract further expressions.

In a similar way, Hough's work on *understand* (Hough 2004) shows how an approach which draws from cognitive linguistic theory, etymology and comparative evidence can solve linguistic puzzles about the origins of expressions.

One point that has not been discussed at length in the main section of the book is the assumption that metaphorical sources tend to be concrete, and to map onto abstract targets. As described in the introduction, my approach in analysing the INTELLIGENCE data was to look first at the etymology of each term, and to determine in this way if any mapping from one concept to another had occurred. This was important in avoiding preconceptions about terms assumed to be (or not to be) figurative, and in several cases turned up unexpected results. While cases of concrete to abstract metaphorical mapping are undoubtedly more common, an increasing number of semantic shifts in the opposite direction have been documented, and these present a strong argument in favour of diachronic language study. One of the most surprising groups in the INTELLIGENCE corpus is made up of 17 entries that derive from *dull*. Folk etymology seems to attribute the meaning 'stupid' to a source meaning connected with SHARP/PIERCING, but the evidence of the *OED* suggests that in fact the opposite transfer of meaning has occurred. The earliest meaning for *dull* is defined as 'Not quick in intelligence or mental perception; slow of understanding; not sharp of wit; obtuse, stupid, inapprehensive. In early use, sometimes: Wanting wit, fatuous, foolish'. This is supported by quotations as early as the tenth century, and has a cognate in Germanic. The concrete meaning of the term, 'Not sharp or keen; blunt (in *lit.* sense)', seems to be much later, and the earliest supporting quotation for this dates to c.1440 (one earlier quotation dating to c.1400 is also listed in the *OED*, but this is marked as dubious).[4] *Keen* appears to develop in a similar way, with the abstract sense evidenced earlier than the concrete; this is also observed by Shindo in a discussion of the semantic development of this item alongside that of *eager*

---

[4] Interestingly, the definitions for this item supplied in the *OED* use the same metaphor, and perhaps show how deep-rooted the connection between the two concepts has become. Part of one earlier definition uses the word 'obtuse'; another, also with earlier supporting quotations than the concrete sense, is 'Having the natural vivacity or cheerfulness blunted'.

and *clear*. She concludes: 'There exist some semantic changes running in the opposite direction to the widely recognized tendency from concrete to abstract meanings' (Shindo 2003).

Another alternative to the traditionally assumed concrete-to-abstract mapping seems to exist in cases where the concepts held to be the source and target of a mapping do not appear to have been separate historically. In Chapter 2, where the SENSES data is discussed, I have shown that some of the most central vision-perception vocabulary in English may not result from semantic transfer from an earlier physical sense to a later mental one. Instances of this kind of linguistic item, which has a conflated meaning that subsequently splits into two senses (or is at least regarded as having a 'literal' and a 'figurative' denotation), challenge traditional ideas about metaphorical mappings, and as I suggest in the conclusion to Chapter 2, these must be accommodated in any theory of metaphor. Again, I would argue that this supports the case for a flexible view of metaphor and metonymy, in which diversity of this kind does not appear 'anomalous'.

## 5.5 AN INTERDISCIPLINARY APPROACH

I have tried to approach the data by using material from a range of disciplines, depending on what seemed most appropriate to a particular group of entries; this has resulted in a study that draws from reconstructive etymology, psychology, archeology, comparative linguistics, history and semantics. I thus hope to have shown the variety of influences that can be involved in the coining and conventionalisation of mappings, and potential reasons for the success of some mappings and the failures of others that are outwardly very similar. An interdisciplinary approach can also be useful in evaluating theories of metaphor and metonymy that have been posited at various times. For example, one relatively recent theory of metaphor, which is appealing in its simplicity, is based on prototype theory:

> the basic mechanism behind metaphor is straightforward. It is sim-
> ply the use of a word with one or more of the 'typicality conditions'
> attached to it broken. As we noted in Chapter 5, words have fuzzy
> edges, in that for the majority of words it is impossible to specify a
> hard-core meaning at all. Humans understand words by referring to
> a prototypical usage, and they match a new example against the
> characteristics of the prototype. A tiger can still be a tiger even
> though it might have three legs and no stripes: it just wouldn't be a
> prototypical tiger. (Aitchison 1987: 144–5)

Aitchison's suggestion is basically that metaphor involves the recategorisa-
tion of any referent as a marginal member of a new group. She goes on to say that in the same way that a tiger missing one leg and stripes is still a

member of the category, describing a person as a tiger involves the same kind of recategorisation. The same idea was proposed by Morse Peckham in 1970: 'We perceive a metaphor as metaphoric ...when we encounter words ...which conventionally do not belong to the same category. A metaphor ... is an assertion that they do' (Peckham 1970: 405). However, whilst this may be helpful in offering a different perspective on the metaphor, it cannot account for the complexities involved in all mappings. As I have shown, ANIMAL metaphors arise out of a tradition of human–animal thought, and this appears to be one part of what makes them 'successful' as a group. Saying that metaphor simply amounts to recategorisation cannot by itself account for the varying likelihood of different mappings, some of which are constrained and will not occur.

More generally, I would argue that a diachronic approach which takes advantage of an interdisciplinary perspective, and which is firmly based on a large corpus of real data, can cast fresh light on current issues in cognitive linguistics. This kind of approach can be useful in evaluating both established and more recently proposed theories of semantics, and opens up new avenues for future research.

## 5.6 ISSUES FOR FUTURE RESEARCH: SAPIR–WHORF, PC LANGUAGE AND THE INFLUENCE OF METAPHOR

I would suggest that the approach I have taken could valuably be widened further, and it would be interesting to link up my own analysis of the target concept INTELLIGENCE with work on related topics. One particularly interesting issue is the debate surrounding linguistic relativism, and I would contend that empirical work of this kind could provide valuable new material for the further consideration of the connection between thought and language.

The question of whether language can influence thought is one that has been discussed within linguistics for decades, and which has remained wholly unresolved. In its strongest form, what has come to be termed the Sapir–Whorf hypothesis – the idea that thought is conditioned and even constrained by language – has been discredited, but the weaker form of the hypothesis, linguistic relativism, continues to be taken seriously by many linguists, particularly in the cognitive linguistics tradition (see e.g. Marmaridou 2006: 396; Wierzbicka 2006: 5; Levinson 2003: 18ff.). This holds that language can influence thought to some degree, but is not the only factor in the way speakers of different languages construct varying world views. The comments of Sweetser represent one of the more moderate views of this kind, and one which accepts the possibility of, if not the evidence for, relativism.

Perhaps ... the issue of language shaping cognition is a little less thorny than we thought. For example, few linguists or anthropologists would be upset by the hypothesis that learning a word for a culturally important category could linguistically reinforce the learning of a category itself. There seem to be areas, at least, of interdependency between cognition and language. Likewise, it would be hard to deny that much of the basic cognitive apparatus of humans is not dependent on language, and that humans therefore share a great deal of prelinguistic and extralinguistic experience which is likely to shape language rather than to be shaped by it. (Sweetser 1990: 7)

In recent years, the possible influence of language on thought has been an important issue amongst non-linguists too. While some people believe that different languages influence speakers' thoughts differently, it is perhaps more generally accepted that the linguistic choices that are made within one language can have a significant effect on how a situation or concept is perceived and understood by other speakers of that language. In the media, particularly, there is an implicit belief that the way in which an idea is framed linguistically is crucially important. This has fed into the idea of 'political correctness' that has been contentious in the last two decades, which is specifically concerned with the way social groups of various kinds are labelled, and the way in which labels can perpetuate particular attitudes. It has become unacceptable to use outdated terminology that might cause offence in official matters, and generally even those who do not subscribe to the use of politically correct (PC) language would judge certain expressions to be inappropriate.

In my opinion, it is important to view the INTELLIGENCE data in the context of these issues, since they provide a background and justification for considering the various metaphors and metonymies involved in the way intelligence is conceptualised. Even before PC language became a fashionable topic of debate, the terminology used to indicate the level of an individual's mental capacities was much discussed within educational theory and was subject to frequent changes in practice. Table 5.1 lists some of the terms that have been considered acceptable at different times, and gives dates of official usage for each; this clearly illustrates the speed with which terms can fall out of acceptability within one register and even become taboo items.

It is impossible to assess conclusively whether or not significance should be attached to terminology, or to evaluate the practice of changing labels in response to more progressive attitudes in order to minimise stigma. However, the impressions of those working in education – even those who are initially sceptical – seem to support the idea that terminology can have an effect on people's perceptions, and can be more or less helpful in the way in which it presents those of varying mental capabilities. In an informal interview I conducted in 2002 with a group of around 20 student teachers in the final stage of a Post-Graduate Certificate of Education (PGCE), most of the group admitted that although they considered some terms like *stupid*, *slow* and *thick* to be inappropriate in describing pupils, they did find themselves using these occasionally outside the classroom. There were mixed feelings about whether or not using 'unofficial' terms related to intelligence had any effect, but several of those taking part in the discussion felt strongly that the way in which another teacher described pupils in a class – for example, labelling them *thick* rather than referring to their ability level – did influence the attitude that other teachers had towards them. One member of the group described her experience of a school in which one teacher refused to teach a class because of the way the students had been described, and the way he had come to talk about them, and she felt very strongly that this was a direct result of pejorative terminology. Though this kind of anecdotal evidence cannot be accepted as proof of the effect of language, it does seem to be mirrored in educational policies, and reflects the general feeling that labels can create stigma and must be monitored carefully.

If it is true that presentation can affect perception in this area, then it must equally be advisable to consider the possible implications of particular metaphors. In turn, it is critical to be aware of what motivates these metaphors. In order to gain some sense of what might be involved in the creation and 'survival' of any metaphorical mapping, its source and development must be explored.

Table 5.1 (From Tomlinson 1982: 61.)

| Statutory categories | | | | | | | Suggested descriptive categories |
|---|---|---|---|---|---|---|---|
| *1886* | *1899* | *1913* | *1945* | *1962* | *1970* | *1981* | |
| Idiot | Idiot | Idiot | Severely sub-normal (SSN) | Severely sub-normal (SSN) | Educationally sub-normal (severe) | | Child with learning difficulties (severe) |
| Imbecile | Imbecile | Imbecile | | Psychopathic | | | |
| | | Moral imbecile | | | | | |
| | Blind | Blind | Blind | | Blind | | Blind |
| | | | Partially sighted | | Partially sighted | | Partially sighted |
| | Deaf | Deaf | Deaf | | Deaf | | Deaf |
| | | | Partially deaf | Partial hearing | Partial hearing | Special Educational Needs | Partial hearing |
| | Epileptic | Epileptic | Epileptic | | Epileptic | | Epileptic |
| | Defecive | Mental defective (feeble-minded) | Educationally subnormal | | Educationally subnormal (mild or moderate) | | Child with learning difficulty (mild or moderate) |
| | | | Maladjusted | | Maladjusted | | Maladjusted disruptive |
| | | Physical defective | Physically handicapped | | Physically handicapped | | Physically handicapped |
| | | | Speech defect | | Speech defect | | Speech defect |
| | | | Delicate | Delicate | Delicate | | Delicate |
| | | | Diabetic | | | | |
| | | | | | | | Dyslexic? |
| | | | | | | | Autistic? |

*Note* Categories suggested but never adopted include: the neuropathic child, the inconsequential child, the psychiatrically crippled child, the aphasic child and others. Autism and dyslexia were recognised under the 1970 Chronically Sick and Disabled Persons Act.

# 6
# APPENDIX

## 6.1 AGE

### Table 1

| Record no. | Meaning | Word | Part of speech | OE? | Plus/ and | a/c1 | Date 1 | +/− | a/c2 | Date 2 | −/+ | a/c3 | Date 3 | Current? | Label | Derivation |
|---|---|---|---|---|---|---|---|---|---|---|---|---|---|---|---|---|
| 4 | clever-wise | fyrnwita | n | OE | | | | | | | | | | | | fyrn wit < *weid- |
| 54 | clever-wise | ealdwita | n | OE | | | | | | | | | | | | eald < *al- wit < *weid- |
| 387 | stupid | mossy | aj | | | | 1597 | − | | 1602 | | | | | sl&jo | moss |
| 681 | stupid | green goose | n | | | | 1768 | + | | 1877 | | | | | | goose |
| 803 | clever-precocious | old-fashioned | aj | | | | 1844 | | | | | | ^ | | cf dl | old < eald < *al- fashion |
| 960 | clever-wise | elder statesman | n | | | | 1921 | | | | | | ^ | | | elder statesman |
| 985 | clever-wise | adult | aj | | | | 1929 | | | | | | ^ | | | adult < *al- |

## 6.2 ALIVE/ANIMATE

### Table 2

| Record no. | Meaning | Word | Part of speech | OE? | Plus/ and | a/c1 | Date 1 | +/− | a/c2 | Date 2 | −/+ | a/c3 | Date 3 | Current? | Label | Derivation |
|---|---|---|---|---|---|---|---|---|---|---|---|---|---|---|---|---|
| 211 | clever-sharp | quick in | aj | | c | | 1449 | − | | 1588 | | | | | | quick |
| 224 | clever-sharp | quick | aj | | | | 1484 | | | | | | | ^ | | quick |
| 251 | clever-sharp | quick-witted | aj | | | | 1530 | | | | | | | ^ | | quick wit < *weid- |
| 281 | clever-sharp | quick-sighted | aj | | | | 1552 | | | | | | | ^ | | quick see |
| 342 | stupid | wooden | aj | | a | | 1586 | | | | | | | ^ | | < sekw- wood |

Table 2 (contd.)

| Record no. | Meaning | Word | Part of speech | OE? | Plus/ and | a/c1 | Date 1 | +/- | a/c2 | Date 2 | -/+ | a/c3 | Date 3 | Current? | Label | Derivation |
|---|---|---|---|---|---|---|---|---|---|---|---|---|---|---|---|---|
| 476 | clever-sharp | quick-eyed | aj | | | a | 1616 | | | | | | | | > | | quick eye <*okw- |
| 687 | stupid | unelectric | aj | | | | 1775 | + | | 1876 | | | | | | | electric |
| 763 | stupid | stookie | n | | | a | 1828 | | | | | | | | > | sc&no dl | stookie |
| 829 | clever-sharp | quick-minded | aj | | | | 1852 | – | | -1908 | | | | | | | quick mind <*men- |
| 860 | stupid | dolly | aj | | | | 1865 | – | | 1922 | | | | | > | | doll |
| 904 | stupid | josser | n | | | | 1886 | | | | | | | | > | | joss |
| 911 | stupid | josser | aj | | | | 1891 | – | | 1893 | | | | | | | joss |
| 988 | stupid | dead from the neck up | aj | | | | 1930 | | | | | | | | > | cq | dead |
| 1064 | stupid | tat(t)ie-bogle | n | | | | 1969 | | | | | | | | > | | tattie |

6.3 BEAUTY

Table 3

| Record no. | Meaning | Word | Part of speech | OE? | Plus/ and | a/c1 | Date 1 | +/- | a/c2 | Date 2 | -/+ | a/c3 | Date 3 | Current? | Label | Derivation |
|---|---|---|---|---|---|---|---|---|---|---|---|---|---|---|---|---|
| 859 | clever-intelligent | beautiful-minded | aj | | | | 1865 | | | | | | | | | | beauty <*deu- mind <*men- |

6.4 BIRTH/CREATION

Table 4

| Record no. | Meaning | Word | Part of speech | OE? | Plus/ and | a/c1 Date 1 | +/- | a/c2 Date 2 | -/+ | a/c3 Date 3 | Current? | Label | Derivation |
|---|---|---|---|---|---|---|---|---|---|---|---|---|---|
| 195 | clever-intelligent | pregnant | aj | | | 1413 | – | 1853 | | | | | pregnant < pregnatus < *genf- |
| 223 | clever-genius | ingenious | aj | | | 1483 | – | 1807 | | | | | genius < *genf- |
| 292 | clever-precocious | pregnant | aj | | | 1557 | – | 1707 | | | | | pregnant < pregnatus < *genf- |
| 309 | clever-intelligent | ingenious | aj | | | 1571 | – | 1824 | | | | | genius < *genf- |
| 349 | clever-intelligent | ingenuous | aj | | | 1588 | – | 1795 | | | | | genius < *genf- |
| 359 | stupid | barren | aj | | | 1590 | – | 1866 | | | | | barren |
| 372 | clever-intelligent | conceited | aj | | | 1593 | – | 1594 | | | | fg | conceive < con capere < *kap- |
| 374 | stupid | unconceiving | aj | | | 1593 | – | 1740 | | | | | conceive < con capere < *kap- |
| 377 | clever-intelligent | conceitful | aj | | | 1594 | – | 1607 | | | | | conceive < con capere < *kap- |
| 424 | stupid | barren-spirited | aj | | | 1601 | | | | | | | barren spirit < spirare |
| 498 | clever-genius | ingenuities | n | | | 1628 | – | 1648 | | | | | genius < *genf- |
| 535 | clever-genius | genius | n | | | 1647 | | | | | | > | genius < *genf- |
| 584 | clever-genius | genie | n | | | 1676 | – | 1687 | | | | | genius < *genf- |
| 631 | clever-genius | genio | n | | | 1709 | | | | | | | genius < *genf- |
| 714 | stupid | barren-brained | aj | | | 1798 | | | | | | | barren brain |
| 869 | stupid | barren-witted | aj | | | 1870 | | | | | | | barren wit < *weid- |
| 1038 | clever-highbrow | eggheaded | aj | | | 1957 | | | | | | > | egg head? |

## 6.5 BODY PART-SEXUAL

### Table 5

| Record no. | Meaning | Word | Part of speech | OE? | Plus/and | a/c1 | Date 1 | +/- | a/c2 | Date 2 | -/+ | a/c3 | Date 3 | Current? | Label | Derivation |
|---|---|---|---|---|---|---|---|---|---|---|---|---|---|---|---|---|
| 997 | stupid | berk/burk | n | | | | 1936 | | | | | | | ^ | sl (rhyming - ie Berkeley Hunt) | berk/burk |
| 1010 | stupid | Berkeley (Hunt) | n | | | | 1940 | | | | | | | ^ | sl (rhyming) | berk/burk |
| 1025 | stupid | tit | n | | | | 1947 | | | | | | | ^ | sl | tit |
| 1026 | stupid | schmo | n | | | | 1948 | | | | | | | ^ | us sl | schmo |
| 1042 | stupid | Berkshire Hunt | n | | | | 1960 | | | | | | | ^ | sl (rhyming) | berk/burk |
| 1050 | stupid | putz | n | | | | 1964 | | | | | | | ^ | us sl | putz |
| 1058 | stupid | pillock | n | | | | 1967 | | | | | | | ^ | | pillock cock |
| 1059 | stupid | prat | n | | | | 1968 | | | | | | | ^ | | prat |
| 1062 | stupid | jerk-off | n | | | | 1968/70 | | | | | | | ^ | | jerk |
| 1063 | stupid | dick-head | n | | | | 1969 | | | | | | | ^ | vu sl | dick head |

## 6.6 BRAIN

### Table 6

| Record no. | Meaning | Word | Part of speech | OE? | Plus/and | a/c1 | Date 1 | +/- | a/c2 | Date 2 | -/+ | a/c3 | Date 3 | Current? | Label | Derivation |
|---|---|---|---|---|---|---|---|---|---|---|---|---|---|---|---|---|
| 218 | stupid | brainless | aj | | | c | 1470 | | | | | | | ^ | | brain |
| 261 | stupid | weak-brained | aj | | | | 1535 | | | | | | | ^ | | weak brain |
| 354 | clever-wise derog | tire-brain | n | | | | 1589 | | | | | | | | | tire brain |

Table 6 (contd.)

| Record no. | Meaning | Word | Part of speech | OE? | Plus/ and | a/c1 | Date 1 | +/- | a/c2 | Date 2 | -/+ | a/c3 | Date 3 | Current? | Label | Derivation |
|---|---|---|---|---|---|---|---|---|---|---|---|---|---|---|---|---|
| 362 | stupid | frost-brained | aj | | | | 1592 | | | | | | | | | frost brain |
| 365 | stupid | shallow-brained | aj | | | | 1592 | – | | 1810 | | | | | | shallow brain |
| 379 | stupid | clay-brained | aj | | | | 1596 | | | | | | | | | clay brain |
| 436 | stupid | beetle-brain | n | | a | | 1604 | | | | | | | | | beetle brain |
| 481 | stupid | thick-brained | aj | | | | 1619 | | | | | | | | | thick brain |
| 496 | stupid | beef-brained | aj | | | | 1627 | | | | | | | | | beef brain |
| 562 | stupid | whey-brained | aj | | | | 1660 | | | | | | | | | whey brain |
| 624 | stupid | shallow-brains | n | | | | 1707 | | | | | | | | | shallow brain |
| 714 | stupid | barren-brained | aj | | | | 1798 | | | | | | | | | barren brain |
| 789 | clever-sharp | nimble-brained | aj | | | | 1836/48 | | | | | | | | | nimble < numol <*nem- brain |
| 809 | clever-intelligent | brainy | aj | | | | 1845 | | | | | | | ^ | | brain |
| 856 | stupid | scant-brain | n | | | | 1864 | | | | | | | | | scant brain |
| 885 | clever-intelligent | brain-worker | n | | | | 1878 | | | | | | | | | brain work |
| 948 | clever-intelligent | brain | n | | | | 1914 | | | | | | | ^ | cq | brain |
| 959 | stupid | suet-brained | aj | | | | 1921 | | | | | | | ^ | | suet brain |
| 961 | stupid | peanut-brained | aj | | | | 1922 | | | | | | | ^ | | peanut brain |
| 970 | clever-genius | master-brain | n | | | | 1923 | | | | | | | ^ | | master brain |
| 977 | clever-genius | the brains | n | | | | 1925 | | | | | | | ^ | | brain |
| 984 | stupid | lame-brained | aj | | | | 1929 | | | | | | | ^ | | lame brain |
| 989 | stupid | sparrow-brain | n | | | | 1930 | | | | | | | ^ | | brain |
| 1017 | clever-intellectual | cerebralist | n | | | | 1943 | | | | | | | ^ | cq | cerebrum <*ker- brain |
| 1018 | stupid | bird-brain | n | | | | 1943 | | | | | | | ^ | | brain |
| 1023 | stupid | lame-brain | n | | | | 1945 | | | | | | | ^ | | lame brain |
| 1032 | stupid | lobotomized | aj | | | | 1953 | | | | | | | ^ | cq | lobotomized |
| 1049 | stupid | pin-brained | aj | | | | 1964 | | | | | | | ^ | | pin brain |
| 1067 | stupid | thimble-brain | n | | | | 1971 | | | | | | | ^ | | brain |

## 6.7 COLOUR

### Table 7

| Record no. | Meaning | Word | Part of speech | OE? | Plus/and | a/c1 | Date 1 | +/- | a/c2 | Date 2 | -/+ | a/c3 | Date 3 | Current? | Label | Derivation |
|---|---|---|---|---|---|---|---|---|---|---|---|---|---|---|---|---|
| 681 | stupid | green goose | n | | | | 1768 | + | | 1877 | | | | | | goose |

## 6.8 COMPLETION

### Table 8

| Record no. | Meaning | Word | Part of speech | OE? | Plus/and | a/c1 | Date 1 | +/- | a/c2 | Date 2 | -/+ | a/c3 | Date 3 | Current? | Label | Derivation |
|---|---|---|---|---|---|---|---|---|---|---|---|---|---|---|---|---|
| 36 | stupid | samwis | aj | OE | | | | | | | | | | | | wise < *weid- |
| 60 | stupid | medwis | aj | OE | | | | | | | | | | | | wise < *weid- |
| 122 | clever-wise | well(-)done | aj | | | c | 1200 | – | c | 1205 | | | | | | well done |
| 126 | clever-wise | ripe | aj | | | c | 1200 | | | | | | > | | | ripe |
| 161 | clever-intelligent | fine | aj | | | | 1377 | – | | 1766 | | | | | | fine |
| 210 | stupid | want-wit | n | | | | 1448/9 | – | | 1610 | + | 1900 | | | | want wit < *weid- |
| 320 | clever-intelligent | fine-headed | aj | | | | 1579 | – | | 1603 | | | | | | fine head |
| 432 | stupid | partless | aj | | | | 1603 | | | | | | | | | part |
| 465 | clever-intelligent | solert | aj | | | | 1612 | – | a | 1680 | | | | | | solert |
| 485 | stupid | half-headed | aj | | | | 1621/31 | | | | | | > | | | half head |
| 487 | clever-intelligent | solertic | aj | | | | 1623 | | | | | | | | | solert |
| 516 | stupid | ungifted | aj | | | | 1637 | | | | | | > | | | gift |
| 532 | stupid | half-witted | aj | | | c | 1645 | | | | | | > | | | half wit < *weid- |
| 572 | stupid | lack-wit | n | | | | 1667 | | | | | | > | | | lack wit < *weid- |
| 673 | stupid | half-wit | n | | | | 1755 | | | | | | > | | | half wit < *weid- |

Table 8 (contd.)

| Record no. | Meaning | Word | Part of speech | OE? | Plus/ and | a/c1 | Date 1 | +/− | a/c2 | Date 2 | −/+ | a/c3 | Date 3 | Current? | Label | Derivation |
|---|---|---|---|---|---|---|---|---|---|---|---|---|---|---|---|---|
| 784 | stupid | half-saved | aj | | | | 1834 | + | | 1871 | | | | | dl | half save |
| 797 | stupid | wanting | aj | | | | 1839 | | | | | | | ^ | cq | want |
| 836 | stupid | (only) half-baked^ | aj | | | | 1855 | + | | 1864 | | | | ^ | 185dl 1864cq | half bake |
| 847 | stupid | tenpence in the shilling | aj | | | | 1860 | | | | | | | ^ | sl | ten pence shilling |
| 863 | stupid | lean-minded | aj | | | | 1866 | | | | | | | | | lean mind < *men-half |
| 865 | stupid | half-baked | n | | | | 1866 | | | | | | | ^ | cq&dl | half |
| 917 | stupid | want-wit | aj | | | | 1894 | | | | | | | | | want wit < *weid- |
| 963 | stupid | nitwit | aj | | | | 1922 | | | | | | | ^ | cq | nit wit < *weid- |
| 965 | stupid | nitwit | n | | | | 1922 | | | | | | | ^ | cq | wit < *weid- |
| 985 | clever-wise | adult | aj | | | | 1929 | | | | | | | ^ | | adult < *al- |
| 991 | stupid | nitwitted | aj | | | | 1931 | | | | | | | ^ | | nit wit < *weid- |
| 1004 | stupid | half-wit | aj | | | | 1938 | | | | | | | ^ | | half wit < *weid- |
| 1024 | stupid | (a proper/right) Charlie/Charley | n | | | | 1946 | | | | | | | ^ | sl | proper right < *reg- charlie |

## 6.9 CONTAINER

Table 9

| Record no. | Meaning | Word | Part of speech | OE? | Plus/ and | a/c1 | Date 1 | +/− | a/c2 | Date 2 | −/+ | a/c3 | Date 3 | Current? | Label | Derivation |
|---|---|---|---|---|---|---|---|---|---|---|---|---|---|---|---|---|
| 9 | stupid | idel | aj | OE | | | | | | | | | | | | idle |
| 137 | stupid | fool | n | | c | 1275 | | | | | | | | ^ | | fool |

Table 9 (contd.)

| Record no. | Meaning | Word | Part of speech | OE? | Plus/ and | a/c1 Date 1 | +/- | a/c2 Date 2 | -/+ | a/c3 Date 3 | Current? | Label | Derivation |
|---|---|---|---|---|---|---|---|---|---|---|---|---|---|
| 255 | stupid | pot-headed | aj | | | 1533 | | | | | | | | pot head |
| 297 | stupid | tom-fool | n | | | 1565 | + | | | | | | | tom fool |
| 434 | clever-common sense | unfoolish | aj | | | 1603 | | 1885 | | | | ∧ | | fool |
| 455 | stupid | fooliaminy | n | | | 1607 | – | 1622 | | | | | | fool |
| 501 | stupid | toom-headed | aj | | | 1629 | | | | | | | | toom head |
| 540 | stupid | fool's head | n | | | 1650 | | | | | | | | fool head |
| 553 | stupid | bottlehead | n | | | 1654 | + | 1815 | | | | | | beetle head |
| 636 | stupid | vacant | aj | | | 1712 | | | | | | | | vacant |
| 656 | stupid | pitcher-souled | aj | | a | 1739 | | | | | | | | pitcher soul |
| 716 | stupid | tom-foolish | aj | | | 1799 | | | | | | | | tom fool |
| 817 | stupid | vacuous | aj | | | 1848 | | | | | | ∧ | | vacuum |
| 831 | stupid | fiddle-headed | aj | | | 1854 | | | | | | | | fiddle head |
| 834 | stupid | pot-head | n | | | 1855 | | | | | | | cq | pot head |
| 843 | stupid | mug | n | | | 1859 | + | 1861 | | | | ∧ | | mug |
| 860 | stupid | dolly | aj | | | 1865 | – | 1922 | | | | | | doll |
| 964 | stupid | mug | aj | | | 1922 | | | | | | ∧ | | mug |
| 969 | clever-shrewd | nobody's fool | n | | | 1923 | | | | | | ∧ | | nobody fool |
| 971 | stupid | stone jug | n | | | 1923 | | | | | | ∧ | sl (rhyming) | mug |
| 992 | stupid | steamer | n | | | 1932 | | | | | | ∧ | sl (rhyming - ie 'steam tug') | mug |
| 1036 | stupid | out to lunch | aj | | | 1955 | | | | | | ∧ | nr sl | out |
| 1067 | stupid | thimble-brain | n | | | 1971 | | | | | | ∧ | | brain |

6.9.1 CONTAINER-EMPTY/FULL OF NOTHING

Table 10

| Record no. | Meaning | Word | Part of speech | OE? | Plus/ and | a/c1 | Date 1 | +/− | a/c2 | Date 2 | −/+ | a/c3 | Date 3 | Current? | Label | Derivation |
|---|---|---|---|---|---|---|---|---|---|---|---|---|---|---|---|---|
| 9 | stupid | idel | aj | OE | | | | | | | | | | | | idle |
| 137 | stupid | fool | n | | | c | 1275 | | | | | | | ^ | | fool |
| 297 | stupid | tom-fool | n | | | | 1565 | | | | | | | ^ | | tom fool |
| 434 | clever-common sense | unfoolish | aj | | | | 1603 | + | | 1885 | | | | | | fool |
| 455 | stupid | fooliaminy | n | | | | 1607 | − | | | | | | | | fool |
| 501 | stupid | toom-headed | aj | | | | 1629 | | | 1622 | | | | | | toom head |
| 540 | stupid | fool's head | n | | | | 1650 | | | | | | | | | fool head |
| 636 | stupid | vacant | aj | | | | 1712 | | | | | | | | | vacant |
| 716 | stupid | tom-foolish | aj | | | | 1799 | | | | | | | | | tom fool |
| 817 | stupid | vacuous | aj | | | | 1848 | | | | | | | ^ | | vacuum |
| 831 | stupid | fiddle-headed | aj | | | | 1854 | − | | | | | | | | fiddle head |
| 860 | stupid | dolly | aj | | | | 1865 | | | 1922 | | | | | | doll |
| 969 | clever-shrewd | nobody's fool | n | | | | 1923 | | | | | | | ^ | nr sl | nobody fool |
| 1036 | stupid | out to lunch | aj | | | | 1955 | | | | | | | ^ | | out |

## 6.10 FAT

### Table 11

| Record no. | Meaning | Word | Part of speech | OE? | Plus/and | a/c1 | Date 1 | +/- | a/c2 | Date 2 | -/+ | a/c3 | Date 3 | Current? | Label | Derivation |
|---|---|---|---|---|---|---|---|---|---|---|---|---|---|---|---|---|
| 348 | stupid | fat | aj | | | | 1588 | | | | | | | | | fat |
| 354 | clever-wise derog | tire-brain | n | | | | 1589 | | | | | | | | | tire brain |
| 384 | stupid | fat-witted | aj | | | | 1596 | | | | | | | ∧ | | fat wit < *weid- |
| 435 | stupid | fat-headed | aj | | | | 1603 | | | | | | | ∧ | | fat head |
| 800 | stupid | fat-head | n | | | | 1842 | | | | | | | ∧ | | fat head |
| 1061 | stupid | flake | n | | | | 1968 | | | | | | | ∧ | | flake |

## 6.11 FRUIT/VEG

### Table 12

| Record no. | Meaning | Word | Part of speech | OE? | Plus/and | a/c1 | Date 1 | +/- | a/c2 | Date 2 | -/+ | a/c3 | Date 3 | Current? | Label | Derivation |
|---|---|---|---|---|---|---|---|---|---|---|---|---|---|---|---|---|
| 290 | stupid | funge | n | | | | 1556 | + | | | | | | | | fungus |
| 591 | stupid | cabbage-head | n | | | | 1682 | | | 1621 | | | | | | cabbage head |
| 780 | stupid | potato-headed | aj | | | | 1832 | | | | | | | | | potato head |
| 786 | stupid | pumpkin-headed | aj | | | | 1835/40 | | | | | | | ∧ | cq | pumpkin head |
| 790 | stupid | turnip | n | | | | 1837 | | | | | | | | | turnip |
| 870 | stupid | cabbage | n | | | | 1870 | | | | | | | ∧ | | cabbage |
| 880 | stupid | pumpkin-head | n | | | | 1876 | + | | 1898 | | | | | | head |
| 888 | stupid | tattie | n | | | | 1879 | | | | | | | | us cq | potato |
| 925 | stupid | turnip-headed | aj | | | | 1898 | | | | | | | ∧ | | turnip head |

Table 12 (contd.)

| Record no. | Meaning | Word | Part of speech | OE? | Plus/ and | a/c1 | Date 1 | +/- | a/c2 | Date 2 | -/+ | a/c3 | Date 3 | Current? | Label | Derivation |
|---|---|---|---|---|---|---|---|---|---|---|---|---|---|---|---|---|
| 926 | stupid | turnip-head | n | | | | 1898 | | | | | | | > | | turnip head |
| 1053 | stupid | nana | n | | | | 1965 | | | | | | | > | sl | banana |

6.12 GOOD/HAPPY

Table 13

| Record no. | Meaning | Word | Part of speech | OE? | Plus/ and | a/c1 | Date 1 | +/- | a/c2 | Date 2 | -/+ | a/c3 | Date 3 | Current? | Label | Derivation |
|---|---|---|---|---|---|---|---|---|---|---|---|---|---|---|---|---|
| 1 | clever-intelligent | gleaw | aj | OE | | | | | | | | | | | | gleaw < *ghel- |
| 7 | clever-wise | gleawlic | aj | OE | | | | | | | | | | | | gleaw < *ghel- |
| 46 | clever-wise | freagleaw | aj | OE | | | | | | | | | | | | gleaw < *ghel- |
| 59 | clever-wise | gleawmod | aj | OE | | | | | | | | | | | | gleaw < *ghel- mod |
| 66 | clever-wise | modgleaw | aj | OE | | | | | | | | | | | | mod gleaw < *ghel- |
| 67 | clever-wise | gleawferhþ | aj | OE | | | | | | | | | | | | gleaw < *ghel- ferhþ |
| 68 | clever-wise | ferhþgleaw | aj | OE | | | | | | | | | | | | ferhþ gleaw < *ghel- |
| 70 | clever-wise | hreþergleaw | aj | OE | | | | | | | | | | | | hreþer gleaw < *ghel- |
| 72 | clever-wise | gleawhydig | aj | OE | | | | | | | | | | | | gleaw < *ghel- hyge |
| 79 | stupid | ungleaw | aj | OE | | | | | | | | | | | | gleaw < *ghel- |
| 81 | clever-wise | hygegleaw | aj | OE | | | | | | | | | | | | hyge gleaw < *ghel- |
| 95 | clever-wise | glew < gleaw | aj | OE | - | c | 1290 | | | | | | | | | gleaw < *ghel- |

6.13 HARD/SOFT

Table 14

| Record no. | Meaning | Word | Part of speech | OE? Plus/ and | a/c1 Date 1 | +/– a/c2 Date 2 | –/+ a/c3 Date 3 | Current? | Label | Derivation |
|---|---|---|---|---|---|---|---|---|---|---|
| 254 | stupid | hammer-head | n | | 1532 | – 1628 | + 1947 | | | hammer head |
| 282 | stupid | hammer-headed | aj | | 1552 | | | > | | hammer head |
| 367 | stupid | ninny-hammer | n | | 1592 | – 1853 | | | | innocent < nocere <*nek- hammer |
| 396 | stupid | stone | n | | 1598 | | | | | stone |
| 422 | stupid | woollen-witted | aj | c | 1600 | – 1635 | | | | wool wit < *weid- |
| 492 | stupid | sop | n | a | 1625 | + 1859 | | | | sop |
| 529 | stupid | as sad as any mallet | aj | | 1645 | | | | | sad mallet |
| 543 | stupid | soft-head | n | | 1650 | | | > | | soft head |
| 571 | stupid | soft-headed | aj | | 1667 | | | > | | soft head |
| 663 | clever-shrewd | hard | aj | | 1747 | | | > | | hard |
| 675 | stupid | woollen-head | n | | 1756 | | | > | | wool head |
| 690 | clever-common sense | hard-headed | aj | | 1779 | | | > | | hard head |
| 701 | stupid | stunpoll | n | a | 1794 | | | > | dl | stone poll |
| 763 | stupid | stookie | n | a | 1828 | | | > | sc&no dl | stookie |
| 785 | stupid | soft | aj | | 1835 | | | > | dl&cq | soft |
| 837 | stupid | putty-head | n | | 1856 | | | | us | putty head |
| 895 | stupid | woolly-headed | aj | | 1883 | | | > | | wool head |
| 914 | stupid | barmy | aj | | 1892 | | | > | | balm |
| 930 | stupid | bone-headed | aj | | 1903 | | | > | fg sl | bone head |
| 934 | stupid | wool-witted | aj | | 1905 | | | > | sl og us | wool wit < *weid- |
| 942 | stupid | bonehead | n | | 1908 | | | > | sl og us | bone head |
| 949 | clever-sharp | hard-boiled | aj | | 1915 | | | > | og us | hard boiled |
| 968 | stupid | ivory dome | n | | 1923 | | | > | us sl | ivory dome |
| 975 | stupid | cloth-headed | aj | | 1925 | | | > | | cloth head |
| 980 | stupid | cloth-head | n | | 1927 | | | > | | head |
| 1021 | stupid | knuckle-head | n | | 1944 | | | > | | knuckle head |

6.14 HEAD

Table 15

| Record no. | Meaning | Word | Part of speech | OE? | Plus/ and | a/c1 | Date 1 | +/− | a/c2 | Date 2 | −/+ | a/c3 | Date 3 | Current? | Label | Derivation |
|---|---|---|---|---|---|---|---|---|---|---|---|---|---|---|---|---|
| 2 | clever-wise | heafod | n | OE | | | | | | | | | | | | head |
| 175 | stupid | noll | n | | | | 1399 | + | | 1566 | | | | | | noll |
| 193 | stupid | doddypoll | n | | | | 1401 | − | | 1767 | | | | | | doddy poll |
| 228 | stupid | doddy-pate | n | | c | | 1500 | | | | | | | | | doddy pate |
| 239 | stupid | hoddypoll | n | | | | 1522 | − | | 1589 | | | | | | hoddy poll |
| 242 | stupid | headless | aj | | | | 1526 | | | | | | | ^ | | head |
| 245 | stupid | daw pate/dawpate | n | | a | | 1529 | − | | 1562 | | | | | | daw pate |
| 247 | stupid | noddypoll | n | | a | | 1529 | + | | 1598 | | | | | | noddy poll |
| 253 | stupid | ass-headed | aj | | | | 1532 | + | | 1609 | | | | | | ass head |
| 254 | stupid | hammer-head | n | | | | 1532 | + | + | 1628 | | | 1947 | | | hammer head |
| 255 | stupid | pot-headed | aj | | | | 1533 | − | | | | | | | | pot head |
| 266 | stupid | sheep's head | n | | | | 1542 | | | | | | | ^ | | sheep head |
| 273 | stupid | dull-head | n | | | | 1549 | − | | 1624 | | | | | | dull head |
| 275 | stupid | blockheaded | aj | | | | 1549 | − | | 1860 | | | | | | block head |
| 276 | stupid | blockhead | n | | | | 1549 | | | | | | | ^ | | block head |
| 277 | stupid | ass-head | n | | | | 1550 | − | | 1601 | | | | | | ass head |
| 278 | stupid | grout-head | n | | | | 1550 | − | | 1649 | | | | | | grout head |
| 280 | stupid | dull-headed | aj | | | | 1552 | − | | 1840 | | | | | | dull head |
| 282 | stupid | hammer-headed | aj | | | | 1552 | | | | | | | ^ | | hammer head |
| 287 | stupid | beetle-headed | aj | | | | 1553/87 | − | + | 1596 | | | 1870 | | | beetle head |
| 300 | stupid | cod's-head | n | | | | 1566 | | | 1708 | | | | | | cod head |
| 310 | stupid | log-headed | aj | | | | 1571 | + | | 1926 | | | | | | log head |
| 311 | stupid | jolt(-)head | n | | | | 1573 | − | | 1767 | | | | | | jolt head |
| 313 | stupid | dorhead | n | | | | 1577 | | | | | | | ^ | | dor head |
| 316 | stupid | beetle-head | n | | | | 1577 | − | | 1656 | | | | | | beetle head |
| 318 | stupid | groutnoll | n | | | | 1578 | − | | 1658 | | | | | | grout noll |
| 319 | stupid | grout-headed | aj | | | | 1578 | − | + | 1694 | | | 1847/78 | | dl | grout head |

| Record no. | Meaning | Word | Part of speech | OE? | Plus/and | a/c1 | Date 1 | +/- | a/c2 | Date 2 | -/+ | a/c3 | Date 3 | Current? | Label | Derivation |
|---|---|---|---|---|---|---|---|---|---|---|---|---|---|---|---|---|
| 324 | stupid | grosshead | n | | | | 1580 | – | | 1606 | | | | | | gross head |
| 325 | stupid | dull-pated | aj | | | | 1580 | – | | 1668 | | | | | | dull pate |
| 330 | stupid | niddipol | n | | | | 1582 | | | | | | | | | noddy poll |
| 331 | stupid | nodcoke | n | | | | 1582 | | | | | | | | | noddy coke <? |
| 339 | stupid | plain-headed | aj | | | | 1586 | | | | | | | | | plain head |
| 351 | stupid | loggerhead | n | | | | 1588 | – | | 1821 | | | 1892 | | | log head |
| 355 | stupid | goose-cap | n | | | | 1589 | – | | 1828 | | | | | | goose cap |
| 361 | stupid | heavy-headed | aj | | | | 1590 | | | | | | | > | | heavy <*kap- head |
| 368 | stupid | jobbernowl | n | | | | 1592 | | | | | | | > | | jobber noll |
| 380 | stupid | knotty-pated | aj | | | | 1596 | | | | | | | | | knot pate |
| 381 | stupid | logger-headed | aj | | | | 1596 | – | | 1831 | | | | | | log head |
| 395 | stupid | block-pate | n | | | | 1598 | | | | | | | | | block pate |
| 413 | stupid | dull-pate | n | | a | | 1600 | – | | 1705 | | | | | | dull pate |
| 416 | stupid | shallow-pate | n | | | | 1600 | – | a | 1700 | + | | 1930 | > | nn ai | shallow pate |
| 428 | stupid | clod-poll/clod pole | n | | | | 1601 | | | | | | | > | | clod poll |
| 433 | stupid | thin-headed | aj | | | | 1603 | | | | | | | | | thin head |
| 435 | stupid | fat-headed | aj | | | | 1603 | | | | | | | > | | fat head |
| 440 | stupid | ram-head | n | | | | 1605 | | | | | | | | | ram head |
| 447 | stupid | blockhead | aj | | | | 1606 | – | | 1630 | | | | | | block head |
| 449 | stupid | clot-poll/-pole | n | | | | 1606 | – | | 1719 | | | | | | clot poll |
| 459 | stupid | puppy-headed | aj | | | | 1610 | | | | | | | > | | puppy head |
| 464 | stupid | dosser-head | n | | | | 1612 | | | | | | | | | head |
| 468 | stupid | wattle-head | n | | | | 1613 | | | | | | | | | wattle head |
| 470 | stupid | wattle-headed | aj | | | | 1613 | + | | 1866 | | | | | | wattle head |
| 478 | stupid | shallow-pated | aj | | | | 1616 | + | | 1870 | | | | | | shallow pate |
| 482 | stupid | jolter(-)head | n | | | | 1620 | – | | 1897 | | | | | | jolt head |
| 485 | stupid | half-headed | aj | | | | 1621/31 | | | | | | | > | | half head |
| 488 | clever-sharp | nimble-headed | aj | | | | 1624 | | | | | | | | | nimble < numol <*nem- head |
| 489 | stupid | sheep's head | aj | | | | 1624 | | | | | | | | | sheep head |
| 491 | stupid | bullhead | n | | | | 1624 | + | | 1840 | | | | | | bull head |

Table 15 (contd.)

| Record no. | Meaning | Word | Part of speech | OE? | Plus/ and | a/c1 | Date 1 | +/− | a/c2 | Date 2 | −/+ | a/c3 | Date 3 | Current? | Label | Derivation |
|---|---|---|---|---|---|---|---|---|---|---|---|---|---|---|---|---|
| 493 | stupid | dunderhead | n | | | a | 1625 | | | | | | | | ∨ | | ?dun dunder <*(s)tenʒ- head |
| 501 | stupid | toom-headed | aj | | | | 1629 | | | | | | | | | | toom head |
| 503 | clever-intelligent | pate | n | | | | 1630 | | | | | | | | ∨ | | pate |
| 510 | stupid | ox-head | n | | | a | 1634 | | | | 1806 | | | | | | ox head |
| 513 | stupid | clod-pate | n | | | | 1636 | + | a | | 1679 | | c | 1690 | | c1690sl | clod pate |
| 515 | stupid | squirrel-headed | aj | | | | 1637 | + | | | 1953 | | | | ∨ | | squirrel head |
| 518 | stupid | clod-pated | aj | | | | 1638 | − | | | 1822 | | | | | | clod pate |
| 520 | stupid | clot-pate | n | | | | 1640 | − | | | 1654 | | | | | | clot pate |
| 523 | stupid | muddy-headed | aj | | | | 1642 | − | | | 1815 | | | | | | mud head |
| 524 | stupid | underhead | n | | | | 1643 | + | | | 1686 | | | | | | under head |
| 527 | stupid | clod-head | n | | | | 1644 | | | | | | | | | | clod head |
| 533 | stupid | under-headed | aj | | | | 1646 | | | | | | | | | | under head |
| 540 | stupid | fool's head | n | | | | 1650 | | | | | | | | | | fool head |
| 543 | stupid | soft-head | n | | | | 1650 | | | | | | | | ∨ | | soft head |
| 546 | stupid | nodhead | n | | | | 1652 | | | | | | | | | | noddy head |
| 548 | stupid | thick-skulled | aj | | | a | 1653 | | | | | | | | ∨ | | thick skull |
| 553 | stupid | bottlehead | n | | | | 1654 | + | | | 1815 | | | | | | beetle head |
| 556 | clever-intelligent | head-piece | n | | | | 1656 | | | | | | | | ∨ | | head piece |
| 560 | stupid | bufflehead | n | | | | 1659 | | | | | | | | ∨ | | buffalo head |
| 566 | stupid | sap-head | aj | | | | 1665 | − | | | 1902 | | | | | | sap head |
| 567 | stupid | timber-headed | aj | | | | 1666 | | | | | | | | | | timber head |
| 571 | stupid | soft-headed | aj | | | | 1667 | | | | | | | | ∨ | | soft head |
| 573 | stupid | leather-headed | aj | | | a | 1668 | | | | | | | | | | leather head |
| 582 | stupid | buffle-headed | aj | | | | 1675 | + | | | 1871 | | | | | | buffalo head |
| 587 | stupid | dolt-head | aj | | | | 1679 | | | | | | | | | | dull head |
| 589 | stupid | totty-head | n | | | | 1680 | | | | | | | | | | tot head |
| 591 | stupid | cabbage-head | n | | | | 1682 | | | | | | | | | | cabbage head |
| 594 | stupid | loggerhead | aj | | | | 1684 | | | | | | | | | | log head |
| 612 | stupid | hulver-head | n | | | a | 1700 | | | | | | | | | | hulver head |

| Record no. | Meaning | Word | Part of speech | OE? Plus/ and | Date 1 +/- a/c1 | Date 2 -/+ a/c2 | Date 3 a/c3 | Current? | Label | Derivation |
|---|---|---|---|---|---|---|---|---|---|---|
| 614 | stupid | leather-head | n | | a 1700 | | | | sl | leather head |
| 615 | stupid | sap-pate | n | | 1700 | | | | | sap pate |
| 619 | clever-sharp | long-headed | aj | | a 1700 + | 1711 − | 1864 | | a1700 ca di | long head |
| 623 | stupid | numskulled | aj | | 1706 | | | > | | numb<*nem- skull |
| 625 | stupid | clod-skull | n | | 1707 | | | | | clod skull |
| 626 | stupid | cod's-headed | aj | | 1708 | | | | | cod head |
| 627 | stupid | doddy-polled | aj | | 1708 | | | | | doddy poll |
| 632 | clever-sharp | clear-headed | aj | | 1709 | | | > | | clear<clarus head |
| 645 | stupid | numskull | n | | 1724 | | | > | | numb<*nem- skull |
| 648 | stupid | pudding-headed | aj | | 1726 − | 1867 | | | | pudding head |
| 655 | stupid | sapskull | n | | 1735 | | | > | | sap skull |
| 671 | stupid | thick-skull | n | | 1755 − | 1894 | | | | thick skull |
| 675 | stupid | woollen-head | n | | 1756 | | | | | wool head |
| 676 | clever-wise derog | wisehead | n | | 1764 | | | > | | wise<*weid- head |
| 678 | stupid | chuckle-headed | aj | | 1768 | | | > | | chuckle head |
| 680 | stupid | mutton-headed | aj | | 1775 | | | | sl&dl | mutton head |
| 685 | stupid | beef-head | n | | 1779 | | | | | beef head |
| 690 | clever-common sense | hard-headed | aj | | 1793 | | | > | | hard head |
| 700 | stupid | mud-headed | aj | | a 1794 | | | | | mud head |
| 701 | stupid | stunpoll | n | | 1794 | | | > | dl | stone poll |
| 702 | stupid | bluff-head | n | | 1798 − | 1884 | | | | bluff head |
| 713 | stupid | sap-head | n | | 1800 | | | > | | sap head |
| 718 | stupid | nog-head | n | | c 1801 − | | | | dl | nog head |
| 719 | stupid | thick-headed | aj | | 1803 − | 1891 | | | | thick head |
| 721 | stupid | mutton-head | n | | 1809 | | | > | | mutton head |
| 728 | stupid | dunderpate | n | | 1809 + | 1829 | | | | ?dun dunder <*(s)tenf- pate |
| 729 | stupid | dummkopf | n | | 1813 | | | > | cq og us | dumb kopf |
| 734 | stupid | ram-headed | aj | | 1816 | | | | | ram head |
| 737 | stupid | tup-headed | aj | | 1820 | | | | | tup head |
| 743 | stupid | chuckle-pate | aj | | | | | | | chuckle pate |

Table 15 (contd.)

| Record no. | Meaning | Word | Part of speech | OE? | Plus/ and | Date 1 | +/− a/c1 | Date 2 | −/+ a/c2 | Date 3 | Current? a/c3 | Label | Derivation |
|---|---|---|---|---|---|---|---|---|---|---|---|---|---|
| 756 | stupid | thick-head | n | | | 1824 | | | | | ^ | | thick head |
| 758 | stupid | dunder-headed | aj | | | 1825 | | | | | ^ | | ?dun dunder < *(s)tenf- head |
| 766 | stupid | jobbernowl | aj | | | 1828 | + | 1838 | | | | | jobber nowl |
| 768 | stupid | beef-headed | aj | | | 1828 | + | 1900 | | | | | beef head |
| 775 | stupid | log-head | n | | | 1831 | | | | | | | log head |
| 777 | stupid | woodenhead | n | | | 1831 | | | | | ^ | | wood head |
| 780 | stupid | potato-headed | aj | | | 1832 | | | | | | | potato head |
| 782 | stupid | blockheadish | aj | | | 1833 | + | | | | | | block head |
| 786 | stupid | pumpkin-headed | aj | | | 1835/40 | | 1863 | | | ^ | cq | pumpkin head |
| 796 | stupid | stupid-head | n | | | 1838 | | | | | | | stupid head |
| 800 | stupid | fat-head | n | | | 1842 | | | | | ^ | | fat head |
| 812 | stupid | lubber-head | n | | | 1847 | + | 1849 | | | | 1847dl di | head |
| 819 | clever-wise | strongheaded | aj | | | 1849 | | | | | | | strong head |
| 821 | stupid | timber-head | n | | | 1849 | | | | | | sl | timber head |
| 826 | stupid | pudding head | n | | | 1851 | | | | | ^ | | pudding head |
| 828 | stupid | numbheaded | aj | | a | 1852 | | | | | | us cq | numb < *nem- head |
| 831 | stupid | fiddle-headed | aj | | | 1854 | | | | | | | fiddle head |
| 834 | stupid | pot-head | n | | | 1855 | | | | | | cq | pot head |
| 837 | stupid | putty-head | n | | | 1856 | | | | | | us | putty head |
| 839 | stupid | mullet-headed | aj | | | 1857 | | | | | ^ | us | mullet head |
| 854 | stupid | flat-head | n | | | 1862 | | | | | ^ | dl&sl | flat head |
| 858 | stupid | wooden-headed | aj | | | 1865 | | | | | | | wood head |
| 867 | stupid | wether head | n | | | 1869 | | | | | | | head |
| 876 | stupid | thick-head | aj | | | 1873 | − | 1894 | | | | dl | thick head |
| 879 | stupid | cholter-headed | aj | | | 1876 | | | | | | | cholter? < jolt head |
| 880 | stupid | pumpkin-head | n | | | 1876 | + | 1898 | | | | us cq | head |
| 882 | stupid | numbhead | n | | | 1876 | | | | | ^ | us cq | numb < *nem- head |
| 889 | stupid | mudhead | n | | | 1882 | − | 1886 | | | | sl | mud head |
| 895 | stupid | woolly-headed | aj | | | 1883 | | | | | ^ | | wool head |

| Record no. | Meaning | Word | Part of speech | Part of OE? Plus/ and | a/c1 Date 1 +/− | a/c2 Date 2 −/+ | a/c3 Date 3 | Current? | Label | Derivation |
|---|---|---|---|---|---|---|---|---|---|---|
| 899 | stupid | lunkhead | n | | 1884 | | | ^ | cq og us | lunk head |
| 903 | stupid | cod's-head-and-shoulders | n | | 1886 | | | ^ | | cod head |
| 906 | stupid | dumbhead | n | | 1887 | | | ^ | us | dumb head |
| 910 | stupid | nog-headed | aj | | 1891 − | 1893 | | ^ | | nog head |
| 923 | stupid | pinhead | n | | 1896 | | | ^ | | head |
| 925 | stupid | turnip-headed | aj | | 1898 | | | ^ | | turnip head |
| 926 | stupid | turnip-head | n | | 1898 | | | ^ | | turnip head |
| 927 | stupid | pin-headed | aj | | 1901 | | | ^ | | pin head |
| 928 | stupid | touched in the head | aj | | 1902 | | | ^ | | touch head |
| 930 | stupid | bone-headed | aj | | 1903 | | | ^ | sl og us | bone head |
| 938 | clever-common sense | level head | n | | 1906 | | | ^ | | level head |
| 942 | stupid | bonehead | n | | 1908 | | | ^ | sl og us | bone head |
| 952 | stupid | mullet-head | n | | 1916 | | | ^ | us | head |
| 962 | stupid | sappyhead | n | | 1922 | | | ^ | | sap head |
| 968 | stupid | ivory dome | n | | 1923 | | | ^ | us sl | ivory dome |
| 975 | stupid | cloth-headed | aj | | 1925 | | | ^ | | cloth head |
| 980 | stupid | cloth-head | n | | 1927 | | | ^ | | head |
| 1000 | stupid | square-headed | aj | | 1936 | | | ^ | | square head |
| 1001 | stupid | suet-headed | aj | | 1937 | | | ^ | | suet head |
| 1021 | stupid | knuckle-head | n | | 1944 | | | ^ | | knuckle head |
| 1022 | stupid | meat-head | n | | 1945 | | | ^ | sl cf us | meat head |
| 1027 | stupid | meat-headed | aj | | 1949 | | | ^ | | meat head |
| 1030 | clever-highbrow | egghead | n | | 1952 | | | ^ | cq og us | egg head |
| 1038 | clever-highbrow | eggheaded | aj | | 1957 | | | ^ | | egg head |
| 1044 | stupid | knot-head | n | | 1961 | | | ^ | nr | knot head |
| 1048 | clever-highbrow | eggheadish | aj | | 1963 | | | ^ | | egg head |
| 1063 | stupid | dick-head | n | | 1969 | | | ^ | vu sl | dick head |
| 1073 | stupid | poophead | n | | 1977 | | | ^ | us | poop head |
| 1075 | stupid | woodentop | n | | 1983 | | | ^ | sl | wood top |

6.15 HEALTH-PHYSICAL/MENTAL

Table 16

| Record no. | Meaning | Word | Part of speech | OE? | Plus/a/c1 and | Date 1 +/−a/c2 | Date 2 −/+a/c3 | Date 3 | Current? | Label | Derivation |
|---|---|---|---|---|---|---|---|---|---|---|---|
| 155 | stupid | sick | aj | | c | 1340 − | | 1817 | | | sick |
| 174 | stupid | kime | n | | | 1395 | | | | | kime |
| 226 | stupid | dotty | aj | | a | 1500 + | | 1885 | | cq&dl | dot or dote |
| 238 | stupid | wearish | aj | | | 1519 − | | 1537 | ^ | | wearish |
| 475 | clever-common sense | sound | aj | | | 1615 | | | ^ | | sound |
| 477 | stupid | moonling | n | | | 1616 | | | | | moon |
| 659 | stupid | sickly | aj | | | 1741/2 − | | 1781 | | | sick |
| 770 | stupid | poggle | n | | | 1829 − | | 1886 | | og ab cq | poggle |
| 801 | clever-common sense | sane | aj | | | 1843 | | | ^ | | sane |
| 808 | stupid | as crazy as a loon | aj | | | 1845 | | | ^ | | crazy < crassen loon |
| 984 | stupid | lame-brained | aj | | | 1929 | | | ^ | | lame brain |
| 1023 | stupid | lame-brain | n | | | 1945 | | | ^ | cq | lame brain |
| 1035 | stupid | silly/crazy as a two-bob watcha | aj | | | 1954 | | | ^ | au sl | silly/crazy < crassen |

6.16 HIT/STUNNED

Table 17

| Record no. | Meaning | Word | Part of speech | OE? | Plus/ and | a/c1 | Date 1 | +/− | a/c2 | Date 2 | −/+ | a/c3 | Date 3 | Current? | Label | Derivation |
|---|---|---|---|---|---|---|---|---|---|---|---|---|---|---|---|---|
| 91 | stupid | stuntly < stuntlic | aj | OE | − | c | 1175 | | | | | | | | | stun < *(s)tenf- |
| 94 | stupid | stunt | aj | OE | − | c | 1200 | | | | | | | | | stun < *(s)tenf- |
| 156 | stupid | astoned | aj | | | c | 1374 | | | | | | | | | stun < *(s)tenf- |
| 265 | stupid | stupid | aj | | | | 1541 | | | | | | | ^ | | stupid |
| 386 | stupid | stupidous | aj | | | | 1597 | | | | | | | | | stupid |
| 425 | stupid | obstupefact | n | | | | 1601 | | | | | | | | | stupid |
| 473 | stupid | stupidious | aj | | | | 1615 | | | | | | | | | stupid |
| 637 | stupid | stupid | n | | | | 1712 | | | | | | | ^ | | stupid |
| 677 | stupid | stupe | n | | | | 1762 | | | | | | | ^ | | stupid |
| 725 | stupid | stupidish | aj | | | | 1806 | | | | | | | ^ | | stupid |
| 796 | stupid | stupid-head | n | | | | 1838 | | | | | | | | | stupid head |
| 866 | stupid | touched in the upper storey | aj | | | | 1867 | | | | | | | | | touch |
| 902 | stupid | loon | n | | | | 1885 | | | | | | | ^ | | loon |
| 928 | stupid | touched in the head | aj | | | | 1902 | | | | | | | ^ | | touch head |
| 1003 | stupid | slappy | n | | | | 1937 | | | | | | | | us sl | slap |
| 1034 | stupid | like a stunned mullet | aj | | | | 1953 | | | | | | | ^ | | stun < *(s) tenf- mullet |
| 1057 | stupid | stupe | aj | | | | 1967 | | | | | | | ^ | | stupid |

## 6.17 HUMAN

### Table 18

| Record no. | Meaning | Word | Part of speech | OE? | Plus/and | a/c1 | Date 1 | +/- | a/c2 | Date 2 | -/+ | a/c3 | Date 3 | Current? | Label | Derivation |
|---|---|---|---|---|---|---|---|---|---|---|---|---|---|---|---|---|
| 897 | stupid | cretin | n | | | | 1884 | + | a | 1930 | | | | > | al tf | cretin |

## 6.18 HUMBLE/ORDINARY

### Table 19

| Record no. | Meaning | Word | Part of speech | OE? | Plus/and | a/c1 | Date 1 | +/- | a/c2 | Date 2 | -/+ | a/c3 | Date 3 | Current? | Label | Derivation |
|---|---|---|---|---|---|---|---|---|---|---|---|---|---|---|---|---|
| 153 | stupid | simple | aj | | | | 1340 | | | | | | | | | | simple |
| 190 | stupid | simple-hearted | aj | | | c | 1400 | - | | 1711 | | | | > | | simple heart |
| 423 | stupid | simplician | n | | | | 1600/9 | - | | 1662 | | | | | | simple |
| 508 | stupid | simplicity | n | | | | 1633 | + | | 1860 | | | | | | simple |
| 525 | stupid | simple | n | | | | 1643 | - | | 1654 | + | | 1894 | | | simple |
| 542 | stupid | simpleton | n | | | | 1650 | | | | | | | | > | | simple -ton |
| 661 | stupid | simple-minded | aj | | | | 1744 | | | | | | | | > | | simple mind < *men- |
| 694 | stupid | Simple Simon | n | | | | 1785 | | | | | | | | > | | simple simon |
| 811 | stupid | simpletonish | aj | | | | 1847 | | | | | | | | | | simple -ton |
| 814 | stupid | simply disposed | aj | | | | 1848 | | | | | | | | | | simple dispose |
| 815 | stupid | simpletonian | aj | | | | 1848 | | | | | | | | | | simple -ton |
| 844 | stupid | simpletonic | aj | | | | 1860 | | | | | | | | | | simple -ton |
| 929 | stupid | simp | n | | | | 1903 | | | | | | | | > | | simple |
| 1014 | stupid | simpy | aj | | | | 1942 | | | | | | | | > | us cq | simple |

6.19 INTELLIGENCE

Table 20

| Record no. | Meaning | Word | Part of speech | OE? | Plus/ and | a/c1 | Date 1 | +/- | a/c2 | Date 2 | -/+ | a/c3 | Date 3 | Current? | Label | Derivation |
|---|---|---|---|---|---|---|---|---|---|---|---|---|---|---|---|---|
| 10 | clever-wise | snotorlic | aj | OE | | | | | | | | | | | | snotor |
| 11 | clever-wise | snytre | aj | OE | | | | | | | | | | | | snotor |
| 12 | clever-wise | forþsnotter | aj | OE | | | | | | | | | | | | forth snotor |
| 13 | clever-shrewd | woruldsnotor | aj | OE | | | | | | | | | | | | world snotor |
| 14 | clever-wise | gerad | aj | OE | | | | | | | | | | | | rad |
| 16 | clever-wise | rædsnottor | aj | OE | | | | | | | | | | | | ræd snotor |
| 17 | clever-wise | infrod | aj | OE | | | | | | | | | | | | frod |
| 28 | clever-intelligent | modcræftig | aj | OE | | | | | | | | | | | | mod craft |
| 33 | stupid | (ge)dwæs | aj | OE | | | | | | | | | | | | dwæs |
| 34 | stupid | dwæslic | aj | OE | | | | | | | | | | | | dwæs |
| 35 | stupid | yfeldysig | aj | OE | | | | | | | | | | | | evil dizzy |
| 38 | clever-wise | hygecræftig | aj | OE | | | | | | | | | | | | hyge craft |
| 39 | clever-sharp | horsc | aj | OE | | | | | | | | | | | | horsc |
| 40 | clever-wise | frod | aj | OE | | | | | | | | | | | | frod |
| 56 | clever-wise | lytig | aj | OE | | | | | | | | | | | | lytig |
| 62 | clever-wise | hygesnottor | aj | OE | | | | | | | | | | | | hyge snotor |
| 63 | clever-wise | foresnotor | aj | OE | | | | | | | | | | | | fore snotor |
| 64 | clever-wise | þancsnot(t)or | aj | OE | | | | | | | | | | | | think snotor |
| 65 | clever-wise | modsnotor | aj | OE | | | | | | | | | | | | mod snotor |
| 74 | clever-wise | hygefrod | aj | OE | | | | | | | | | | | | hyge frod |
| 92 | clever-wise | snoter < snotor | aj | OE | - | c | 1200 | | | | | | | | | snotor |
| 110 | clever-intelligent | crafty < cræftig | aj | OE | - | | 1791 | + | | 1876 | | | | ^ | 1876 > ai&dl | craft |
| 111 | stupid | slow < slaw | aj | OE | | | | | | | | | | ^ | | slow |
| 117 | stupid | dull < dol | aj | OE | | | | | | | | | | ^ | | dull |
| 123 | stupid | dill | aj | | | c | 1200 | - | c | 1440 | | | | | | ?dull |
| 125 | clever-sharp | spack | aj | | | c | 1200 | - | a | 1400 | + | | 1674 | ^ | 1674 > dl | spack |
| 134 | stupid | dult | aj | | | c | 1225 | | | | | | | | | dull |

Table 20 (contd.)

| Record no. | Meaning | Word | Part of speech | OE? | Plus/ and | a/c1 | Date 1 | +/– | a/c2 | Date 2 | –/+ | a/c3 | Date 3 | Current? | Label | Derivation |
|---|---|---|---|---|---|---|---|---|---|---|---|---|---|---|---|---|
| 140 | clever-wise | sage | aj | | | | 1297 | – | a | 1872 | | | | | | sapere < *sap- |
| 142 | stupid | boinard | n | | a | | 1300 | + | | 1399 | | | | | | boinard -ard |
| 150 | stupid | nice | n | | c | | 1330 | – | c | 1430 | | | | | | nice |
| 171 | stupid | dull-witted | aj | | | | 1387 | | | | | | | ^ | | dull wit < *weid- |
| 172 | stupid | stulty | aj | | | | 1387/8 | | | | | | | | | stultus |
| 176 | stupid | dullish | aj | | | | 1399 | | | | | | | ^ | | dull |
| 182 | clever-wise | sage | n | | a | | 1400 | – | | 1862 | | | | | | sapere < *sap- |
| 193 | stupid | doddypoll | n | | | | 1401 | – | | 1767 | | | | | | doddy poll |
| 205 | stupid | dullard | n | | c | | 1440 | | | | | | | | | dull -ard |
| 206 | stupid | deaf | aj | | c | | 1440 | – | | 1482 | | | | | | deaf |
| 208 | stupid | dotterel | n | | c | | 1440 | – | | 1681 | | | | | | dote -rel |
| 219 | clever-wise | sapient | aj | | | | 1471 | – | | 1868 | | | | | | sapere < *sap- |
| 225 | stupid | jobard | n | | a | | 1500 | + | a | 1500 | | | | | | jobard -ard |
| 228 | stupid | doddy-pate | n | | c | | 1500 | | | | | | | | | doddy pate |
| 233 | clever-intelligent | craftly | aj | | | | 1509 | | | | | | | | | craft |
| 268 | stupid | doltish | aj | | | | 1543 | | | | | | | ^ | | dull |
| 273 | stupid | dull-head | n | | | | 1549 | – | | 1624 | | | | | | dull head |
| 274 | clever-wise | sapient | n | | | | 1549 | – | | 1600 | + | | 1827 | | 1827jo | sapere < *sap- |
| 279 | stupid | dolt | n | | | | 1551 | | | | | | | | | dull |
| 280 | stupid | dull-headed | aj | | | | 1552 | – | | 1840 | | | | ^ | | dull head |
| 296 | stupid | dunstical | aj | | | | 1563/87 | – | | 1674 | | | | | | dunce |
| 301 | stupid | sottish | aj | | | | 1566 | – | | 1796 | | | | | | sot |
| 302 | stupid | deaf/dumb as a beetle | aj | | | | 1566 | | | | | | | ^ | | deaf dumb beetle |
| 307 | stupid | dummel | n | | | | 1570 | | | | | | | | | dumb |
| 317 | stupid | dunce | n | | | | 1577/87 | | | | | | | ^ | | dunce |
| 325 | stupid | dull-pated | aj | | | | 1580 | – | | 1668 | | | | | | dull pate |
| 334 | stupid | dullard | aj | | | | 1583 | – | | 1894 | | | | | | dull -ard |
| 347 | clever-wise | sophy | n | | | | 1587 | – | | 1678 | | | | | | sophi |
| 350 | stupid | duncical | aj | | | | 1588 | – | | 1841 | | | | | | dunce |

| Record no. | Meaning | Word | Part of speech | OE? | Plus/ and | a/c1 Date 1 | +/- | a/c2 Date 2 | -/+ | a/c3 Date 3 | Current? | Label | Derivation |
|---|---|---|---|---|---|---|---|---|---|---|---|---|---|
| 357 | stupid | doddy | n | | a | 1590 | | | | | | | doddy |
| 361 | stupid | heavy-headed | aj | | | 1590 | | | | | > | | heavy < *kap-head |
| 363 | stupid | dorbellical | aj | | | 1592 | + | 1603 | | | | | dorbel |
| 364 | stupid | dorbel | n | | | 1592 | – | 1621 | | | | | dorbel |
| 368 | stupid | jobbernowl | n | | | 1592 | | | | | > | | jobber noll |
| 378 | stupid | stock | n | | | 1594 | | | | | > | | stock |
| 389 | stupid | duncified | aj | | | 1597 | + | 1759 | | | | | dunce |
| 392 | clever-wise | sophi | n | | | 1598 | | | | | | | sophi |
| 407 | stupid | dorbellist | n | | | 1599 | | | | | | | dorbel |
| 413 | stupid | dull-pate | n | | a | 1600 | – | 1705 | | | | | dull pate |
| 457 | clever-wise derog | nod-crafty | aj | | | 1608 | | | | | | | nod craft |
| 472 | stupid | fondrel | n | | | 1614 | | | | | | | fond -rel |
| 474 | stupid | dulman | n | | | 1615 | – | | a | 1666 | | | dull |
| 480 | stupid | buzzard-blind | aj | | | 1619 | | | | | | | buzzard -ard blind < *bhlendh- |
| 502 | stupid | duncecomb | n | | | 1630 | | | | | | | dunce |
| 512 | clever-wise | grand sophy | n | | a | 1635 | – | 1688 | | | | | grand sophi |
| 536 | clever-wise derog | grand sophy | n | | | 1649 | | | | | | | grand sophi |
| 537 | clever-wise derog | sophy | n | | | 1649 | | | | | | | sophi |
| 541 | clever-sharp | sagacious | aj | | | 1650 | – | 1863 | | | | | sagire |
| 555 | clever-wise | sapientipotent | aj | | | 1656 | | | | | | | sapere < *sap-potent |
| 580 | clever-wise | sapientipotent | n | | | 1675 | | | | | | | sapere < *sap-potent |
| 587 | stupid | dolt-head | n | | | 1679 | | | | | | | dull head |
| 595 | stupid | nizy | n | | c | 1684/6 | – | a | 1814 | | | | nice |
| 617 | stupid | insipid | n | | a | 1700 | – | a | 1834 | | | | sapere < *sap- |
| 627 | stupid | doddy-polled | aj | | | 1708 | | | | | > | | doddy poll |
| 635 | stupid | dolt | aj | | | 1711 | | | | | | | dull |
| 657 | clever-wise | sophical | aj | | | 1739 | | | | | | | sophi |

Table 20 (contd.)

| Record no. | Meaning | Word | Part of speech | OE? | Plus/ and | a/c1 | Date 1 | +/− | a/c2 | Date 2 | −/+ | a/c3 | Date 3 | Current? | Label | Derivation |
|---|---|---|---|---|---|---|---|---|---|---|---|---|---|---|---|---|
| 660 | stupid | hebete | aj | | | | 1743 | | | | | | | ^ | | hebete |
| 667 | clever-wise derog | sage | n | | | | 1751 | − | | 1893 | | | | | | sapere < *sap- |
| 684 | clever-wise | sophic | aj | | a | | 1773 | | | | | | | ^ | | sophi |
| 711 | stupid | dummy | n | | | | 1796 | | | | | | | | | dumb |
| 729 | stupid | dummkopf | n | | | | 1809 | | | | | | | ^ | cq og us | dumb kopf |
| 749 | stupid | dumb | aj | | | | 1823 | | | | | | | ^ | | dumb |
| 755 | stupid | ill-informed | aj | | | | 1824 | | | | | | | ^ | | ill inform |
| 760 | stupid | duncely | aj | | | | 1826 | | | | | | | | | dunce |
| 766 | stupid | jobbernowl | aj | | | | 1828 | + | | 1838 | | | | | | jobber nowl |
| 776 | stupid | duncish | aj | | | | 1831 | − | | 1833 | | | | | | dunce |
| 872 | clever-intelligent | opening | aj | | | | 1872 | | | | | | | | | open |
| 877 | clever-wise | unbesotted | aj | | | | 1875 | | | | | | | | | sot |
| 887 | clever-wise | sage-like | aj | | | | 1879 | + | | 1887 | | | | | | sapere < *sap- |
| 891 | stupid | dully | n | | | | 1883 | | | | | | | | cq | dull |
| 906 | stupid | dumbhead | n | | | | 1887 | | | | | | | ^ | us&sc sl | dumb head |
| 919 | clever-shrewd | sophisticated | aj | | | | 1895 | | | | | | | ^ | | sophi |
| 946 | stupid | goop | n | | | | 1914 | | | | | | | ^ | sl og us | goop |
| 953 | stupid | rumdum(b) | n | | | | 1916 | | | | | | | ^ | nr | rum dumb |
| 957 | stupid | dumb-bell | n | | | | 1920 | | | | | | | ^ | sl og us | dumb |
| 967 | stupid | moron | n | | | | 1922 | | | | | | | ^ | | moron |
| 976 | clever-shrewd | sophisticate | n | | | | 1925 | | | | | | | ^ | og us | sophi |
| 986 | stupid | dumb-cluck | n | | | | 1929 | | | | | | | ^ | sl og us | dumb cluck |
| 1041 | stupid | dumbo | n | | | | 1960 | | | | | | | ^ | sl og us | dumb |
| 1052 | stupid | right one | n | | | | 1965 | | | | | | | ^ | sl og us | right < *reg- |

6.20 LIQUID/SEMI-LIQUID

Table 21

| Record no. | Meaning | Word | Part of speech | OE? | Plus/ and | a/c1 | Date 1 | +/− | a/c2 | Date 2 | −/+ | a/c3 | Date 3 | Current? | Label | Derivation |
|---|---|---|---|---|---|---|---|---|---|---|---|---|---|---|---|---|
| 557 | stupid | vappe | n | | | | 1657 | | | | | | | | | vappe |
| 562 | stupid | whey-brained | aj | | | | 1660 | | | | | | | | | whey brain |
| 566 | stupid | sap-headed | aj | | | | 1665 | − | | 1902 | | | | | | sap head |
| 574 | stupid | sappy | aj | | | | 1670 | | | | | | | > | | sap |
| 615 | stupid | sap-pate | n | | | a | 1700 | | | | | | | | | sap pate |
| 655 | stupid | sapskull | n | | | | 1735 | | | | | | | > | | sap skull |
| 713 | stupid | sap-head | n | | | | 1798 | − | | 1884 | | | | | | sap head |
| 736 | stupid | sap | n | | | | 1815 | | | | | | | > | | sap |
| 827 | stupid | dope | n | | | | 1851 | | | | | | | > | cq og dl | dope |
| 921 | stupid | dopey | aj | | | | 1896 | | | | | | | > | sl og us | dope |
| 962 | stupid | sappyhead | n | | | | 1922 | | | | | | | > | | sap head |
| 973 | stupid | barm-stick | n | | | | 1924 | | | | | | | > | dl | stick |
| 998 | stupid | mess | n | | | | 1936 | | | | | | | > | sl | mess |

6.21 LOOSE TEXTURE

Table 22

| Record no. | Meaning | Word | Part of speech | OE? | Plus/ and | a/c1 | Date 1 | +/− | a/c2 | Date 2 | −/+ | a/c3 | Date 3 | Current? | Label | Derivation |
|---|---|---|---|---|---|---|---|---|---|---|---|---|---|---|---|---|
| 918 | stupid | fozy | aj | | | | 1894 | | | | | | | > | sc&dl | fozy |

## 6.22 LUMP

### Table 23

| Record no. | Meaning | Word | Part of speech | OE? | Plus/ and | a/c1 | Date 1 | +/− | a/c2 | Date 2 | −/+ | a/c3 | Date 3 | Current? | Label | Derivation |
|---|---|---|---|---|---|---|---|---|---|---|---|---|---|---|---|---|
| 226 | stupid | dotty | aj | | a | | 1500 | + | | 1885 | | | | > | cq&dl | dot or dote |
| 380 | stupid | knotty-pated | aj | | | | 1596 | | | | | | | | | knot pate |
| 449 | stupid | clot-poll/-pole | n | | | | 1606 | | | | | | | > | | clot poll |
| 506 | stupid | clot | n | | | | 1632 | + | 1876 | | | | 1942 | > | 1876dl 1942 > cq clot | clot |
| 520 | stupid | clot-pate | n | | | | 1640 | − | 1654 | | | | | > | | clot pate |
| 648 | stupid | pudding-headed | aj | | | | 1726 | | 1867 | | | | | | | pudding head |
| 678 | stupid | chuckle-headed | aj | | | | 1764 | | | | | | | > | | chuckle head |
| 743 | stupid | chuckle-pate | aj | | | | 1820 | | | | | | | | | chuckle pate |
| 826 | stupid | pudding head | n | | | | 1851 | | | | | | | > | | pudding head |
| 1029 | stupid | clottish | aj | | | | 1952 | | | | | | | > | cq | clot |
| 1044 | stupid | knot-head | n | | | | 1961 | | | | | | | > | nr | knot head |

## 6.23 MIND

### Table 24

| Record no. | Meaning | Word | Part of speech | OE? | Plus/ and | a/c1 | Date 1 | +/− | a/c2 | Date 2 | −/+ | a/c3 | Date 3 | Current? | Label | Derivation |
|---|---|---|---|---|---|---|---|---|---|---|---|---|---|---|---|---|
| 3 | clever-wise | runwita | n | OE | | | | | | | | | | | | rune wit < *weid- |
| 4 | clever-wise | fyrnwita | n | OE | | | | | | | | | | | | fyrn wit < *weid- |
| 5 | clever-wise | Þeodwita | n | OE | | | | | | | | | | | | Þeod wit < *weid- |
| 8 | stupid | unandgittol | aj | OE | | | | | | | | | | | | andgit |
| 18 | clever-wise | rædhycgende | aj | OE | | | | | | | | | | | | ræd hyge |

| Record no. | Meaning | Word | Part of speech | OE? | Plus/and | a/c1 | Date 1 | +/- | a/c2 | Date 2 | -/+ | a/c3 | Date 3 | Current? | Label | Derivation |
|---|---|---|---|---|---|---|---|---|---|---|---|---|---|---|---|---|
| 23 | clever-wise | hygefæst | aj | OE | | | | | | | | | | | | hyge fæst |
| 24 | clever-mind | hohfæst | aj | OE | | | | | | | | | | | | hoh fæst |
| 28 | clever-intelligent | modcræftig | aj | OE | | | | | | | | | | | | mod craft |
| 29 | stupid | ungewitful | aj | OE | | | | | | | | | | | | wit < *weid- |
| 38 | clever-wise | hygecræftig | aj | OE | | | | | | | | | | | | hyge craft |
| 44 | clever-wise | wissefa | n | OE | | | | | | | | | | | | wise < *weid- sefa |
| 45 | clever-wise | andgietful | aj | OE | | | | | | | | | | | | andgit |
| 48 | clever-wise | (ge)wittig | aj | OE | | | | | | | | | | | | wit < *weid- |
| 50 | clever-intelligent | gemyndig | aj | OE | | | | | | | | | | | | mind < *men- |
| 51 | clever-sharp | gearowitol | aj | OE | | | | | | | | | | | | gearo wit < *weid- |
| 52 | clever-intelligent | andgitol | aj | OE | | | | | | | | | | | | andgit |
| 53 | clever-intelligent | Pancolmod | aj | OE | | | | | | | | | | | | think mod |
| 54 | clever-wise | ealdwita | n | OE | | | | | | | | | | | | eald < *al- wit < *weid- |
| 55 | clever-wise | witega | n | OE | | | | | | | | | | | | wit < *weid- |
| 58 | clever-wise | forewitig | aj | OE | | | | | | | | | | | | fore wit < *weid- |
| 59 | clever-wise | gleawmod | aj | OE | | | | | | | | | | | | gleaw < *ghel- mod |
| 62 | clever-wise | hygesnottor | aj | OE | | | | | | | | | | | | hyge snotor |
| 65 | clever-wise | modsnotor | aj | OE | | | | | | | | | | | | mod snotor |
| 66 | clever-wise | modgleaw | aj | OE | | | | | | | | | | | | mod gleaw < *ghel- |
| 67 | clever-wise | gleawferhp | aj | OE | | | | | | | | | | | | gleaw < *ghel- ferhp |
| 68 | clever-wise | ferhpgleaw | aj | OE | | | | | | | | | | | | ferhp gleaw < *ghel- |
| 69 | clever-wise | hygepancol | aj | OE | | | | | | | | | | | | hyge think |
| 72 | clever-wise | gleawhydig | aj | OE | | | | | | | | | | | | gleaw < *ghel- hyge |
| 73 | clever-wise | wishydig | aj | OE | | | | | | | | | | | | wise < *weid- hyge |
| 74 | clever-wise | hygefrod | aj | OE | | | | | | | | | | | | hyge frod |
| 75 | clever-wise | wiswylle | aj | OE | | | | | | | | | | | | wise < *weid- will |
| 78 | stupid | modigleas | aj | OE | | | | | | | | | | | | mod |
| 80 | clever-wise | wishycgende | aj | OE | | | | | | | | | | | | wise < *weid- hyge |
| 81 | clever-wise | hygegleaw | aj | OE | | | | | | | | | | | | hyge gleaw < *ghel- |
| 82 | stupid | unandgitfull | aj | OE | | | | | | | | | | | | andgit |
| 83 | stupid | unwita | n | OE | | | | | | | | | | | | wit < *weid- |

Table 24 (contd.)

| Record no. | Meaning | Word | Part of speech | OE? | Plus/ and | a/c1 | Date 1 | +/− a/c2 | Date 2 | −/+ a/c3 | Date 3 | Current? | Label | Derivation |
|---|---|---|---|---|---|---|---|---|---|---|---|---|---|---|
| 93 | clever-wise | uÞwite < uÞwita | n | OE | – | c | 1200 | | | | | | | uÞ wit < *weid- |
| 97 | clever-wise | witter < witter- | aj | OE | – | a | 1400/50 | | | | | | | wit < *weid- |
| 105 | clever-wise | wite < wita | n | OE | – | c | 1315 | + | 1701 | | 1762 | | | wit < *weid- |
| 106 | stupid | unwitty < unwittig | aj | OE | – | | 1670 | + | 1859 | – | | | | wit < *weid- |
| 107 | clever-intelligent | witty < (ge)wittig | aj | OE | – | | 1784 | + | 1886 | | | | 1886dl | wit < *weid- |
| 112 | stupid | witless < gewitleas | aj | OE | | | | | | | | ^ | | wit < *weid- |
| 116 | stupid | mindless < gemyndleas | aj | OE | | | | | | | | ^ | | mind < *men- |
| 128 | clever-sharp | yare-witel | aj | | | c | 1205 | | | | | | | ?yare wit < *weid- |
| 131 | clever-wise | witful | aj | | | c | 1205 | – | 1614 | | | | | wit < *weid- |
| 152 | clever-wise | witty | aj | | | | 1340 | – | 1611 | | | | | wit < *weid- |
| 162 | clever-intelligent | witted (with prec. modifier) | aj | | | | 1377 | | | | | ^ | | wit < *weid- |
| 165 | clever-wise | hearty | aj | | | | 1382 | | | | | | | heart |
| 167 | stupid | heartless | aj | | | | 1382 | – | | | | | | heart |
| 171 | stupid | dull-witted | aj | | | | 1387 | | | | | ^ | | dull wit < *weid- |
| 183 | clever-common sense | reasonable | aj | | | a | 1400 | | | | | ^ | | rational |
| 190 | stupid | simple-hearted | aj | | | c | 1400 | – | 1711 | | | | | simple heart |
| 210 | stupid | want-wit | n | | | | 1448/9 | – | 1610 | + | 1900 | | | want wit < *weid- |
| 212 | clever-intelligent | well-witted | aj | | | c | 1450 | – | 1552 | | | | | well wit < *weid- |
| 217 | clever-genius and intelligent | wit | n | | | c | 1470 | | | | | ^ | nn ai&hs | wit < *weid- |
| 221 | stupid | short-witted | aj | | | | 1477 | – | 1513 | | | | | short wit < *weid- |
| 230 | clever-intelligent | sententious | aj | | | | 1503 | | | | | ^ | | sense < *sent- |
| 231 | stupid | insensuat | aj | | | | 1508 | | | | | | | sense < *sent- |
| 244 | clever-intelligent | witted | aj | | | | 1528 | – | 1606 | | | | | wit < *weid- |
| 248 | stupid | insensate | aj | | | a | 1529 | | | | | | | sense < *sent- |

| Record no. | Meaning | Word | Part of speech | OE? | Plus/ and | a/c1 | Date 1 | +/- | a/c2 | Date 2 | -/+ | a/c3 | Date 3 | Current? | Label | Derivation |
|---|---|---|---|---|---|---|---|---|---|---|---|---|---|---|---|---|
| 251 | clever-sharp | quick-witted | aj | | | | 1530 | | | | | | | ∧ | | quick wit < *weid- |
| 256 | stupid | insensible | aj | | | a | 1533 | – | | 1794 | | | | | | sense < *sent- |
| 257 | stupid | feeble-minded | aj | | | | 1534 | | | | | | | ∧ | | feeble mind < *men- |
| 263 | clever-intelligent | wits | n | | | | 1536 | | | | | | | ∧ | nn ai | wit < *weid- |
| 328 | clever-sharp | ready-witted | aj | | | | 1581 | – | | 1869 | | | | | | ready wit < *weid- |
| 337 | clever-common sense | sensible | aj | | | | 1584 | | | | | | | ∧ | | sense < *sent- |
| 341 | clever-sharp | sharp-witted | aj | | | a | 1586 | | | | | | | ∧ | | sharp wit < *weid- |
| 358 | clever-wise | wittiful | aj | | | | 1590 | | | | | | | | | wit < *weid- |
| 369 | stupid | lean-witted | aj | | | | 1593 | | | | | | | | | lean wit < *weid- |
| 370 | clever-common sense | mother witted | aj | | | | 1593 | | | | | | | | | mother wit < *weid- |
| 371 | stupid | blunt-witted | aj | | | | 1593 | | | | | | | | | blunt wit < *weid- |
| 384 | stupid | fat-witted | aj | | | | 1596 | | | | | | | ∧ | | fat wit < *weid- |
| 400 | clever-intelligent | senseful | aj | | | c | 1598 | – | | 1700 | | | | | | sense < *sent- |
| 406 | stupid | wit-lost | aj | | | | 1599 | | | | | | | | | wit < *weid- lose |
| 422 | stupid | woollen-witted | aj | | | c | 1600 | – | | 1635 | | | | | | wool wit < *weid- |
| 424 | stupid | barren-spirited | aj | | | | 1601 | | | | | | | | | barren spirit < spirare |
| 444 | stupid | beef-witted | aj | | | | 1606 | | | | | | | | | beef wit < *weid- |
| 471 | clever-sharp | nimble-witted | aj | | | | 1613/6 | | | | | | | ∧ | | nimble < numol < *nem- wit < *weid- |
| 505 | clever-common sense | rational | aj | | | | 1632 | – | | 1856 | | | | | | rational |
| 511 | stupid | thickwitted | aj | | | | 1634 | | | | | | | ∧ | | thick wit < *weid- |
| 517 | stupid | lean-souled | aj | | | | 1638 | | | | | | | | | lean soul |
| 532 | stupid | half-witted | aj | | | c | 1645 | | | | | | | ∧ | | half wit < *weid- |
| 544 | clever-wise | cordate | aj | | | | 1651 | – | | 1734 | a | | | | | cord < *ghert- |
| 565 | clever-genius | eagle-wit | n | | | | 1665 | | | | | | | | | eagle wit < *weid- |
| 572 | stupid | lack-wit | n | | | | 1667 | | | | | | | ∧ | | lack wit < *weid- |
| 593 | stupid | under-witted | aj | | | | 1683 | + | | 1856 | | | | | | under wit < *weid- |

Table 24 (contd.)

| Record no. | Meaning | Word | Part of speech | OE? Plus/ and | a/c1 Date 1 | +/- a/c2 Date 2 | -/+ a/c3 Date 3 | Current? Label | Derivation |
|---|---|---|---|---|---|---|---|---|---|
| 639 | clever-sharp derog | over-witted | aj | a | 1716 | | | | over wit < *weid- |
| 643 | clever-genius | master-mind | n | | 1720 | | | ^ | master mind < *men- |
| 656 | stupid | pitcher-souled | aj | a | 1739 | | | | pitcher soul |
| 661 | stupid | simple-minded | aj | | 1744 | | | ^ | simple mind < *men- |
| 662 | clever-common sense | sensible | n | | 1747 | | | | sense < *sent- |
| 673 | stupid | half-wit | n | | 1755 | | | ^ | half wit < *weid- |
| 698 | clever-intelligent | spiritual | aj | | 2791/23 – | 1872 | | | spirit < spirare |
| 712 | clever-common sense | sensical | aj | | 1797 – | 1839 | | | sense < *sent- |
| 765 | stupid | unwitted | aj | | 1828 | | | | wit < *weid- |
| 791 | stupid | squirrel-minded | aj | | 1837 | | | | squirrel mind < *men- |
| 820 | stupid | ninny-minded | aj | | 1849 | | | | innocent < nocere < *nek- mind < *men- |
| 825 | clever-common sense | common(-)sensible | aj | | 1851 | | | ^ | common sense < *sent- |
| 829 | clever-sharp | quick-minded | aj | | 1852 – | -1908 | | | quick mind < *men- |
| 846 | clever-common sense | common(-)sensical | aj | | 1860 | | | ^ | common sense < *sent- |
| 859 | clever-intelligent | beautiful-minded | aj | | 1865 | | | | beauty < *deu- mind < *men- |
| 863 | stupid | lean-minded | aj | | 1866 | | | | lean mind < *men- |
| 869 | stupid | barren-witted | aj | | 1870 | | | | barren wit < *weid- |
| 878 | clever-common sense | common-sensed | aj | | 1875 | | | ^ | common sense < *sent- |
| 893 | stupid | weak-minded | aj | | 1883 | | | ^ | weak mind < *men- |
| 917 | stupid | want-wit | aj | | 1894 | | | | want wit < *weid- |
| 931 | stupid | thickwit | n | | 1904 | | | | thick wit < *weid- |

| Record no. | Meaning | Word | Part of speech | OE? | Plus/ and | a/c1 | Date 1 | +/- | a/c2 | Date 2 | -/+ | a/c3 | Date 3 | Current? | Label | Derivation |
|---|---|---|---|---|---|---|---|---|---|---|---|---|---|---|---|---|
| 934 | stupid | wool-witted | aj | | | | 1905 | | | | | | | | | wool wit < *weid- |
| 944 | stupid | torpid-minded | aj | | | | 1909 | | | | | | | > | | torpid mind < *men- |
| 954 | clever-genius | supermind | n | | | | 1918 | | | | | | | > | | super mind < *men- |
| 963 | stupid | nitwit | aj | | | | 1922 | | | | | | | > | cq | nit wit < *weid- |
| 965 | stupid | nitwit | n | | | | 1922 | | | | | | | > | cq | wit < *weid- |
| 966 | stupid | dim-wit | n | | | | 1922 | | | | | | | > | og us | dim wit < *weid- |
| 991 | stupid | nitwitted | aj | | | | 1931 | | | | | | | > | | nit wit < *weid- |
| 1004 | stupid | half-wit | aj | | | | 1938 | | | | | | | > | | half wit < *weid- |
| 1011 | stupid | dim-witted | aj | | | | 1940 | | | | | | | > | | dim wit < *weid- |

## 6.24 OBJECT

Table 25

| Record no. | Meaning | Word | Part of speech | OE? | Plus/ and | a/c1 | Date 1 | +/- | a/c2 | Date 2 | -/+ | a/c3 | Date 3 | Current? | Label | Derivation |
|---|---|---|---|---|---|---|---|---|---|---|---|---|---|---|---|---|
| 254 | stupid | hammer-head | n | | | | 1532 | - | | 1628 | + | | 1947 | | | hammer head |
| 255 | stupid | pot-headed | aj | | | | 1533 | | | | | | | | | | pot head |
| 282 | stupid | hammer-headed | aj | | | | 1552 | | | | | | | | > | | hammer head |
| 367 | stupid | ninny-hammer | n | | | | 1592 | | | 1853 | | | | | | | innocent < nocere < *nek- hammer |
| 656 | stupid | pitcher-souled | aj | | a | | 1739 | | | | | | | | | | pitcher soul |
| 707 | stupid | spoony | n | | | | 1795 | | | | | | | | > | | spoon |
| 717 | stupid | spoon | n | | | | 1799 | | | | | | | | > | sl&cq | spoon |
| 834 | stupid | pot-head | n | | | | 1855 | | | | | | | | | cq | pot head |
| 843 | stupid | mug | n | | | | 1859 | + | | 1861 | | | | | > | | mug |
| 957 | stupid | dumb-bell | n | | | | 1920 | | | | | | | | > | sl og us | mug |

Table 25 (contd.)

| Record no. | Meaning | Word | Part of speech | OE? | Plus/ and | a/c1 | Date 1 | +/- | a/c2 | Date 2 | -/+ | a/c3 | Date 3 | Current? | Label | Derivation | dumb |
|---|---|---|---|---|---|---|---|---|---|---|---|---|---|---|---|---|---|
| 964 | stupid | mug | aj | | | | 1922 | | | | | | | > | sl (rhyming) | mug | |
| 971 | stupid | stone jug | n | | | | 1923 | | | | | | | > | sl (rhyming) | mug | |
| 992 | stupid | steamer | n | | | | 1932 | | | | | | | > | ie 'steam tug' | mug | |
| 1035 | stupid | silly/crazy as a two-bob watch | aj | | | | 1954 | | | | | | | > | au sl | silly/crazy < crassen | |
| 1049 | stupid | pin-brained | aj | | | | 1964 | | | | | | | > | | pin brain | |
| 1064 | stupid | tat(t)ie-bogle | n | | | | 1969 | | | | | | | > | | tattie | |
| 1067 | stupid | thimble-brain | n | | | | 1971 | | | | | | | > | | brain | |

6.25 PURE/CLEAN

Table 26

| Record no. | Meaning | Word | Part of speech | OE? | Plus/ and | a/c1 | Date 1 | +/- | a/c2 | Date 2 | -/+ | a/c3 | Date 3 | Current? | Label | Derivation |
|---|---|---|---|---|---|---|---|---|---|---|---|---|---|---|---|---|
| 192 | clever-intelligent | clean | aj | | | c | 1400 | | | | | | | | | clean |
| 264 | clever-intelligent | cleanly | aj | | | c | 1540 | - | | 1712 | | | | > | | clean |

## 6.26 SENSE/FEELING

### Table 27

| Record no. | Meaning | Word | Part of speech | OE? Plus/and | a/c1 | Date 1 | +/– | a/c2 | Date 2 | –/+ | a/c3 | Date 3 | Current? | Label Derivation |
|---|---|---|---|---|---|---|---|---|---|---|---|---|---|---|
| 230 | clever-intelligent | sententious | aj | | | 1503 | - | | 1513 | | | | | sense <*sent- |
| 332 | stupid | thick(-)skin | n | | | 1582 | – | | 1893 | | | | | thick |
| 337 | clever-common sense | sensible | aj | | | 1584 | | | | | | | ^ | sense <*sent- |
| 362 | stupid | frost-brained | aj | | | 1592 | | | | | | | | frost brain |
| 378 | stupid | stock | n | | | 1594 | | | | | | | ^ | stock |
| 400 | clever-intelligent | senseful | aj | | | 1598 | – | c | 1700 | | | | | sense <*sent- |
| 623 | stupid | numskulled | aj | | | 1706 | | | | | | | ^ | numb <*nem- skull |
| 645 | stupid | numskull | n | | | 1724 | | | | | | | ^ | numb <*nem- skull |
| 662 | clever-common sense | sensible | n | | | 1747 | | | | | | | | sense <*sent- |
| 693 | stupid | insensible | n | | | 1785 | | | | | | | | sense <*sent- |
| 712 | clever-common sense | sensical | aj | | | 1797 | – | | 1839 | | | | | sense <*sent- |
| 726 | stupid | num | n | | | 1807 | | | | | | | | numb <*nem- |
| 825 | clever-common sense | common(-)sensible | aj | | | 1851 | | | | | | | ^ | common sense <*sent- |
| 828 | stupid | numbheaded | aj | | a | 1852 | | | | | | | | us cq numb <*nem- head |
| 846 | clever-common sense | common(-)sensical | aj | | | 1860 | | | | | | | ^ | common sense <*sent- |
| 878 | clever-common sense | common-sensed | aj | | | 1875 | | | | | | | ^ | common sense <*sent- |
| 882 | stupid | numbhead | n | | | 1876 | | | | | | | ^ | us cq numb <*nem- head |
| 883 | stupid | insensate | n | | | 1877 | – | | 1878 | | | | | sense <*sent- |
| 944 | stupid | torpid-minded | aj | | | 1909 | | | | | | | ^ | torpid mind <*men- |

## 6.27 SHAPE

### Table 28

| Record no. | Meaning | Word | Part of speech | OE? | Plus/and | a/c1 | Date 1 | +/- | a/c2 | Date 2 | -/+ | a/c3 | Date 3 | Current? | Label | Derivation |
|---|---|---|---|---|---|---|---|---|---|---|---|---|---|---|---|---|
| 100 | clever-sharp | yepe < yeap | aj | OE | - | c | 1485 | | | | | | | | | yepe |
| 179 | clever-sharp | yap/yaup | aj | | | a | 1400 | | | | | | | | cf sc&no | yepe |
| 974 | stupid | loopy | aj | | | | 1925 | | | | | | | ^ | sl | loop |
| 1000 | stupid | square-headed | aj | | | | 1936 | | | | | | | ^ | | square head |
| 1030 | clever-highbrow | egghead | n | | | | 1952 | | | | | | | ^ | cq og us | egg head |
| 1038 | clever-highbrow | eggheaded | aj | | | | 1957 | | | | | | | ^ | | egg head |
| 1048 | clever-highbrow | eggheadish | aj | | | | 1963 | | | | | | | ^ | | egg head |

## 6.28 SHARP/PIERCING

### Table 29

| Record no. | Meaning | Word | Part of speech | OE? | Plus/and | a/c1 | Date 1 | +/- | a/c2 | Date 2 | -/+ | a/c3 | Date 3 | Current? | Label | Derivation |
|---|---|---|---|---|---|---|---|---|---|---|---|---|---|---|---|---|
| 42 | clever-sharp | scearpþancol | aj | OE | | | | | | | | | | | | sharp think |
| 57 | clever-intelligent | cene | aj | OE | | | | | | | | | | | | keen |
| 96 | clever-wise | keen < cene | aj | OE | - | a | 1400 | | | | | | | | | keen |
| 103 | clever-sharp | sharp < scearp | aj | OE | - | | 1705 | | | | | | | | | sharp |
| 117 | stupid | dull < dol | aj | OE | | c | 1200 | - | c | 1440 | | | | ^ | | dull |
| 123 | stupid | dill | aj | OE | | c | 1200 | | | | | | | | | ?dull |

| Record no. | Meaning | Word | Part of speech | OE? | Plus/and | a/c1 | Date 1 | +/- | a/c2 | Date 2 | -/+ | a/c3 | Date 3 | Current? | Label | Derivation |
|---|---|---|---|---|---|---|---|---|---|---|---|---|---|---|---|---|
| 134 | stupid | dult | aj | | | | 1225 | | | | | | | | | dull |
| 171 | stupid | dull-witted | aj | | | | 1387 | | | | | | | ^ | | dull wit < *weid- |
| 176 | stupid | dullish | aj | | | | 1399 | | | | | | | ^ | | dull |
| 205 | stupid | dullard | n | | c | | 1440 | | | | | | | | | dull -ard |
| 235 | stupid | obtuse | aj | | | | 1509 | | | | | | | ^ | | obtuse |
| 268 | stupid | doltish | aj | | | | 1543 | | | | | | | ^ | | dull |
| 273 | stupid | dull-head | n | | | | 1549 | − | | 1624 | | | | | | dull head |
| 279 | stupid | dolt | n | | | | 1551 | | | | | | | ^ | | dull |
| 280 | stupid | dull-headed | aj | | | | 1552 | − | | 1840 | | | | | | dull head |
| 325 | stupid | dull-pated | aj | | | | 1580 | − | | 1668 | | | | | | dull pate |
| 334 | stupid | dullard | aj | | | | 1583 | − | | 1894 | | | | | | dull -ard |
| 335 | clever-sharp | sharpsighted | aj | | | | 1583 | | | | | | | ^ | | sharp see < sekw- |
| 341 | clever-sharp | sharp-witted | aj | | a | | 1586 | | | | | | | ^ | | sharp wit < *weid- |
| 353 | clever-sharp | acute | aj | | | | 1588 | | | | | | | ^ | | acute < acuere |
| 371 | stupid | blunt-witted | aj | | | | 1593 | | | | | | | | | blunt wit < *weid- |
| 410 | clever-sharp | penetrant | aj | | | | 1599 | − | | 1836 | | | | | | penetrate |
| 413 | stupid | dull-pate | n | | a | | 1600 | − | | 1705 | | | | | | dull pate |
| 474 | stupid | dulman | n | | | | 1615 | − | a | 1666 | | | | | | dull |
| 479 | clever-sharp | acuminous | aj | | | | 1618 | − | | 1810 | | | | | | acumen < acuere |
| 499 | clever-shrewd | smart | aj | | | | 1628 | | | | | | | ^ | | smart |
| 551 | clever-sharp | acuminate | aj | | | | 1654 | | | | | | | | | acumen < acuere |
| 587 | stupid | dolt-head | n | | | | 1679 | | | | | | | | | dull head |
| 588 | clever-sharp | penetrating | aj | | a | | 1680 | | | | | | | ^ | | penetrate |
| 606 | clever-shrewd | sharp | aj | | | | 1697 | | | | | | | ^ | | sharp |
| 622 | clever-sharp | keen | aj | | | | 1704 | | | | | | | ^ | | keen |
| 635 | stupid | dolt | aj | | | | 1711 | | | | | | | ^ | | dull |
| 649 | clever-sharp | penetrative | aj | | a | | 1727 | | | | | | | ^ | | penetrate |
| 653 | clever-sharp | cute | aj | | | | 1731 | + | | 1756 | − | | 1848 | | 1731di 1848cq | acute < acuere |
| 654 | clever-sharp | penetrant | n | | a | | 1734 | | | | | | | | | penetrate |
| 664 | stupid | unpenetrating | aj | | | | 1748 | | | | | | | | | penetrate |

Table 29 (contd.)

| Record no. | Meaning | Word | Part of speech | OE? Plus and | a/c1 Date 1 | +/- a/c2 Date 2 | -/+ a/c3 Date 3 | Current? | Label | Derivation |
|---|---|---|---|---|---|---|---|---|---|---|
| 666 | clever-intelligent | smartish | aj | | 1748 | | | ^ | | smart |
| 686 | stupid | unacute | aj | | 1775 | | | | | acute < acuere |
| 705 | clever-sharp derog | over-sharp | aj | | 1795 | | | | | over sharp |
| 778 | clever-sharp | acuminated | aj | | 1831 | | | ^ | | acumen < acuere |
| 794 | clever-precocious | sharp | aj | | 1837 | | | ^ | | sharp |
| 798 | clever-sharp | sharp | n | | 1840 | − | | | | sharp |
| 822 | clever-sharp | incisive | aj | | 1850 | a | −1885 | ^ | | incisive |
| 849 | stupid | unsmart | aj | | 1861 | | | | | smart |
| 851 | clever-smart aleck derog | smarty/smartie | n | | 1861 | | | ^ | | smart |
| 861 | clever-smart aleck derog | smart alec/aleck/alick | n | | 1865 | | | ^ | cq og us smart alec | smart alec |
| 891 | stupid | dully | n | | 1883 | + | 1887 | | cq | dull |
| 892 | clever-smart aleck derog | smarty | aj | | 1883 | | | ^ | | smart |
| 896 | clever-sharp and precocious (?appears derog) | sharpshins | n | | 1883/6 | | | ^ | dl | sharp shins |
| 935 | clever-smart aleck derog | smart-alecky | aj | | 1905 | | | ^ | cq og us smart alec | |
| 972 | clever-sharp | needle-sharp | aj | | 1923 | | | ^ | | needle sharp |
| 1012 | clever-smart aleck derog | smarty-pants/smarti-pants | n | | 1941 | | | ^ | | smart pants |
| 1013 | clever-sharp | sharpie | n | | 1942 | | | ^ | cq og us sharp | |
| 1015 | clever-sharp | sharpshooter | n | | 1942 | | | ^ | us cq | sharp shoot |
| 1037 | clever-smart aleck derog | smart alec/aleck/alick | aj | | 1956 | | | ^ | cq og us smart alec | |
| 1043 | clever-smart aleck derog | smart-arsed/-assed | aj | | 1960 | | | ^ | sl | smart arse |

| Record no. | Meaning | Word | Part of speech | OE? | Plus/ and | a/c1 | Date 1 | +/- | a/c2 | Date 2 | -/+ | a/c3 | Date 3 | Current? | Label | Derivation |
|---|---|---|---|---|---|---|---|---|---|---|---|---|---|---|---|---|
| 1045 | clever-smart aleck derog | smart-arse/-ass | n | | | | 1962 | | | | | | | ∧ | sl | smart arse |
| 1046 | clever-smart aleck derog | smarty-boots/smarti-boots | aj | | | | 1962 | | | | | | | ∧ | cq | smart boots |
| 1047 | clever-smart aleck derog | smarty-boots/smarti-boots | n | | | | 1962 | | | | | | | ∧ | cq | smart boots |
| 1065 | clever-smart aleck derog | smarty-pants/smarti-pants | aj | | | | 1969 | | | | | | | ∧ | | smart pants |
| 1074 | clever-shrewd | smart money | n | | | | 1977 | | | | | | | ∧ | | smart money |

## 6.29 SIZE

### Table 30

| Record no. | Meaning | Word | Part of speech | OE? | Plus/ and | a/c1 | Date 1 | +/- | a/c2 | Date 2 | -/+ | a/c3 | Date 3 | Current? | Label | Derivation |
|---|---|---|---|---|---|---|---|---|---|---|---|---|---|---|---|---|
| 85 | clever-wise | gebeorglic | aj | OE | | | | | | | | | | | | beorg |
| 241 | stupid | gross | aj | | | | 1526 | – | | 1844 | | | | | | gross |
| 258 | clever-intelligent | large | aj | | | | 1535 | – | | 1667 | | | | | | large |
| 310 | stupid | log-headed | aj | | | | 1571 | + | | 1926 | | | | ∧ | | log head |
| 351 | stupid | loggerhead | n | | | | 1588 | – | | 1821 | + | | 1892 | | | log head |
| 381 | stupid | logger-headed | aj | | | | 1596 | – | | 1831 | | | | | | log head |
| 433 | stupid | thin-headed | aj | | | | 1603 | | | | | | | | | thin head |
| 517 | stupid | lean-souled | aj | | | | 1638 | | | | | | | | | lean soul |
| 581 | stupid | logger | aj | | | | 1675 | – | | 1781 | + | | 1812 | | 1812dl | log |
| 594 | stupid | loggerhead | aj | | | | 1684 | | | | | | | | | log head |
| 702 | stupid | bluff-head | n | | | | 1794 | | | | | | | | | bluff head |
| 775 | stupid | log-head | n | | | | 1831 | | | | | | | | | log head |

Table 30 (contd.)

| Record no. | Meaning | Word | Part of speech | OE? | Plus/ and | a/c1 | Date 1 | +/- | a/c2 | Date 2 | -/+ | a/c3 | Date 3 | Current? | Label | Derivation |
|---|---|---|---|---|---|---|---|---|---|---|---|---|---|---|---|---|
| 856 | stupid | scant-brain | n | | | | 1864 | | | | | | | | | scant brain |
| 923 | stupid | pinhead | n | | | | 1896 | | | | | | | ^ | | head |
| 927 | stupid | pin-headed | aj | | | | 1901 | | | | | | | ^ | | pin head |
| 961 | stupid | peanut-brained | aj | | | | 1922 | | | | | | | ^ | | peanut brain |
| 1049 | stupid | pin-brained | aj | | | | 1964 | | | | | | | ^ | | pin brain |
| 1055 | stupid | schmoll | n | | | | 1967 | | | | | | | ^ | sl | schmoll |
| 1067 | stupid | thimble-brain | n | | | | 1971 | | | | | | | ^ | | brain |

## 6.30 SOUND

Table 31

| Record no. | Meaning | Word | Part of speech | OE? | Plus/ and | a/c1 | Date 1 | +/- | a/c2 | Date 2 | -/+ | a/c3 | Date 3 | Current? | Label | Derivation |
|---|---|---|---|---|---|---|---|---|---|---|---|---|---|---|---|---|
| 91 | stupid | stuntly<stuntlic | aj | OE | - | c | 1175 | | | | | | | | | stun<*(s)ten£- |
| 94 | stupid | stunt | aj | OE | - | c | 1200 | | | | | | | | | stun<*(s)ten£- |
| 156 | stupid | astoned | aj | | | c | 1374 | | | | | | | | | stun<*(s)ten£- |
| 250 | clever-sharp | clear-eyed | aj | | | | 1530 | | | | | | ^ | | | clear<clarus eye<*okw- |
| 311 | stupid | jolt(-)head | n | | | | 1573 | - | | | | | | | | jolt head |
| 345 | clever-sharp | clear-sighted | aj | | | | 1586 | - | | | | | ^ | | | clear<clarus |
| 482 | stupid | jolter(-)head | n | | | | 1620 | - | | 1897 | | | | | | jolt head |
| 483 | stupid | dunderwhelp | n | | | | 1621 | + | a | 1625 | | | | | | ?dun dunder <*(s)ten£- whelp |

Table 31 (contd.)

| Record no. | Meaning | Word | Part of speech | OE? | Plus/ and | a/c1 | Date 1 | +/- | a/c2 | Date 2 | -/+ | a/c3 | Date 3 | Current? | Label | Derivation |
|---|---|---|---|---|---|---|---|---|---|---|---|---|---|---|---|---|
| 493 | stupid | dunderhead | n | | a | | 1625 | | | | | | | > | | ?dun dunder <*(s)tenʒ- head |
| 632 | clever-sharp | clear-headed | aj | | | | 1709 | | | | | | | > | | clear <clarus head |
| 728 | stupid | dunderpate | n | | | | 1809 | + | | 1829 | | | | | | ?dun dunder <*(s)tenʒ- pate |
| 758 | stupid | dunder-headed | aj | | | | 1825 | | | | | | | > | | ?dun dunder <*(s)tenʒ- head |
| 879 | stupid | cholter-headed | aj | | | | 1876 | | | | | | | | dl | cholter? <jolt head |
| 979 | stupid | gawp | n | | | | 1926 | | | | | | | > | cq&dl | gawp |
| 982 | stupid | cluck | n | | | | 1928 | | | | | | | > | sl og us | cluck |
| 986 | stupid | dumb-cluck | n | | | | 1929 | | | | | | | > | sl og us | dumb cluck |
| 1009 | stupid | ding(-)a(-)ling | n | | | | 1940 | | | | | | | > | nr sl | ding |
| 1034 | stupid | like a stunned mullet | aj | | | | 1953 | | | | | | | > | sl | stun <*(s)tenʒ- mullet |

6.31 SPEECH

Table 32

| Record no. | Meaning | Word | Part of speech | OE? | Plus/ and | a/c1 | Date 1 | +/- | a/c2 | Date 2 | -/+ | a/c3 | Date 3 | Current? | Label | Derivation |
|---|---|---|---|---|---|---|---|---|---|---|---|---|---|---|---|---|
| 15 | clever-wise | wiswyrde | aj | OE | | | 1530 | | | | | | | > | | wise <*weid- word |
| 250 | clever-sharp | clear-eyed | aj | | | | | | | | | | | | | clear <clarus eye <*okw- |
| 270 | stupid | momish | aj | | | | 1546 | – | | 1592 | | | | | | mome |
| 286 | stupid | mome | n | | | | 1553 | – | | 1923 | | | | | ob ex ai | mome |

Table 32 (contd.)

| Record no. | Meaning | Word | Part of speech | OE? | Plus/ and | a/c1 | Date 1 | +/− | a/c2 | Date 2 | −/+ | a/c3 | Date 3 | Current? | Label | Derivation |
|---|---|---|---|---|---|---|---|---|---|---|---|---|---|---|---|---|
| 302 | stupid | deaf/dumb as a beetle | aj | | | | 1566 | | | | | | | ^ | | deaf dumb beetle |
| 307 | stupid | dummel | n | | | | 1570 | | | | | | | | | dumb |
| 314 | clever-wise | bilwise | aj | | | | 1577 | | | | | | | | | bill wise < *weid- |
| 345 | clever-sharp | clear-sighted | aj | | | | 1586 | | | | | | | ^ | | clear < clarus |
| 383 | clever-wise | oracle | n | | | | 1596 | | | | | | | ^ | | oracle |
| 426 | stupid | surd | aj | | | | 1601 | − | a | 1676 | | | | | | surd |
| 559 | clever-precocious | prodigy | n | | | | 1658 | | | | | | | ^ | | pro- *agiom |
| 632 | clever-sharp | clear-headed | aj | | | | 1709 | | | | | | | ^ | | clear < clarus head |
| 638 | stupid | boobily | aj | | | | 1714 | + | | 1740 | | | | | | booby < bobo < balbus |
| 696 | stupid | staumrel | aj | | | | 1787 | | | | | | | ^ | sc | stammer -rel |
| 711 | stupid | dummy | n | | | | 1796 | | | | | | | ^ | | dumb |
| 720 | stupid | staumrel | n | | | | 1802 | | | | | | | ^ | sc | stammer -rel |
| 729 | stupid | dummkopf | n | | | | 1809 | | | | | | | ^ | cq og us | dumb kopf |
| 749 | stupid | dumb | aj | | | | 1823 | | | | | | | ^ | | dumb |
| 906 | stupid | dumbhead | n | | | | 1887 | | | | | | | ^ | us&sc sl | dumb head |
| 953 | stupid | rumdum(b) | n | | | | 1916 | | | | | | | ^ | nr | rum dumb |
| 957 | stupid | dumb-bell | n | | | | 1920 | | | | | | | ^ | sl og us | dumb |
| 986 | stupid | dumb-cluck | n | | | | 1929 | | | | | | | ^ | sl og us | dumb cluck |
| 1041 | stupid | dumbo | n | | | | 1960 | | | | | | | ^ | sl og us | dumb |

6.32 SPEED

Table 33

| Record no. | Meaning | Word | Part of speech | OE? | Plus/ and | a/c1 | Date 1 | +/- | a/c2 | Date 2 | -/+ | a/c3 | Date 3 | Current? | Label | Derivation |
|---|---|---|---|---|---|---|---|---|---|---|---|---|---|---|---|---|
| 111 | stupid | slow < slaw | aj | OE | | | | | | | | | | ^ | | slow |
| 125 | clever-sharp | spack | aj | | | c | 1200 | – | a | 1400 | + | | | 1674 | ^ | 1674>dl | spack |
| 128 | clever-sharp | yare-witel | aj | | | c | 1205 | | | | | | | | ^ | | ?yare wit < *weid- |
| 199 | clever-sharp | snell | aj | | | c | 1425 | – | a | 1450 | + | | | 1719 | ^ | 1719>sc&no | snell |
| 211 | clever-sharp | quick in | aj | | | c | 1449 | – | | 1588 | | | | | | | quick |
| 214 | stupid | sluggish | aj | | | c | 1450 | | | | | | | | ^ | | slug |
| 224 | clever-sharp | quick | aj | | | c | 1484 | | | | | | | | ^ | | quick |
| 251 | clever-sharp | quick-witted | aj | | | | 1530 | | | | | | | | ^ | | quick wit < *weid- |
| 281 | clever-sharp | quick-sighted | aj | | | | 1552 | | | | | | | | ^ | | quick see < sekw- |
| 476 | clever-sharp | quick-eyed | aj | | | a | 1616 | | | | | | | | ^ | | quick eye < *okw- |
| 488 | clever-sharp | nimble-headed | aj | | | | 1624 | | | | | | | | | | nimble < numol < *nem- head |
| 697 | clever-sharp | snap | aj | | | | 1790 | | | | | | | | ^ | sc | snap |
| 764 | clever-wise | expedient | aj | | | | 1828 | | | | | | | | | | ex- pedem |
| 789 | clever-sharp | nimble-brained | aj | | | | 1836/48 | | | | | | | | | | nimble < numol < *nem- brain |
| 829 | clever-sharp | quick-minded | aj | | | | 1852 | – | | -1908 | | | | | | | quick mind < *men- |
| 871 | clever-sharp | snappy | aj | | | | 1871 | | | | | | | | ^ | cq | snap |
| 995 | stupid | schlepper | n | | | | 1934 | | | | | | | | ^ | cq cf us | schlep |
| 1007 | stupid | schlep | n | | | | 1939 | | | | | | | | ^ | us cq | schlep |

## 6.33 STRENGTH/WEAKNESS

### Table 34

| Record no. | Meaning | Word | Part of speech | OE? | Plus/ and | a/c1 | Date 1 | +/- | a/c2 | Date 2 | -/+ | a/c3 | Date 3 | Current? | Label | Derivation |
|---|---|---|---|---|---|---|---|---|---|---|---|---|---|---|---|---|
| 28 | clever-intelligent | modcræftig | aj | OE | | | | | | | | | | | | mod craft |
| 38 | clever-wise | hygecræftig | aj | OE | | | | | | | | | | | | hyge craft |
| 110 | clever-intelligent | crafty < cræftig | aj | OE | — | | 1791 | + | | 1876 | | | | > | 1876 > ai&dl | craft |
| 233 | clever-intelligent | craftly | aj | | | | 1509 | | | | | | | | | craft |
| 457 | clever-wise derog | nod-crafty | aj | | | | 1608 | — | | | | | | | | nod craft |
| 561 | clever-genius | pancratic | aj | | | a | 1660 | | | 1848 | | | | > | | pan- cratos |
| 722 | stupid | imbecile | aj | | | | 1804 | | | | | | | > | | imbecile |
| 744 | stupid | imbecile | n | | | | 1820 | | | | | | | > | | imbecile |
| 783 | clever-sharp | wide(-)awake | aj | | | | 1833 | | | | | | | > | cq og sl | awake < *weg- |
| 819 | clever-wise | strongheaded | aj | | | | 1849 | | | | | | | | | strong head |
| 908 | clever-sharp | wide-awake | n | | | | 1890 | | | | | | | | | awake < *weg- |
| 947 | stupid | feeb | n | | | | 1914 | | | | | | | > | us sl | feeble |
| 984 | stupid | lame-brained | aj | | | | 1929 | | | | | | | > | | lame brain |
| 1023 | stupid | lame-brain | n | | | | 1945 | | | | | | | > | cq | lame brain |

## 6.34 VALUE

### Table 35

| Record no. | Meaning | Word | Part of speech | OE? | Plus/ and | a/c1 | Date 1 | +/- | a/c2 | Date 2 | -/+ | a/c3 | Date 3 | Current? | Label | Derivation |
|---|---|---|---|---|---|---|---|---|---|---|---|---|---|---|---|---|
| 600 | stupid | Tom Farthing | n | | | | 1689 | | | | | | | > | | tom |
| 951 | stupid | gubbins | n | | | | 1916 | | | | | | | | cq | gubbins |

## 6.35 WEALTH/PROSPERITY

### Table 36

| Record no. | Meaning | Word | Part of speech | OE? | Plus/ and | a/c1 | Date 1 | +/- | a/c2 | Date 2 | -/+ | a/c3 | Date 3 | Current? | Label | Derivation |
|---|---|---|---|---|---|---|---|---|---|---|---|---|---|---|---|---|
| 601 | clever-common sense | sonsy | aj | | | a | 1689 | - | | 1720 | | | | | 1720sc | sonsy |
| 824 | clever-intelligent | opulent | aj | | | | 1851 | - | | 1867 | | | | | 1867fg | opulentus < *op-lourd |
| 853 | stupid | boodle | n | | | | 1862 | | | | | | | | sl | boodle <?*bheuf- |
| 1074 | clever-shrewd | smart money | n | | | | 1977 | | | | | > | | | | smart money |

## 6.36 WEIGHT

### Table 37

| Record no. | Meaning | Word | Part of speech | OE? | Plus/ and | a/c1 | Date 1 | +/- | a/c2 | Date 2 | -/+ | a/c3 | Date 3 | Current? | Label | Derivation |
|---|---|---|---|---|---|---|---|---|---|---|---|---|---|---|---|---|
| 146 | stupid | heavy | aj | | | c | 1300 | | | | | | | > | | heavy < *kap-lourd |
| 173 | stupid | lourd | aj | | | | 1390 | - | | | | | | | | lourd |
| 287 | stupid | beetle-headed | aj | | | | 1553/87 | - | | 1596 | + | | 1870 | | fg | beetle head |
| 299 | stupid | beetle | aj | | | | 1566 | | | | | | | > | | beetle |
| 302 | stupid | deaf/dumb as a beetle | aj | | | | 1566 | | | | | | | | | deaf dumb beetle |
| 310 | stupid | log-headed | aj | | | | 1571 | + | | 1926 | | | | > | | log head |
| 316 | stupid | beetle-head | n | | | | 1577 | - | | 1656 | | | | | | beetle head |
| 351 | stupid | loggerhead | n | | | | 1588 | - | | 1821 | + | | 1892 | | | log head |
| 361 | stupid | heavy-headed | aj | | | | 1590 | | | | | | | > | | heavy < * kap- head |

Table 37 (contd.)

| Record no. | Meaning | Word | Part of speech | OE? | Plus/ and | a/c1 | Date 1 | +/− | a/c2 | Date 2 | −/+ | a/c3 | Date 3 | Current? | Label | Derivation |
|---|---|---|---|---|---|---|---|---|---|---|---|---|---|---|---|---|
| 381 | stupid | logger-headed | aj | | | | 1596 | − | | 1831 | | | | | | log head |
| 415 | stupid | lourdish | aj | | | | 1600 | | | | | | | | | lourd |
| 436 | stupid | beetle-brain | n | | | a | 1604 | | | | | | | | | beetle brain |
| 529 | stupid | as sad as any mallet | aj | | | | 1645 | | | | | | | | | sad mallet |
| 530 | clever-wise | weighed | aj | | | c | 1645 | − | | 1689 | | | | | | weigh |
| 553 | stupid | bottlehead | n | | | | 1654 | + | | 1815 | | | | | | beetle head |
| 581 | stupid | logger | aj | | | | 1675 | − | | 1781 | + | | 1812 | | 1812dl | log |
| 594 | stupid | loggerhead | aj | | | | 1684 | | | | | | | | | log head |
| 775 | stupid | log-head | n | | | | 1831 | | | | | | | | | log head |

# BIBLIOGRAPHY

ACHTEMEIER, P. J. (ed.), 1985. *Harper's Bible Dictionary*, San Francisco: Harper & Row.

AITCHISON, J., 1987. *Words in the Mind: An Introduction to the Mental Lexicon*, Oxford: Blackwell.

ALLEN, R. E. (ed.), 1990. *The Concise Oxford Dictionary*, 8th edn, Oxford: Clarendon Press.

ALLEN, R. E., 1999. 'Lumping and splitting', *English Today* 60, 61–3.

BARCELONA, A., 2000a. 'On the plausibility of claiming a metonymic motivation for conceptual metaphor', in Barcelona (2002b: 31–58).

BARCELONA, A. (ed.), 2000b. *Metaphor and Metonymy at the Crossroads: A Cognitive Perspective*, Berlin: Mouton de Gruyter.

BARCELONA, A., 2002. 'Clarifying and applying the notions of metaphor and metonymy within cognitive linguistics: an update', in R. Dirven & R. Pörings (eds.), *Metaphor and Metonymy in Comparison and Contrast*, Berlin: Mouton de Gruyter, 207–78.

BARNDEN, J., 1997. *ATT-Meta Project Databank: Examples of Usage of Metaphors of Mind*. http://www.cs.bham.ac.uk/~jab/ATT-Meta/Databank/

BARROW, R., 1993. *Language, Intelligence, and Thought*, Aldershot: Elgar.

BENSON, L. D., 1987. *The Riverside Chaucer*, Oxford: Oxford University Press.

BLACK, M., 1962. *Models and Metaphors: Studies in Language and Philosophy*, Ithaca, NY: Cornell University Press.

BLACK, M., 1993. 'More about metaphor', in A. Ortony (ed.), *Metaphor and Thought*, Cambridge: Cambridge University Press, 19–41.

BLANK, A. & KOCH, P., 1999a. 'Introduction', in Blank & Koch (1999b: 1–14).

BLANK, A. & KOCH, P. (eds.), 1999b. *Historical Semantics and Cognition*, Berlin: Mouton de Gruyter.

BLOOMFIELD, L., 1933. *Language*, London: Allen & Unwin.

BOLTON, G., 1901. *The Animals of the Bible*, London: Newnes.

BORODITSKY, L., 2000. 'Metaphoric structuring: understanding time through spatial metaphors', *Cognition* 75, 1–28.

BOSWORTH, J. & TOLLER, N. T. (eds.), 1898. *An Anglo-Saxon Dictionary*, London: Oxford University Press.

BREWER, C., 2000. '*OED* sources', in L. Mugglestone (ed.), *Lexicography and the OED: Pioneers in the Untrodden Forest*, Oxford: Oxford University Press, 40–58.

BROWN, R., 1958. *Words and Things*, Glencoe, Ill.: Free Press.

BUCK, C. D., 1949. *A Dictionary of Selected Synonyms in the Principal Indo-European Languages: A Contribution to the History of Ideas*, Chicago: University of Chicago Press.

CAMPBELL, A. (ed.), 1972. *An Anglo-Saxon Dictionary: enlarged addenda and corrigenda*, London: Oxford University Press.

CHARTERIS-BLACK, J., 2003. 'Cross-linguistic differences in the use of metaphor and metonymy in English and Malay phraseology', paper presented at International Cognitive Linguistics Conference 12, University of Logroño.

CRIST, E., 1999. *Images of Animals: Anthropomorphism and the Animal Mind*, Philadephia: Temple University Press.

CROFT, W., 2002. 'The role of domains in the interpretation of metaphors and metonymies', in R. Dirven & R. Pörings (eds.), *Metaphor and Metonymy in Comparison and Contrast*, Berlin: Mouton de Gruyter, 161–205.

CUYCKENS, H., BERG, T., DIRVEN, R. & PANTHER, K.-U. (eds.), 2003. *Motivation in Language: Studies in Honor of Günther Radden*, Amsterdam: Benjamins.

DAVIDSON, D., 1996. 'What metaphors mean', in A. P. Martinich (ed.), *The Philosophy of Language*, 3rd edn, New York: Oxford University Press, 415–26.

DE LA CRUZ CABANILLAS, I. & TEJEDOR MARTÍNEZ, C., 2002. 'The HORSE family: on the evolution of the field and its metaphorization process', in J. E. Diaz-Vera (ed.), *A Changing World of Words: Studies in English Historical Lexicography, Lexicology and Semantics*, Amsterdam: Rodopi, 229–54.

DENNET, D. C., 1987. *The Intentional Stance*, Cambridge, Mass.: MIT Press.

DIRVEN, R., 2002a. 'Introduction', in R. Dirven & R. Pörings (eds.), *Metaphor and Metonymy in Comparison and Contrast*, Berlin: Mouton de Gruyter, 1–38.

DIRVEN, R., 2002b. 'Metonymy and metaphor: different mental strategies of conceptualisation', in R. Dirven & R. Pörings (eds.), *Metaphor and Metonymy in Comparison and Contrast*, Berlin: Mouton de Gruyter, 75–111.

DOBROVOL'SKIJ, D. & PIIRAINEN, E., 2005. *Figurative Language: Cross-Cultural and Cross-Linguistic Perspectives*, Amsterdam: Elsevier.

DOUGLAS, J. D. (ed.), 1982. *New Bible Dictionary*, 2nd edn, Leicester: Inter-Varsity Press.

DUNBAR, R., 1984. 'Learning the language of primates' (review of Harré & Reynolds 1984), *New Scientist* 104, 45.

DURKIN, P., 2002. 'Changing documentation in the third edition of the *Oxford English Dictionary*: sixteenth-century vocabulary as a test case', in T. Fanego & S. Seoane (eds.), *Sounds, Words and Change: Selected Papers from 11 ICEHL, Santiago de Compostela, 7–11 September 2000*, Amsterdam: Benjamins, 65–81.

EHRET, C., 1995. *Reconstructing Proto-Afroasiatic (Proto-Afrasian): Vowels, Tone, Consonants, and Vocabulary*, Berkeley: University of California Press.

FAUCONNIER, G. & TURNER, M., 1998. 'Conceptual integration networks', *Cognitive Science* 22, 133–87.

FAUCONNIER, G. & TURNER, M., 2002. *The Way We Think: Conceptual Blending and the Mind's Hidden Complexities*, New York: Basic Books.

FEYAERTS, K., 1999. 'Metonymic hierarchies: the conceptualization of stupidity in German idiomatic expressions', in K.-U. Panther & G. Radden (eds.), *Metonymy in Language and Thought*, Amsterdam: Benjamins, 309–32.

FEYAERTS, K., 2000. 'Refining the inheritance hypothesis: interaction between metaphoric and metonymic hierarchies', in Barcelona (2000b: 59–78).

GEERAERTS, D., 1997. *Diachronic Prototype Semantics: A Contribution to Historical Lexicology*, Oxford: Oxford University Press.

GEERAERTS, D. & GRONDELAERS, S., 1995. 'Looking back at anger: cultural traditions and metaphorical patterns', in J. R. Taylor & R. E. MacLaury (eds.), *Language and the Cognitive Construal of the World*, Berlin: Mouton de Gruyter, 153–80.

GIBBS, L., 2002. *Aesop's Fables*, Oxford: Oxford University Press.

GIBBS JR., R., 2000. 'Making good psychology out of blending theory', *Cognitive Linguistics* 11, 347–58.

GLARE, P. G. W., 1982. *Oxford Latin Dictionary*, Oxford: Clarendon Press.

GLUCKSBERG, S. (with a contribution from Matthew S. McGlone), 2001. *Understanding Figurative Language: From Metaphors to Idioms*, Oxford: Oxford University Press.

GLUCKSBERG, S. & KEYSAR, B., 1993. 'How metaphors work', in A. Ortony (ed.), *Metaphor and Thought*, 2nd edn, Cambridge: Cambridge University Press, 401–24.

GOOSSENS, L., 2002. 'Metaphtonomy: the interaction of metaphor and metonymy in expressions for linguistic action', in R. Dirven & R. Pörings (eds.), *Metaphor and Metonymy in Comparison and Contrast*, Berlin: Mouton de Gruyter, 349–77.

GRADY, J. E., 1997. 'Foundations of meaning : primary metaphors and primary scenes', Ph.D. thesis, University of California.

GRADY, J., OAKLEY, T. & COULSON, S., 1999. 'Blending and metaphor', in G. Steen & R. Gibbs (eds.), *Metaphor in Cognitive Linguistics*, Philadelphia: Benjamins, 101–24.

GRADY, J., TAUB, S. & MORGAN, P., 1996. 'Primitive and compound metaphors', in A. Goldberg (ed.), *Conceptual Structure, Discourse and Language*, Stanford, Calif.: CSLI, 177–87.

HARRÉ, V. & REYNOLDS, R., 1984. *The Meaning of Primate Signals*, Cambridge: Cambridge University Press.

HASER, V., 2005. *Metaphor, Metonymy and Experientialist Philosophy*, Berlin: Mouton de Gruyter.

HASSIG, D. (ed.), 1999. *The Mark of the Beast: The Medieval Bestiary in Art, Life and Literature*, New York: Garland.

HERTZ, R., 1960. *Death and the Right Hand*, trans. from the French by Rodney & Claudia Needham, Aberdeen: Cohen & West.

HOLLAND, D. & QUINN, N., 1987. *Cultural Models in Language and Thought*, Cambridge: Cambridge University Press.

HOLTHAUSEN, F., 1934. *Altenglisches etymologisches wörterbuch*, Heidelberg: Winter.

HOME, H. (Lord Kames), 1993. *Elements of Criticism*, 6th edn, London: Routledge.

HONECK, R. P., 1980. 'Historical notes on figurative language', in R. P. Honeck & R. R. Hoffman (eds.), *Cognition and Figurative Language*, Hillsdale, NJ: Erlbaum, 25–46.

HOUGH, C. A., 2004. 'New light on the verb "understand"', in C. J. Kay, C. Hough & I. Wotherspoon (eds.), *New Perspectives on English Historical Linguistics: Selected Papers from 12 ICEHL, Glasgow, 21–26 August 2002*, vol. 2: *Lexis and Transmission*, Amsterdam: Benjamins, 139–47.

HSIEH, S., 2003. 'The corpora of Mandarin Chinese and German animal fixed expressions: a cognitive semantic application', in J. Barnden, S. Glasbey, M. Lee, K. Markert & A. Wallington (eds.), *Proceedings of the Interdisciplinary Workshop on Corpus-Based Approaches to Figurative Language, 23rd March 2003*, UCREL Technical Papers vol.18 Special Issue, University Centre for Computer Corpus Research on Language, University of Lancaster.

HSIEH, S., 2006. 'A corpus-based study on animal expressions in Mandarin Chinese and German', *Journal of Pragmatics* 38, 2206–22.

JAY, M., 1993. *Downcast Eyes: The Denigration of Vision in Twentieth-Century French Thought*, Berkeley: University of California Press.

JOHNSON, C., 1999a. 'Constructional grounding: the role of interpretational overlap in lexical and constructional acquisition', Ph.D. thesis, University of California.

JOHNSON, C., 1999b. 'Metaphor vs. conflation in the acquisition of polysemy: the case of *see*', in M. K. Hiraga, C. Sinha & S. Wilcox (eds.), *Cultural, Psychological and Typological Issues in Cognitive Linguistics: Selected Papers of the Bi-annual ICLA Meeting in Albuquerque, July 1995*, Amsterdam: Benjamins, 155–69.

JOHNSON, M., 1980. 'A philosophical perspective on the problems of metaphor', in R. P. Honeck & R. R. Hoffman (eds.), *Cognition and Figurative Language*, Hillsdale, NJ: Erlbaum, 47–67.

JOHNSON, M., 1987. *The Body in the Mind: The Bodily Basis of Meaning, Imagination and Reason*, Chicago: University of Chicago Press.

JOHNSON, M. G. & MALGADY, R. G., 1980. 'Toward a perceptual theory of metaphoric comprehension', in R. P. Honeck & R. R. Hoffman (eds.), *Cognition and Figurative Language*, Hillsdale, NJ: Erlbaum, 259–82.

KASTOVSKY, D., 2006. 'Vocabulary', in R. Hogg & D. Denison (eds.), *A History of the English Language*, Cambridge: Cambridge University Press, 199–270.

KATZ, A. N., 1989. 'On choosing the vehicles of metaphors: referential concreteness, semantic distances, and individual differences', *Journal of Memory and Language* 28, 486–99.

KAY, C. J., 2000. 'Metaphors we lived by: pathways between Old and Modern English', in R. Roberts & J. Nelson (eds.), *Essays on Anglo-Saxon and Related Themes in Memory of Lynne Grundy*, London: King's College London, Centre for Late Antique and Medieval Studies, 273–85.

KAY, C. J., ROBERTS, J., SAMUELS, M. & WOTHERSPOON, I. (eds.), forthcoming. *Historical Thesaurus of English*, Oxford: Oxford University Press.

KENNEDY, J. S., 1992. *The New Anthropomorphism*, Cambridge: Cambridge University Press.

KIRKPATRICK, B. (ed.), 1992. *Brewer's Concise Dictionary of Phrase and Fable*, Oxford: Helicon.

KÖVECSES, Z., 1995. 'Anger: its language, conceptualization, and physiology', in J. R. Taylor & R. E. MacLaury (eds.), *Language and the Cognitive Construal of the World*, Berlin: Mouton de Gruyter, 181–96.

KÖVECSES, Z., 2005. *Metaphor in Culture: Universality and Variation*, Cambridge: Cambridge University Press.

KREBS, J. R. & DAVIES, N. B., 1981. *An Introduction to Behavioural Ecology*, Oxford: Blackwell.

LAKOFF, G., 1987. *Women, Fire, and Dangerous Things: What Categories Reveal about the Mind*, Chicago: University of Chicago Press.

LAKOFF, G., 1993. 'The contemporary theory of metaphor', in A. Ortony (ed.), *Metaphor and Thought*, 2nd edn, Cambridge: Cambridge University Press, 202–51.

LAKOFF, G., 1994. Conceptual metaphor homepage. http://cogsci.berkeley.edu/lakoff/

LAKOFF, G., 1996. 'The metaphor system for morality', in A. Goldberg (ed.), *Conceptual Structure, Discourse and Language*, Stanford, Calif.: CSLI, 249–66.

LAKOFF, G. & JOHNSON, M., 1980. *Metaphors We Live By*, Chicago: University of Chicago Press.

LAKOFF, G. & JOHNSON, M., 1999. *Philosophy in the Flesh: The Embodied Mind and its Challenge to Western Thought*, New York: Basic Books.

LAKOFF, G. & TURNER, M., 1989. *More than Cool Reason: A Field Guide to Poetic Metaphor*, Chicago: University of Chicago Press.

LANDAU, B. & GLEITMAN, L., 1985. *Language and Experience: Evidence from the Blind Child*, Cambridge, Mass.: Harvard University Press.

LANGACKER, R., 1987. *Foundations of Cognitive Grammar*, vol. 1, Stanford, Calif.: Stanford University Press.

LEACH, E., 1964. 'Anthropological aspects of language: animal categories and verbal abuse', in E. H. Lenneberg (ed.), *New Directions in the Study of Language*, Cambridge, Mass.: MIT Press.

LEHMANN, W. P., 1986. *A Gothic Etymological Dictionary*, Leiden: Brill.

LEVINSON, S., 2003. *Space in Language and Cognition*, Cambridge: Cambridge University Press.

LEWIS, C. T. & SHORT, C., 1966. *A Latin Dictionary*, reissue, Oxford: Oxford University Press.

LIDDELL, H. G. & SCOTT, R., 1996. *A Greek–English Lexicon*, revised, Oxford: Clarendon Press.

LIEBERMAN, P., 1998. *Eve Spoke: Human Language and Human Evolution*, London: Picador.

LUCY, J. A., 1992. *Language Diversity and Thought: A Reformulation of the Linguistic Relativity Hypothesis*, Cambridge: Cambridge University Press.

LYONS, J., 1977. *Semantics*, vol. 1, Cambridge: Cambridge University Press.

MACCORMAC, E. R., 1985. *A Cognitive Theory of Metaphor*, Cambridge, Mass.: MIT Press.

MACNEILAGE, P. F. & DAVIS, B. L., 2000. 'Evolution of speech: the relation between ontogeny and phylogeny', in C. Knight, M. Studdert-Kennedy & J. R. Hurford (eds.), *The Evolutionary Emergence of Language: Social Function and the Origins of Linguistic Form*, Cambridge: Cambridge University Press, 146–60.

MARMARIDOU, S., 2006. 'On the conceptual, cultural and discursive motivation of Greek pain lexicalizations', *Cognitive Linguistics* 17, 393–434.

MAY, H. G. & METZGER, B. M. (eds.), 1977. *The New Oxford Annotated Bible with the Apocrypha*, Revised Standard Version, New York: Oxford University Press.

McFARLAND, D. J., 1989. 'The teleological imperative', in A. Montefiore & D. Noble (eds.), *Goals, No-Goals and Own Goals: A Debate on Goal-Directed and Intentional Behaviour*, London: Unwin Hyman, 211–28.

METZGER, B. M. & COOGAN, M. D. (eds.), 1993. *The Oxford Companion to the Bible*, New York: Oxford University Press.

MITCHELL, R.W., THOMPSON, N. S. & MILES, H. L., 1997. *Anthropomorphism, Anecdotes and Animals*, New York: SUNY Press.

MITHEN, S., 1996. *The Prehistory of the Mind: A Search for the Origins of Art, Religion and Science*, London: Phoenix.

MYNORS, R. A. B., 1989. *Collected Works of Erasmus*, vol. 32: *Adages I vi 1 to I x 100*, Toronto: University of Toronto Press.

MYNORS, R. A. B., 1992. *Collected Works of Erasmus*, vol. 34: *Adages II vii 1 to III iii 100*, Toronto: University of Toronto Press.

NARAYANAN, S., 1997. 'Embodiment in language understanding: sensory-motor representations for metaphoric reasoning about event descriptions', Ph.D. thesis, University of California.

ONIONS, C. T., 1966. *The Oxford Dictionary of English Etymology*, Oxford: Clarendon Press.

ORTONY, A., 1993. 'Metaphor, language and thought', in A. Ortony (ed.), *Metaphor and Thought*, 2nd edn, Cambridge: Cambridge University Press, 1–16.

OSGOOD, C. E., 1980. 'The cognitive dynamics of synesthesia and metaphor', in R. P. Honeck & R. R. Hoffman (eds.), *Cognition and Figurative Language*, Hillsdale, NJ: Erlbaum, 203–238.

PALMATIER, R. A., 1995. *Speaking of Animals: A Dictionary of Animal Metaphors*, Westport, Conn.: Greenwood Press.

PANTHER, K.-L. & RADDEN, G., 1999. 'Introduction', in K.-L. Panther & G. Radden (eds.), *Metonymy in Language and Thought*, Amsterdam: Benjamins, 1–14.

PARTRIDGE, E., 1984. *A Dictionary of Slang and Unconventional English: Colloquialisms and Catch Phrases, Fossilised Jokes and Puns, General Nicknames, Vulgarisms and such Americanisms as have been Naturalised*, ed. Paul Beale, London: Routledge & Kegan Paul.

PECKHAM, M., 1970. 'Metaphor: a little plain speaking on a weary subject', in M. Peckham (ed.), *The Triumph of Romanticism: Collected Essays*, Columbia: University of South Carolina Press.

PEIRSMAN, Y. & GEERAERTS, D., 2006. 'Metonymy as a prototypical category', *Cognitive Linguistics* 17, 269–316.

PHILLIPS, M. M. & MYNORS, R. A. B., 1982. *Collected Works of Erasmus*, vol. 31: *Adages I i 1 to I v 100*. Toronto: University of Toronto Press.

PICKETT, J. P. et al. (eds.), 2000. *The American Heritage Dictionary of the English Language*, 4th edn, Boston: Houghton Mifflin.

POKORNY, J., 1959. *Indogermanisches etymologisches Worterbuch*, Bern: Francke.

RADDEN, G., 2000. 'How metonymic are metaphors?', in Barcelona (2000b: 93–108).

RADDEN, G., 2002. 'How metonymic are metaphors?', in R. Dirven & R. Pörings (eds.), *Metaphor and Metonymy in Comparison and Contrast*, Berlin: Mouton de Gruyter, 407–34.

RADDEN, G. & PANTHER, K.-U., 2004. 'Introduction', in G. Radden & K.-U. Panther (eds.), *Studies in Linguistic Motivation*, Berlin: Mouton de Gruyter, 1–46.

REAY, I. E., 1991. 'A lexical analysis of metaphor and phonaestheme', Ph.D. thesis, University of Glasgow.

REDDY, M., 1979. 'The conduit metaphor: a case of frame conflict in our language about language', in A. Ortony (ed.), *Metaphor and Thought*, Cambridge: Cambridge University Press, 284–324.

REICHMANN, P. F. & COSTE, E. L., 1980. 'Mental imagery and the comprehension of figurative language: is there a relationship?', in R. P. Honeck & R. R. Hoffman (eds.), *Cognition and Figurative Language*, Hillsdale, NJ: Erlbaum, 183–200.

RICHARDS, I. A., 1936. *The Philosophy of Rhetoric*, New York: Oxford University Press.

ROBERTS, J. & KAY, C. (eds.), 2000. *A Thesaurus of Old English*, 2 vols, Amsterdam: Rodopi.

ROSCH, E., MERVIS, C. B., GRAY, W. D., JOHNSON, D. M. & BOYES-BRAEM, P., 1976. 'Basic objects in natural categories', *Cognitive Psychology* 8, 382–439.

SAEED, J. I., 1999. *Semantics*, Oxford: Blackwell.

SALISBURY, J. E., 1996. 'Human animals of medieval fables', in N. C. Flores (ed.), *Animals in the Middle Ages: A Book of Essays*, New York: Garland, 49–65.

SALVINI, R., 1969. *Medieval Sculpture*, London: Joseph.

SAMUELS, M., 1972. *Linguistic Evolution*, London: Cambridge University Press.

SCHÖN, D. A., 1993. 'Generative metaphor: a perspective in problem-setting in social policy', in A. Ortony (ed.), *Metaphor and Thought*, 2nd edn. Cambridge: Cambridge University Press, 137–63.

SEARLE, J. R., 1993. 'Metaphor', in A. Ortony (ed.), *Metaphor and Thought*, 2nd edn, Cambridge: Cambridge University Press, 83–111.

SHELLEY, P. B., 1891. *A Defense of Poetry*, ed. with introduction and notes by Albert S. Cook, Boston, Mass.: Ginn.

SHINDO, M., 2003. 'The role of subjectification in semantic extensions of adjectives: a chronological perspective', paper presented at International Cognitive Linguistics Conference 12, University of Logroño.

SILVA, P., 2000. 'Time and meaning: sense and definition in the *OED*', in L. Mugglestone (ed.), *Lexicography and the OED: Pioneers in the Untrodden Forest*, Oxford: Oxford University Press, 77–95.

SIMPSON, J. (ed.), 2000–. *OED Online*, 3rd edn, Oxford: Oxford University Press. http://dictionary.oed.com

SIMPSON, J. & WEINER, E. (eds.), 1989. *The Oxford English Dictionary*, 2nd edn, Oxford: Oxford University Press.

SMITH, J. J., 1996. *An Historical Study of English: Function, Form and Change*, London: Routledge.

SPENCE, N. C. W., 2001. 'The human bestiary', *Modern Language Review* 96, 913–30.

STEEN, G., 1994. *Understanding Metaphor in Literature*, London: Longman.

STEEN, G., 2002. 'Towards a procedure for metaphor identification', *Language and Literature* 11, 17–33.

SWEETSER, E. E., 1984. 'Semantic structure and semantic change: a cognitive linguistic study of modality, perception, speech acts, and logical relations', Ph.D. thesis, University of California, Berkeley.

SWEETSER, E. E., 1990. *From Etymology to Pragmatics: Metaphorical and Cultural Aspects of Semantic Structure*, Cambridge: Cambridge University Press.

SYLVESTER, L., 2006. 'Forces of change: are social and moral attitudes legible in this *Historical Thesaurus of English* classification?', in G. Caie, C. Hough & I. Wotherspoon (eds.), *The Power of Words: Essays in Lexicography, Lexicology and Semantics in honour of Christian J. Kay*, Amsterdam: Rodopi, 185–208.

TALEBINEJAD, M. R. & DASTJERDI, H. V., 2005. 'A cross-cultural study of animal metaphors: when owls are not wise!', *Metaphor and Symbol* 20, 133–50.

TAUB, S., 1996. 'How productive are metaphors? A close look at the participation of a few verbs in the STATES ARE LOCATIONS metaphor (and others)', in A. Goldberg (ed.), *Conceptual Structure, Discourse and Language*, Stanford, Calif.: CSLI, 449–62.

TAYLOR, D., 1993. *Hardy's Literary Language and Victorian Philology*, Oxford: Clarendon Press.

TAYLOR, J., 2002. 'Category extension by metonymy and metaphor', in R. Dirven & R. Pörings (eds.), *Metaphor and Metonymy in Comparison and Contrast*, Berlin: Mouton de Gruyter, 323–47.

THORNTON, F., 1988. 'A classification of the semantic field good and evil in the vocabulary of English', Ph.D. thesis, University of Glasgow.

TILLEY, C., 1999. *Metaphor and Material Culture*, Oxford: Blackwell.

TISSARI, H., 2003. *LOVEscapes: Changes in Prototypical Senses and Cognitive Metaphors since 1500*, Helsinki: Société Néophilologique.

TOLLER, N. T. (ed.), 1921. *An Ango-Saxon Dictionary: Supplement*, London: Oxford University Press.

TOMLINSON, S., 1982. *A Sociology of Special Education*, London: Routledge & Kegan Paul.

TRYON, D. T. (ed.), 1995. *Comparative Austronesian Dictionary: An Introduction to Austronesian Studies*, 4 vols, Berlin: Mouton de Gruyter.

TURBAYNE, C. M., 1962. *The Myth of Metaphor*, New Haven, Conn.: Yale University Press.

ULLMANN, S., 1962. *Semantics: An Introduction to the Science of Meaning*, Oxford: Blackwell.

UNGERER, F. & SCHMID, H., 1996. *An Introduction to Cognitive Linguistics*, London: Longman.

VIBERG, Å., 1983. 'The verbs of perception: a typological study', *Linguistics* 21, 123–61.

WALDRON, R. A., 1979. *Sense and Sense Development*, London: Deutsch.

WARREN, B., 2002. 'An alternative account of the interpretation of referential metonymy and metaphor', in R. Dirven & R. Pörings (eds.), *Metaphor and Metonymy in Comparison and Contrast*, Berlin: Mouton de Gruyter, 114–30.

WATKINS, C., 2000a. 'Indo-European and the Indo-Europeans', in J. P. Pickett et al. (eds.), *The American Heritage Dictionary of the English Language*, 4th edn, Boston: Houghton Mifflin. http://www.bartleby.com/61/8.html

WATKINS, C., 2000b. 'Indo-European roots index', in J. P. Pickett et al. (eds.), *The American Heritage Dictionary of the English Language*, 4th edn, Boston: Houghton Mifflin. http://www.bartleby.com/61/IEroots.html

WHITE, T. H., 1954. *The Book of Beasts*, London: Cape.

WIERZBICKA, A., 2006. *English: Meaning and Culture*, Oxford: Oxford University Press.

# ACKNOWLEDGEMENTS

This book is based on my PhD thesis, completed at the University of Glasgow. I am grateful to everyone at the Department of English Language, and especially the staff of the *Historical Thesaurus of English*, who gave me invaluable help and encouragement as a postgraduate student. In particular, I would like to thank Flora Edmonds, *HTE* database manager, for many hours of practical advice, and Irené and Graham Wotherspoon for their generous support in the final painful stages of thesis writing. Additionally, various scholars made helpful comments and suggestions throughout my research, and I would like to acknowledge the contributions made by Carole Biggam, Isabel de la Cruz Cabanillas, Philip Durkin, Kurt Feyaerts, Sakis Kyratzis, George Lakoff, Jim McGonigal, Jeremy Smith and Gerard Steen.

I greatly appreciate the support I have had from colleagues at the University of Salford throughout the process of researching and writing this book. I would also like to thank the Philological Society and Wiley-Blackwell for advice and guidance in the preparation of the manuscript, in particularly the Publications Secretary, Delia Bentley, and Rachael Farnsworth and Sarah Barrett at Wiley-Blackwell. Two anonymous reviewers made extremely helpful and constructive suggestions on revisions, and I am grateful for their thoroughness and attention to detail, as well as their positive comments.

Finally, this book would never have been finished without the constant support and unlimited patience of my family and friends, Philip Durkin, and my former supervisor, Christian Kay, to whom this book is dedicated.

# GENERAL INDEX

# INDEX OF WORD FORMS AND
# CORE CONCEPT GROUPS

Word form have been italicised and core concept groups are marked by small capitals.

# INDEX OF REFERENCES